AIR WAR
OVER ITALY
1943-1945

ANDREW BROOKES

Ian Allan
PUBLISHING

For Caroline and Damian

First published 2000

ISBN 0 7110 2690 4

Published by Ian Allan Publishing

an imprint of Ian Allan Publishing Ltd,
Terminal House, Shepperton, Surrey TW17 8AS.

Printed by Ian Allan Printing Ltd,
Riverdene Business Park, Hersham, Surrey KT12 4RG.

Code: 0001

Half title page:
Defending the Fatherland – a Bf109 0f II/JG77 patrols over the mountains of northern Italy.
Author's Collection

This page:
Propellers turn on the PSP that served as the all-weather operating strip for the P-51 Mustangs of a Negro Fighter Group. The Group is about to take-off to escort Allied heavy bombers 'on a mission against Nazi military installations'. *IWM*

CONTENTS

Acknowledgements
Grateful thanks to my old friend, Peter Singleton, of the
RAF Air Historical Branch, for helping with so many of
the illustrations.

ABBREVIATIONS & GLOSSARY

AAF	Allied Air Forces
ACM	Air Chief Marshal
AI	Airborne Intercept
Air Cdre	Air Commodore
Air OP	Air observation post
AM	Air Marshal
ANR	Aeronautica Nazionale Repubblicana — the Italian Air Force that fought for the Germans after the surrender of Italy
AOC-in-C	Air Officer Commanding-in-Chief
ASC	Air Support Command
AVM	Air Vice-Marshal
B-17	Boeing B-17 Flying Fortress
B-24	Consolidated B-24 Liberator
B-25	North American B-25 Mitchell
B-26	Martin B-26 Marauder
BAF	Balkan Air Force
BG	Bombardment Group
Bn	Battalion
C-in-C	Commander-in-Chief
CG	Commanding General
CO	Commanding Officer
Col	Colonel
Coy	Company
FAF	French Air Force
FAGr	Fernaufklärungsgruppe (Long-Range — Strategic — Reconnaissance Group)
FG	Fighter Group
GCI	Ground-controlled intercept
Gen	General
GOC	General Officer Commanding
Gp	Group (Br and US)
GrC	Gruppo (plural Gruppi) Caccia — ANR pursuit groups
Groupement	Group (Fr)
Gruppe	Group (Ger)
Gustav	The G model of the Messerschmitt Bf109. The 109E was nicknamed the 'Emil'
Jabo	Jadgbomber — (fighter-bomber)
Jafu	Fighter Leader as in Jafu Oberitalien — Fighter Leader North Italy
JG	Jagdgeschwader (fighter wing)
KG	Kampfflugzeuggeschwader (bomber wing)
Luftflotte(n)	Air Fleet(s)
MAAF	Mediterranean Allied Air Forces

MAC	Mediterranean Air Command
Maj	Major
MATAF	Mediterranean Allied Tactical Air Forces
MORU	Mobile Operations Room Unit
MRAF	Marshal of the RAF
NAAF	Northwest African Air Forces
NAGr	Nahaufklärungsgruppe (Short-Range — Tactical — Reconnaissance Group)
NSGr	Nachtschlachtgruppe (Night ground-attack)
NZ	New Zealand
OKW	Oberkommando der Wehrmacht — High Command of the German Armed Forces
P-38	Lockheed P-38 Lightning
P-40	Curtiss P-40, known as Kittyhawk to the RAF; Warhawk USAAF
P-51	North American P-51 Mustang
PoW	Prisoner of war
PR	Photographic Reconnaissance
PSP	Pierced Steel Plate
Pz	Panzer (tank or Armoured as in 15th Pz Div)
PzGr	Panzergrenadier
RA	Royal Artillery
Ranks	German ranks have been translated into English, with the original German indicated in parentheses
RP	Rocket projectile
RSI	Italian Social Republic
R/T	Radio telegraphy
SG	Schlacht (ground-attack) Geschwader
SKG	Schnellkampfgeschwader, or fast bomber wing
SNCO	Senior Non-Commissioned Officer
Stab	HQ
Staffel(n)	Luftwaffe equivalent to an RAF squadron (see Chapter 3, Note 4)
StG	Stuka (Sturzkampfflugzeug = dive-bomber) Geschwader
TBF	Tactical Bomber Force
Units	Air Forces and Armies written in full; Corps and Commands in Roman; Divisions, Brigades and others in Arabic

INTRODUCTION

The ground phase of the 1991 Gulf War is best remembered for being finished 100 hours after it started, but from the airman's point of view, it was the 1,000 hours of aerial activity beforehand which ensured that it was only a 100-hour conflict. There was nothing serendipitous about this — soon after Iraq invaded Kuwait, ground and air staffs put their heads together to determine when an enemy division would cease to be a fighting force. Opinions varied as to whether this would come with 40 or 60% reductions in manpower and weapons, so they split the difference. Finally General Norman Schwarzkopf's air advisers told him, 'We guarantee we can "attrit" armour, army and people to the 50% level if you give us about 30 days.'[1] Allied air kept its side of the bargain and, in consequence, Allied ground forces were able to free Kuwait expeditiously.

Gen Merrill McPeak (a former USAF Chief of Staff) waxed lyrical about 'Desert Storm' being 'the first time in history that a field army has been defeated by air power'. Yet the liberation of Kuwait was unique in other ways. For example, 'for every Iraqi killed in the air and ground campaign, almost 20 capitulated, most without a fight. This level of demoralisation is unprecedented in modern wars and far surpasses similar ratios for Korea and Vietnam.'[2] It is therefore worth revisiting what one of Ed McBain's 87th Precinct characters termed 'a real war' — the battle for mainland Italy in 1943–45 — to put current air power potential into perspective.

Today, the battle for Italy is largely forgotten. Yet at its inception it was no sideshow. Chronologically, the invasion of Italy was a sequel to the conquest of Sicily, but in grand strategic terms the two events were widely separated. The fall of Sicily marked the end of the opening stage of World War 2. The invasion of mainland Italy initiated a new, offensive phase which climaxed in the final defeat of Germany.

Up to the fall of Rome in June 1944, the Mediterranean was the major theatre of Anglo-American war operations. The emphasis shifted once the Allies landed in Normandy and began island-hopping across the Pacific, but while the struggle for Italy became of secondary importance after 'Overlord', there was nothing second rate about the contest so far as the Allied soldiers were concerned. In just one campaign in 1944, the US Fifth Army sustained 32,000 battle deaths — just short of the number of American servicemen killed during the entire Korean War. It is no coincidence that the most decorated American soldier of World War 2 — Audie Murphy — earned many of his citations in Italy.

That the Allies eventually overcame all adversities in Italy owed much to air power, not least because the theatre served as a laboratory for many of the aerial weapons and techniques that are commonplace today. This book recounts the Italian air story using interviews, diaries, letters, published and unpublished reminiscences, official histories and operational record books. In all of them, it is clear that the exploitation of air power over Italy was intimately linked to the ground battle, and that Allied operational air forces were integrated for all meaningful intents and purposes. Yet in the end it was a close-run thing. For that reason, the air war over Italy offers many pointers to what air power can and cannot do today.

Notes to the Introduction

1. Glosson, B.; The Gulf War and Some Lessons Learned; London, 1993, p.37.
2. Lambert, A.; 'Air Power's Gestation as a Psychological Weapon'; The Journal of the RAF Staff College, 1996, p.25.

Below:
Oops! A B-24 Liberator crew look sheepish after landing at a Luftwaffe airfield. *Author's Collection*

DESERT SONG

'If you knit together the power of the Army on the land and the power of the Air in the sky, then nothing will stand against you and you will never lose a battle.'
Gen Sir Bernard Montgomery

Notwithstanding previous efforts with balloons, aerial warfare only converted from dream to reality during the Italian–Turkish war for Libya in 1911–12. In November 1911, three Italian pilots each carried out 'an aeroplane reconnaissance' to determine the headquarters of Arab and Turkish troops, and in the process four bombs were dropped 'on the enemy with effect'. The enemy in question did not take kindly to such unwelcome attention, and on 15 December an Italian aircraft was hit by anti-aircraft artillery shrapnel. The pilot then swooped low over the battery, as if to congratulate the gun crew, dropping some visiting cards as he flew by.

This gentlemanly approach would survive for some time and it may explain why many regard World War 1 aviation as little more than 'Those Magnificent Men in their Flying Machines'. Yet this is very unfair. Such were developments in aerial expertise that, by the armistice in 1918, the RAF had 22,647 aeroplanes, divided among 188 squadrons and nearly 700 airfields — and this largest air force in the world was not just for posing.

Co-operation with the army was first-rate; between 1915 and 1917, the Royal Flying Corps carried out an aerial survey of the whole British front, enabling the Royal Engineers to produce a really accurate map at last. It would form the basis of the 'artillery boards' supplied to all gun batteries and, consequently, the long preliminary bombardments which had advertised all offensives up to then were no longer necessary. At Cambrai on 20 November 1917, 1,003 guns of the Third Army opened fire at zero hour with a single crash and no warning. Then a line of 378 fighting tanks, under an umbrella of 289 aircraft, led forward eight divisions to attack German positions. Such joint air/land co-operation restored surprise and precision to the battlefield, and in so doing signalled the beginning of the end of the hellish war of attrition that had been the story of World War 1 from when the trench lines had been established in late 1914.

Nor was this just an air/land matter. By November 1918 the strength of the purely maritime side of the RAF in home waters numbered some 685 aircraft and 103 airships. Over 500 of these aircraft were engaged on anti-submarine activities, together with all the airships. No wonder that the redoubtable Adm Jackie Fisher could write in 1917 that the day of the battleship was over, and that sea war in future would be dominated by the submarine and the aircraft!

Above all, World War 1 proved that aeroplanes could reach out over land and sea quickly, justifying H. G. Wells' observation in 1908 that, 'in the air there are no streets, no channels, no point where one can say to an antagonist, "if he wants to reach my capital he must come by here". In the air, all directions lead everywhere.'[1]

The trouble was, that by 1939 the RAF had forgotten how to support the army and navy, and all the lessons had to be relearned in World War 2. Why was this? Quite simply, it all came down to survival. Within months of its formation in 1918, the RAF was forced to reduce from 188 combat squadrons to 25. In an effort to hold onto its hard-won independence, the RAF turned first to imperial policing, and in the long term to strategic bombing, roles that were both cost-effective and less susceptible to military or naval presumption.

Between 1919 and 1938, the RAF was on operations somewhere around the Empire on every day of those so-called peace years. Yet experience built up far afield seemed to get left behind on the troop ship: many in the RAF thought that it could bomb Hitler's Germany into submission without any night, all-weather or precise bomb-aiming capability. The fact that the army, navy and air force drifted far apart in the interwar years was a frightening indictment of political timidity, single-service short-sightedness, and petty rivalries — and Britain was very fortunate indeed to get away with it.

The RAF reinvented the wheel with the Royal Navy during the Battle of the Atlantic, and with the army in North Africa. But it was not until the Battle of Alam el Halfa — seven weeks before the Battle of Alamein and three years to the month after declaring war on Germany — that Britain finally got back to the standard of air-land co-operation enjoyed at Cambrai in 1917. The little-known struggle on the stony brown sands facing the Alam el Halfa ridge saw the RAF assuming practically the whole offensive effort against the enemy. While the army held the line, British air power bombed Axis positions repeatedly.

'These enemy raids,' recorded the Afrika Corps War Diary, 'intensified night after night, are an effective battle technique.' On top of the physical impact, the diarist recorded that 'officers and men were badly shaken and their fighting capacity considerably reduced by the enforced dispersal, lack of sleep, and the strain of waiting for the next bomb'.[2]

For the first time in the war, Rommel tried to fight an armoured battle with absolute inferiority in the air. After his finely honed Afrika Corps was blunted by effective air power, the Desert Fox wrote that 'anyone who has to fight, even with the most modern

Left:
The two British airmen who convinced US air leaders of the validity of the air support principles learned in the Western Desert — Sir Arthur Tedder (left) and Arthur Coningham.
Author's Collection

Below:
Commander of the Northwest African Photographic Wing, and son of the President, Col Elliott Roosevelt, in 1943 with hands on hips (far left). The nonchalant RAF officer at right foreground with hands in pockets is Sqn Ldr A. H. W. 'Freddie' Ball.
Author's Collection

Left:
Lt-Gen Carl 'Tooey' Spaatz,
Commander Northwest African Forces,
presents the US DFC to members of
330 Wing, 205 Group, in August
1943. *RAF Air Historical Branch*

Right:
The Central Mediterranean.

weapons, against an enemy in complete control of the air, fights like a savage against modern European troops, under the same handicaps and with the same chances of success'.[3] With Uncle Sam's arrival in theatre, it was just a matter of time before Axis forces were driven out of North Africa.

Gen Dwight Eisenhower was appointed Allied Commander-in-Chief, and it was under his sensitive leadership that British and Americans in North Africa learnt how to integrate action by land, air and sea. A major architect of such 'jointery' was ACM Sir Arthur Tedder, a former army officer and fighter squadron commander who by early 1943 had become Air C-in-C for the whole Mediterranean theatre.

'Air power,' wrote Tedder afterwards, echoing H. G. Wells, 'cannot be separated into little packets; it knows no boundaries on land and sea other than those imposed by the radius of action of the aircraft; it is a unit and demands unity of command. In the Middle East campaign we were fortunate that all the air forces . . . came under one command, and it was possible to switch and concentrate against the vital target as the day-to-day situation changed.'[4]

The decision to create Mediterranean Air Command (MAC), taking in all the Allied air forces from one end of that sea to the other, made perfect sense as they were all fighting the same war. At the very top, the quiet but tough Tedder set up his small policy-making and planning headquarters side by side with that of the supreme commander, to whom he became deputy for air operations.

By far and away the largest subordinate command in MAC was Northwest African Air Forces (NAAF), reporting to the unassuming but decisive USAAF Lt-Gen Carl Spaatz. 'Tooey' Spaatz had not liked being moved from the Eighth Air Force, but he was partly consoled by becoming Tedder's deputy and being given responsibility for all Allied air assets in Northwest Africa. His powerful force comprised the Northwest African Strategic Air Force under Maj-Gen Jimmy Doolittle, the Northwest African Coastal Air Force under the doughty defender of Malta, AVM Sir Hugh Lloyd, the Northwest African Tactical Air Force under AM Sir Arthur Coningham, Northwest African Air Service Command under Maj-Gen Delmar H. Dunton, the Northwest African Training Command under Brig-Gen John K. Cannon, Northwest African Troop Carrier Command under Brig-Gen Paul L. Williams and the Northwest African Photographic Reconnaissance Wing under the President's son, Col Elliott Roosevelt.

Spaatz, Doolittle, Coningham and Lloyd set up their headquarters close to Tedder's. Coningham's command comprised AVM Harry Broadhurst's Desert Air Force, XII Air Support Command (ASC) under Maj-Gen Edwin House, and Air Cdre Laurence Sinclair's Tactical Bomber Force (TBF). Broadly speaking, XII ASC was American, the Tactical and Strategic Bomber forces were mixed, and the Desert Air Force was British Commonwealth.[5] That said, as the campaign progressed, British flying units working under American control, or vice versa, became accepted practice and presented few problems.

It was interdiction in various forms by heavy bombers, constant attacks by medium bombers to disrupt and demoralise ground forces, close air support from fighter-bombers against pinpoint targets such as tanks, constant photo-reconnaissance, fighters covering the whole thing, and air supply/casualty evacuation — all of these combined to drive the Axis out of North Africa. This use of the whole air force to support the army was to underpin the Normandy invasion in 1944, but there was the small matter of Italy to get out of the way first.

In early 1943 the charming and genial Harold Alexander, fourth son of an earl and youngest general in the British Army back in 1937, was made Eisenhower's deputy and ground commander of Allied armies fighting the North African campaign. Eisenhower and Alexander worked as closely as any allies could, but despite the chemistry and trust that existed from Prime Minister Churchill and President Roosevelt downwards, there were profound differences in national strategic approach.

American forces joined the battle for North Africa because Roosevelt insisted that some sort of operation must be launched in 1942, not only to get the American people emotionally focused on Europe, but also to help avert a total Russian collapse. But while the Americans were hell-bent on invading across the English Channel in 1943, the British preferred to wear down the enemy by naval blockades and strategic bombing until the Third Reich collapsed under external and internal pressures. To be blunt, US planning staffs regarded British plans for the defeat of Germany as leisurely and indecisive. Perhaps the British, haunted by memories of the fearsome slaughter in World War 1, inclined towards caution, but their approach was certainly at variance with the clear and simple principles that guided the US Army: mobilise the greatest possible resources, concentrate them as quickly as possible at the decisive point, and then engage in battle to settle the matter. There was an American suspicion that British operations were geared to maintaining the integrity of their Empire, and that American soldiers would be duped into picking British political chestnuts out of the fire, not least around the Mediterranean and the Balkans.

A compromise was reached at a conference held in Casablanca in January 1943. The Combined Chiefs of Staff agreed that the Mediterranean should be fully opened to release shipping for the

cross-Channel invasion, and to provide bases from which Allied bombers could attack the German-controlled economic base. While it was agreed that operations should be continued to distract German strength from the Russian Front, to wear down the German war machine in general, and to force the collapse of Italy, there was no wish to get drawn into an Italian land campaign. It was assumed that once the Mediterranean had been opened and Sicily taken, the weight of Allied sea and air power would be enough itself to force an Italian collapse.

In the final analysis, there was no alternative to this 'Mediterranean Strategy'. By the time the combined chiefs met again in May 1943, and Gen Alexander's forces had overcome the last Axis resistance in North Africa, there was neither the time nor the shipping available to launch a cross-Channel invasion that year. Unless Mediterranean troops were left to kick their heels for a year while the Russians continued to fight single-handedly, something had to be found for them to do: as Churchill put it so appositely, the Allies would be 'a laughing stock if in the spring and early summer no British or American soldiers were firing at any German or Italian soldiers'. Combatants and statesmen alike were fixated on helping Marshal Stalin to win the war, and in 1943 there was no theatre other than the Mediterranean where this could be done.

Carried away by the euphoria of clearing North Africa, the British cast caution aside and put forward ambitious plans for exploiting success — the invasion of Sicily, they argued, should be followed at once by landings in Calabria. Then, from there, the Allies could go eastwards into the Balkans, or if there were a total collapse of Italian resistance, Italy would be occupied as far north as Rome. Either way, the Germans would be forced to divert forces south, which would do far more to prepare the way for a successful cross-Channel operation in 1944 than simply ferrying Mediterranean troops back to the UK.

These proposals were keenly debated in Eisenhower's headquarters but they were neither endorsed nor rejected. The airmen coveted airfields on the Italian mainland from where they could reach out to attack central and south-eastern Europe, but it was arguable that if Allied strategy aimed to tie Germans down while launching bomber raids, this could be done just as effectively by seizing Corsica and Sardinia. It is hard not to conclude that the impetus to carry the battle into Italy and to free Rome was as much emotional as strategic. Certainly, when the Allied armies landed in Sicily on 10 July, nobody had yet decided where they were to go next.

Notes to Chapter 1

1.   Wells, H. G.; The War in the Air; pp.247–48.
2.   Playfair, I. S. O.; The Mediterranean and Middle East; p.387.
3.   Lewin, R.; Rommel as Military Commander; p.162.
4.   Tedder, Lord; Air Power in War; p.91.
5.   Of the 28 Allied squadrons operating in Italy before 1943 was out, eight were South African.

SICILIAN PRELUDE

'War without allies is bad enough — with allies it is hell.'
MRAF Sir John Slessor

When it came to review the operational history of the Luftwaffe in 1948, the British Air Ministry pulled no punches:

'In the last days of the North African battle, the German Air Force in the Mediterranean, although still comprising over 800 aircraft, was an effete force . . . its influence in the last days of the campaign was nil.' [1]

To stop the rot, reorganisation and strengthening became essential. Luftwaffe operational flying units were subordinated to Luftflotten — air fleets. Each Luftflotte comprised one or more self-contained and balanced striking forces of bomber, fighter, ground-attack and reconnaissance units, known as Fliegerkorps. [2]

After the failings in North Africa, the Mediterranean Air Fleet was divided into two separate commands — Southeast Command covering Greece, Crete and the Balkans, and Luftflotte 2 encompassing Italy, Sicily, Sardinia, Corsica and part of southern France. Simultaneously, Luftflotte 2's HQ, which had shown itself lamentably wanting in ability and energy, was strengthened by the arrival from Russia of the capable but tough Field Marshal Wolfram von Richthofen. [3] Under him, command of II Fliegerkorps was given to Gen Alfred Buelowius, formerly CO of an army co-operation corps in Russia. A new bomber organisation was established within II Fliegerkorps under Col Dietrich Peltz, a Stuka pilot and rising star who had previously been in charge of operations against England. At the same time Gen Adolf Galland, Inspector of Fighters and Ground-Attack Aircraft, was detached from Luftwaffe High Command to the Mediterranean to speed up the supply of fighter pilots and aircraft as well as to restore efficiency and morale.

On 20 May, the Luftwaffe in the Mediterranean had an estimated 989 combat aircraft — 541 fighters and fighter-bombers, 240 bombers, 97 close- and long-range reconnaissance, 58 ground-attack and 53 coastal — of which 578 were serviceable. Their Italian allies had 1,385 combat aircraft — 901 fighters and 484 bombers — of which 698 were serviceable. But this combined Axis strength of 1,276 serviceable aircraft was scattered as far north as the Alps and as far east as Greece.

By early July the Axis had about 775 operational combat aircraft within range of Sicily, and 63 more bombers were on the point of arriving. Three-quarters of the 434 aircraft on the island were fighters and fighter-bombers. The Allies with their 267 available squadrons in the Mediterranean — 146 American and 121 British — had a definite but not overwhelming numerical superiority.

Gen Alexander, Allied Land Force Commander for the invasion of Sicily, was responsible for 115,000 British Empire and over 66,000 American assault troops to be transported by nearly 2,500 naval vessels and landing craft. Signal intercepts indicated that Axis commanders were concentrating their air assets on Sardinia, Sicily and Pantelleria, and that as many as 795 aircraft (545 of which were German) might attack the invasion fleet. [4] Lumbering landing craft and their naval escorts were sitting ducks close inshore, and one opponent particularly feared was the Focke-Wulf FW190. Built as an air defence fighter, the FW190 proved to be so fast and sturdy that it was only a matter of time before it was pressed into service in the Jabo (from Jadgbomber — fighter-bomber) role. A whole Gruppe was based at Comiso in Sicily by the end of 1942 and practised an anti-shipping role. Against shipping an FW190 would approach with its target to one side at about 8,000ft. As the chosen ship disappeared beneath the wing, the pilot would bank into a 50° dive, aiming to reach 500mph by bomb release at around 4,000ft. Immediately after the 1,100lb bomb was sent on its way, the pilot turned to avoid anti-aircraft fire while descending to about 150ft to make a getaway.

ACM Tedder's experience in pursuit of Rommel across the desert had convinced him of two things — the paramount importance of air superiority, and the need for the early capture of enemy airfields to maintain the momentum of an assault. There was a comradely synergy in all this. The air would help the army ashore, whereupon the army must help the air to seize the airfields it needed.

As only Malta was within single-seat fighter range of southern Sicily, some 600 front-line aircraft, plus directing radars and control links, were positioned in Malta and Gozo by June 1943 under the energetic direction of the former Battle of Britain group commander, AVM Sir Keith Park. But Tedder briefed Alexander that single-engined fighters operating out of Malta or Tunisia could only provide an air defence umbrella over the southern half of Sicily: they could not effectively operate over the main Sicilian port of Messina from Malta alone. Alex listened carefully as 'Tedder pointed out that the Comiso-Gela airfield centre, inland from the south coast, had been developed into a first-class air base, and that, unless it could be captured for our own use, our air force would labour under an intolerable handicap'. [5] It was a measure of the role played by air power that the risk of supplying Allied forces across open beaches and through two small ports was accepted as

TABLE 1:
PRINCIPAL UNITS OF NORTHWEST AFRICAN AIR FORCES, 1 JUNE 1943

Strategic Air Force

US 2nd, 97th, 99th, 301st Bomb Groups (B-17s)
US 310th, 321st Bomb Groups (B-25s)
US 17th, 319th, 320th Bomb Groups (B-26s)
US 1st, 14th, 82nd Fighter Groups (P-38s)
US 325th Fighter Group (P-40s)
RAF 205 Group (Wellingtons) (231, 236, 330, 331 Wings)

Tactical Air Force

US 47th Bomb Group (A-20s)
US 12th*, 340th* Bomb Groups (B-25s)
RAF 232, 326 Wings
3 (SAAF) Wing
Two tac/recce squadrons

XII Air Support Command

US 33rd, 324th* Fighter Groups (P-40s)
US 31st Fighter Group (Spitfires)
US 27th, 86th Fighter-Bomber Groups (A-36s)
US 111th Observation Squadron

Western Desert Air Force

RAF and SAAF, but including US 57th* and 79th* Fighter Groups (P-40s)

* Ninth Air Force

Coastal Air Force

US 81st, 350th Fighter Groups (P-39s)
US 52nd Fighter Group (Spitfires)
RAF 323, 328 Wings
1st and 2nd Air Defense Wings
Miscellaneous units, including US 1st and 2nd Anti-submarine Squadrons

Troop Carrier Command

US 51st Wing: 60th, 62nd, 64th Groups (C-47s)
US 52nd Wing: 61st, 313th, 314th, 316th* Groups (C-47s)
RAF 38 Wing

Training Command

Three replacement battalions
US 68th Observation Group
Miscellaneous training units

Photographic Reconnaissance Wing

US 3rd Photo Group
Two RAF squadrons
One FAF squadron

* Ninth Air Force

Assigned Strength of USAAF Groups

1 Heavy bombers: 48 aircraft (4 squadrons, 12 aircraft each)
2 Medium bombers: 57 aircraft (4 squadrons, 13 aircraft each, plus 5 HQ aircraft)
3 Light bombers: 57 aircraft (4 squadrons, 13 aircraft each, plus 5 HQ aircraft)
4 Dive bombers: 57 aircraft (4 squadrons, 13 aircraft each, plus 5 HQ aircraft)
5 Fighters: 75 aircraft (3 squadrons, 25 aircraft each)
6 Troop carrier: 52 aircraft (4 squadrons, 13 aircraft each)

In each instance the strength was normal, except in the case of the heavies where normal equipment was 35 aircraft.

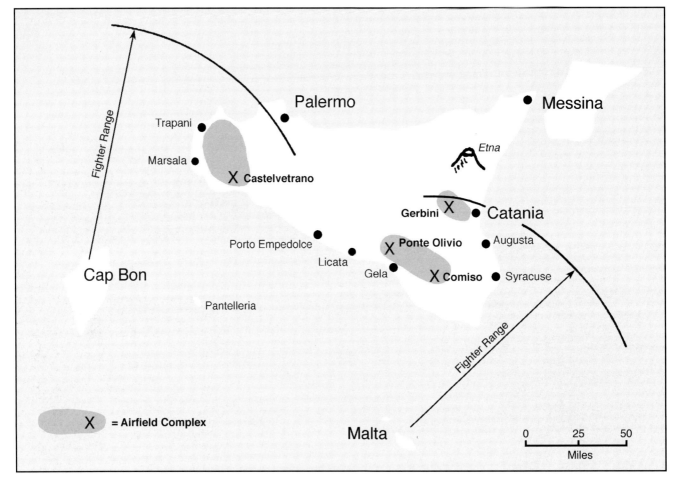

Sicilian airfields and ports, with fighter radii of operations from North Africa and Malta.

the price for the vital Comiso-Gela airfield falling into Allied hands at the earliest opportunity.

Even before Axis forces surrendered in Tunisia, Allied strategic bombers were paving the way for the next move. By day, the B-17s of the US Twelfth Air Force and B-24s of the Ninth, supplemented at night by Wellingtons of the RAF's 205 Group, attacked three main pre-invasion objectives — airfields, in the hope of destroying Axis air assets on the ground, ports and mainland communications to prevent resupply of the island garrison.

Between 8 and 10 May, a few days before the Tunisian surrender, a formidable three-day air attack was made on the small island of Pantelleria athwart the narrows between Tunisia and Sicily. The bombing resumed on 18 May, and from 6 June it was progressively stepped up with all the Northwest African Strategic Air Force squadrons (apart from those flying Wellingtons), the Tactical Bomber Force and the specially reinforced US XII ASC taking part. The TBF operated 'medium' B-25 Mitchells in two US groups and Leo 45s in the 8th French Groupement, plus 'light' Boston IIIs (RAF designation for the Douglas DB-7B) and Baltimore IIIs (RAF designation for the Martin 187) in South African and RAF markings, and A-20 Bostons in one US group.

The TBF specialised in those targets that could be selected more quickly and then be more heavily pounded at shorter notice than by any other means. They were no mean opponents, especially with fighter escorts, and they ranged at will over the Sicilian Channel.

As Roderic Owen wrote most graphically:

'Pantelleria was the Italian equivalent of Heligoland, a forbidden zone since 1926, a volcanic rock pockmarked by 100 or so gun emplacements, supporting an aerodrome with underground hangars and powerful radar apparatus . . . Its 42.5 square miles were defended by some 10,000 men, well provisioned, with sufficient though not ample, supplies of water.

The island functioned chiefly as a gigantic spying glass to keep Rome informed of every movement in the narrow straits, on the North African coast, and in the air above. To mount an invasion of Sicily without first knocking out Pantelleria was to enable the enemy to give a running commentary of top secret news. To leave its 80 aircraft unmolested was to invite attacks on formations bombing in support of the landing on Sicily.' [6]

Above:
Allied air supremacy over Panelleria. *RAF Air Historical Branch*

Between 8 May and 11 June, when the seaborne assault went in, Northwest African Air Forces mounted 154 air attacks (5,218 sorties) to drop 6,400 tons on what the Fascist press termed the 'Italian Gibraltar'. 1,500 tons of bombs fell on 10 June alone, but the first Allied landing in Nazi Europe was still expected to be a tough assignment. Maj Peter Faulks was leading D Company of the 1st Battalion, The Duke of Wellington's Regiment, when at the last minute the landing craft were swung around in the bay. The fighting troops, who had previously been at the front, now had to clamber over the cooks and drivers to lead the way on to the beaches. They need not have worried. The thoroughly demoralised Italian garrison did more than surrender promptly: they welcomed the Allies on the beaches, packed up and ready to go. The only casualty was a British infantryman who was bitten by a local jackal!

Pantelleria became famous as the first instance of a substantial ground force surrendering to massive air power alone. The smaller island of Lampedusa fell likewise after an air attack which started at dawn. By late afternoon, the Allies had flown some 450 sorties and dropped around 270 tons of bombs when the Italian commander tried to surrender to an amazed RAF sergeant who had

been forced to land his air-sea rescue aircraft on the island's airfield with engine trouble. The good SNCO did not want to know, so the garrison put out white flags around 19.00hrs. Negotiations were completed quickly thereafter, although the local commander refused to sign the surrender terms 'until he was reminded that we had another 1,000 bombers at our call, then he borrowed a pen and signed'.[7] Such apparently clear examples of the successful effect of sustained air attack on morale were to be a source of great comfort to the Allies in the coming months.

The Axis had 19 principal airfields in Sicily, plus a dozen newly constructed strips of lesser importance, and from 15 June 1943 in Tedder's words, 'a crescendo of attacks on the enemy's airfields was launched'. The Gerbini complex in the east, home to most of the Luftwaffe fighters, was given special attention by the RAF and AAF's Cyrenaica-based heavies. The bomb types carried on such missions depended on the target. The US 500lb General Purpose bomb was considered best for hangars and installations, while the 100lb demolition and 50lb fragmentation bomb in clusters did best

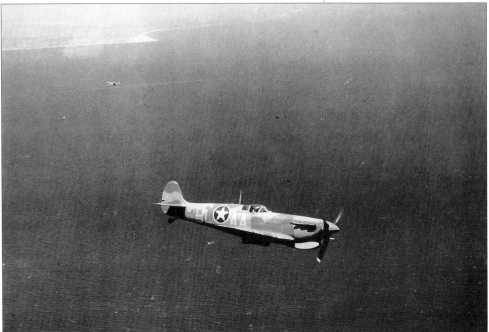

Above:
A B-17 flies over Catania airfield, Sicily, as bombs from Flying Fortresses that have overflown earlier explode below. *IWM*

Left:
A USAAF Spitfire on patrol off Panelleria in June 1943. *RAF Air Historical Branch*

against aircraft parked on dispersal areas. Results everywhere were good, as Tedder noted:

'The movement of the enemy's aircraft from one field to another, the attempts to evade attack by dispersal, the preparation of satellite airstrips; all this was watched from the air. The enemy was harried from field to field. As a result, he was forced to withdraw his bombers to airfields in Italy. This naturally increased the range at which his fighters had to operate over Sicily, and caused the progressive weakening of his opposition. The last serious attempt to interfere with our air operations took place on 5 July.' [8]

This engagement between US B-17s and about 100 German fighters could not disguise the fact that, to all intents and purposes, the Luftwaffe was defeated before the Allied invasion of Sicily began. Allied troops landed on Sicily five days later: above the US 3rd Infantry Division going ashore on the Licata beaches were American P-40s launched from Pantelleria airfield.[9]

On 10 July, in the skies above the convoys of ships, danced the first of the 1,092 sorties flown on beach patrol; in response, the Luftwaffe could mount only 275–300 sorties, half of which were at night. Most fighter aircraft flew three sorties a day, covering not only the ships and beachheads, but also escorting Allied bombers. The aim of all fighter-bomber attacks was to interfere with Axis movements towards the landing areas. Desert Air Force flew more than 3,000 sorties between 10 and 12 July, of which the attached US 31st and 33rd Fighter Groups notched up more than 1,000. By way of comparison, over 1,300 combat sorties were flown by Allied airmen during the first 24 hours of the 1991 Gulf War.

Coastal Air Force, a predominantly British organisation, escorted convoys through the Mediterranean. It did its work so thoroughly that when over 100 Ju88s, FW190s and Cant Z.1007s had tried to hit an eastbound convoy off Cap Bon back on 26 June, Coastal's fighters accounted for six intruders and no vessel suffered serious damage. Yet air superiority is in the eye of the beholder. In so far as the Allies lost only 12 vessels from enemy action during the invasion of Sicily when they feared they might lose 300, it was down to massive air superiority. But if you had been on the US destroyer Maddox, which went down with most of its crew on 10 July after being hit by a Stuka, you might have cried, 'Air superiority? Phooey.'

Having lost over 100 aircraft during the previous week, the Luftwaffe's remaining FW190 fighter-bombers were ordered back to the mainland for safekeeping. As there were no sizeable airfields in the toe of Italy, the FW190s could operate only from the Naples area, some 200 miles from the scene of operations. With a range of less than 500 miles, there was little time for FW190s to hang around looking for good targets before it was time to go back home again.

The Allied counter-air campaign was so successful that only 25 German aircraft remained on Sicily by 18 July. Given free rein, the day-fighters and fighter-bombers of the Twelfth Air Force left the roads of Sicily blocked with burning trucks and seriously hampered Axis movements. Around and about, NAAF flew around 1,000 heavy- and medium-bomber sorties against key supply nodes, terminal ports and Italian west coast marshalling yards, with the aim of blocking Axis efforts to reinforce Sicily.

Nothing appeared to be off-limits any more. Back in January 1943, Foreign Secretary Anthony Eden reminded the House of Commons that Mussolini had sent aircraft to participate in the Battle of Britain and the British had 'as much right to bomb Rome as the Italians had to bomb London.[10] . . . We should not hesitate to do so with the best of our ability and as heavily as possible if the

Left:
Bombs dropped from US aircraft on 19 July 1943 explode on the electrified Littorio railway yards which acted as the central dispatching point for freight traffic between northern and southern Italy.
Author's Collection

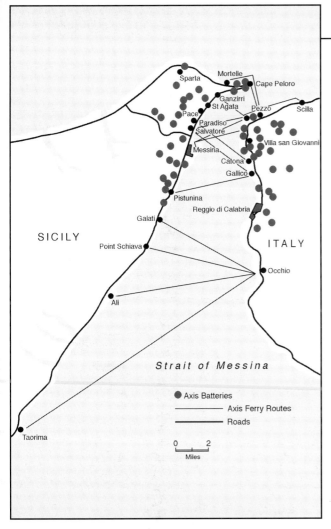

Axis Batteries

——— Axis Ferry Routes

Roads

0   2
Miles

Strait of Messina

SICILY

ITALY

course of the war should render such bombing convenient and helpful.'

On the morning of 19 July, after warning leaflets had been dropped, 156 B-17 Fortresses, 144 B-25 Mitchells and 117 B-24 Liberators bombed the Lorenzo and Littorio railway yards at Rome. In the afternoon, 117 B-26 Marauders escorted by US P-38 Lightnings hit Ciampino North and South airfields. Allied airmen met only feeble fighter opposition and local flak was ineffective. The whole of the morning force returned to bases, but two B-26s were lost in the afternoon. Aerial photographs taken the following day showed 38 aircraft destroyed or damaged at the two airfields, together with 130 direct hits on rolling stock and trucks; five Germans were killed. Churchill had been happy to sanction the bombardment of marshalling yards so close to the Eternal City because daylight precision bombing was portrayed as being quite accurate. Gen George Marshall, the US Army Chief of Staff, agreed, but as with several unfortunate instances in and around Kosovo in 1999, a few bombs fell wide in Rome too. Unintended 'collateral damage' was inflicted on the ancient basilica of San Lorenzo-without-the-walls with its 12th century frescos, and the headstone of the poet John Keats. This prompted much subsequent heartsearching by The New York Times.

By the end of July, the Allies had 21 Sicilian airfields back up and running and 40 squadrons based on the island. The Luftwaffe's response was spasmodic, though in the early hours of 1 August, 25 Ju88s and Do217s made a successful raid on Palermo, putting the largest dock temporarily out of commission, destroying ration and petrol supplies, blowing up an ammunition train and sinking a vessel. But this went against the general trend: Allied success in Sicily by then was a foregone conclusion, though there was a salutary lesson for those shrewd enough to notice. Despite overwhelming Allied superiority on the ground and in the air, Axis forces were able to fight delaying actions so successfully that 39 days were required to complete the occupation of the island.

Over 100,000 Italians became prisoners of war, but the Germans remained skilful and obdurate throughout. Commanders cleverly employed two German and four Italian divisions to delay the passage of two large Allied armies sufficiently to allow an orderly withdrawal into suitable defensive positions in the northeast corner of the island. It soon became clear to everyone that the exit point for remaining Axis troops would be Messina, less than three miles from the Italian mainland. Allied air forces therefore made Messina their prime target, and by 8 August the port was reduced 'to a condition much the same as that in which it had been left by the earthquake of 1909'.[11] Yet in among the rubble, the Germans — well supported by their remaining Italian allies — managed to evacuate an estimated 60,000 men and nearly 10,000 vehicles with 94 guns and even 47 tanks.

This Axis 'Dunkirk' was made possible by a formidable anti-aircraft 'flak' barrier. Although German air elements in Sicily had been neutralised, Luftwaffe ground units — comprising 30,000 personnel — remained largely intact. Among them were some very powerful ground defence units which threw up an intensive wall of metal described as 'heavier than the Ruhr'.[12] Between 112 and 168 88mm guns were placed along both sides of the Straits of Messina, backed by 148 37mm or 20mm guns, with Italian 90mm and 75mm guns mixed in between. On 1 August, AM Coningham told Tedder he 'considered that the Messina area flak was now practically prohibitive for all aircraft except the heavy bombers'.[13] Allied fighter-bombers, which had been attacking the ferries at very low level, were forced to fly higher, which spoiled aiming accuracy and consequently reduced Axis shipping losses drastically.

Nothing less than the use of B-17s with their bombsights was advocated 'if we are to maintain continuous air action to defeat an attempt at evacuation,' but on 11 August Coningham released the B-17s 'in order that they may be freely employed against Strategic [objectives] and exploit the situation in Italy proper'.[14] Translated, this meant that Coningham was responding to pressure to use the big birds for something really meaningful; in particular, Tedder had been pushing for a maximum strength strike on Rome which he believed might drive Italy from the war.[15] In the event, the objective was more prosaic. The Roman marshalling yards, which by then were repaired, needed to be closed again to help isolate Axis forces further south. After two Wellingtons dropped warning leaflets on the city, 106 B-17s, 102 B-26s and 66 B-25s, escorted by 140 P-38s, revisited Lorenzo and Littorio marshalling yards. Post-attack photography showed the damage inflicted to be 'severe and comprehensive'.

As luck would have it, Axis evacuation from Sicily became a daylight operation on 13 August, which was discovered only hours after the entire B-17 force struck Rome's marshalling yards that afternoon. The heavies were then forced to stand down for four days, by which time the evacuation was completed. Axis ground forces in Messina had been mystified by the absence of heavy bomber attacks by day, but they made full use of their good fortune, even though Marauders and Mitchells flew a total of 576 and the fighter-bombers 1,883 sorties between 8 and 17 August on both sides of the Straits. For those who were more attracted to bombing capital cities than exposed lifelines, Gen von Vietinghoff (subsequently supreme commander in Italy) made the telling observation that, without the men rescued from Sicily, 'it would not have been possible to offer effective resistance on the Italian mainland south of Rome'.[16]

*   *   *   *

The fall of Sicily came as the coup de grâce to the Italian third of the Axis. It had seen its overseas empire disappear, its armies humiliated and its homeland increasingly hammered from the air. Once Mussolini made it clear that he would not take Italy out of the war on his own, his subordinates decided to do it for him. The Duce was deposed and arrested on 25 July and, three weeks later, formal negotiations were opened in Lisbon with the Allies on behalf of the new regime. Hitler said to his advisers:

'If the worst comes to the worst, the Italian peninsula can be sealed off somehow. It is of decisive importance for us to hold the Balkans: oil, copper, bauxite, chrome, above all security, so there is not a complete smash there if things get worse in Italy.'[17]

Seventeen days after the clearing of Sicily, the British Eighth Army made its crossing of the Straits of Messina. This was a diversion: the main amphibious assault, by Gen Mark Clark's US Fifth Army, came in the Gulf of Salerno. On 8 September the Italian government surrendered unconditionally. The German C-in-C, Field Marshal Albert Kesselring, was left to pick up the pieces.

Notes to Chapter 2

1. The Rise and Fall of the German Air Force; Air Ministry Pamphlet 248, pp.254–61.
2. While the Air Corps carried out operations, the Air Fleet issued the orders and directed.
3. The Red Baron's cousin had commanded the Condor Legion at the end of the Spanish Civil War, and fought in the Polish, Flanders, Balkan and Russian campaigns.
4. Hinsley, F. H.; British Intelligence in the Second War; vol III, pt I, p.71.
5. North, J. (ed); The Alexander Memoirs; p.106.
6. Owen, R.; The Desert Air Force; p.160.
7. G-2, AFHQ, Intel Notes — Pantelleria and Lampedusa, 3 July 1943.
8. Tedder, Lord; With Prejudice; p.445.
9. While the Curtiss P-40 fighter was never a match for the Bf109, it proved its value as a fighter-bomber in North Africa. It was known as the Warhawk to the Americans, and Kittyhawk to RAF and Commonwealth air forces.
10. Mussolini offered 30 squadrons for this endeavour.
11. Richards, D. and Saunders H. St G.; Royal Air Force 1939–1945; ii, p.322. Denis Richards told the author that while he wrote the Sicilian section, all subsequent sections on the Italian campaign came from Hilary Saunders' pen.
12. Shepperd, G. A.; The Italian Campaign 1943–45; p.69.
13. Air Historical Branch (AHB), The Sicilian Campaign; p.80.
14. Coningham to Tedder, signal of 11 August 1943.
15. Mark, E.; Aerial Interdiction in Three Wars; pp.71–72.
16. Vietinghoff, H.; The Campaign in Italy; Ch 6, p.2.
17. Führer Naval Conference, 14 May 1943.

THE SOFT UNDERBELLY

'Here it is the same every day, up at 04.00hrs, at readiness all day, bombs, air combat, heat, flies and to bed at 10.00 in the evening. It is tremendously wearing and one can't get used to it. I don't enjoy the southern theatre any more. This damned flying over water is no fun . . . if one goes down into it one drowns. Hero's death, lovely words, especially for the newspaper, but the subject is still death.'
Lt Karl Paashaus, 5/JG53

Albert Kesselring was born into good Bavarian bourgeois stock in 1885. He joined the artillery — not the dilettante horse variety but

the Bavarian foot artillery — wherein he gained valuable experience of manoeuvre operations during World War 1. In 1922, Kesselring joined the staff in Berlin which was tasked with organising the postwar German Army. It was there that his natural gifts for administration and organisation came to the fore, such that in 1933 he was moved across to the newly emergent Luftwaffe, to become chief administrator and then chief of staff.

When the Luftwaffe went into action for the first time in Poland, Kesselring was in charge of Luftflotte 1. He went on to command Luftflotte 2 during the invasion of the Low Countries, and his performance was so outstanding that he received his field marshal's baton after the fall of France. In December 1941, he was appointed C-in-C South with a brief to establish air and sea superiority in the Mediterranean. This ostensibly gave him control over all Axis forces, including Rommel's Afrika Corps. While masterminding the first true carpet bombing campaign against Malta, Kesselring capitalised on his friendly and approachable style to sustain a working relationship with all manner of sensitivities and egos.

Kesselring was blessed with a capacity to grasp essentials, plus a simple faith in doing his duty to the best of his ability without complaint. He was always photographed wearing a cheerful grin, and his men responded to their genuine laughing cavalier by nicknaming him 'Smiling Albert'.

In May 1943, Hitler earmarked Rommel for overall command in Italy should the Italians decide to surrender — then at the last minute, Hitler decided that Rommel would command all forces in Greece, Crete and the Aegean instead. However, when Mussolini was overthrown, Hitler changed his mind again and hauled Rommel back to a shadow HQ from where he was to plan to assume responsibility for all German troops in northern Italy.

Overall, Hitler's intention was that Rommel would look after Army Group B (all troops in the north), while Kesselring looked after Army Group C (all units south of Rome plus those evacuated from Sicily). On 17 August, Rommel moved his HQ to Lake Garda but then came the Allied landings. Hitler made a gesture in Kesselring's direction by creating a new Tenth Army of six divisions in central and southern Italy under the panzer leader Gen (Generaloberst) Heinrich von Vietinghoff. Eventually, Hitler decided that all of Italy should be placed under a single command, but he prevaricated between Kesselring — who was keen to fight the Allies as far south as possible — and Rommel — who argued for holding the line much further north. In essence, Rommel was

Left:
Field Marshal 'Smiling Albert' Kesselring. *Author's Collection*

against making a stand where the Allies could exploit their maritime superiority to outflank the German defences, whereas Kesselring, always air-minded, saw the importance of keeping Allied heavy bombers as far away as possible from the Reich. In the end, Hitler opted for Kesselring and his never-failing optimism, leaving Rommel to take-off from Villafranca airfield for a new role in Normandy.

Yet although Kesselring became de facto ruler of the better part of Italy, he appeared to have little or nothing going for him. First, there was the wobbly Axis; according to Kesselring's biographer, 'Germany's military operations in Italy were like isolated rocks surrounded by a quicksand of intrigue and uncertainty.'[1] Then, an Italian Social Republic was set up under Mussolini at Salo on Lake Garda on 15 September 1943, and at first it enjoyed considerable support among local Italians. But Mussolini was given authority only over the Po Valley — six other northern provinces had to accept the authority of German 'High Commissioners' — and it soon became apparent that the Salo Republic was little more than a tool of occupation. Kesselring said:

'There were often times when it would be far easier to fight alone with inadequate forces than to have to accept so bewildering a responsibility for the Italian people's aversion to the war and our ally's lack of fighting qualities and dubious loyalty.'[2]

Eventually, Italian manpower under arms would consist of 100,000 men incorporated into units under Kesselring's command. But the partisan organisation (which Mussolini put at 60 brigades)[3] killed around 13,000 German soldiers and wounded about the same number between June and August 1944. As an indication of the conditions facing Axis aircrew, records of fighter unit JG77[4] refer to nocturnal partisan assaults on aircraft dispersals and crew quarters, and daylight assaults both on leave and on duty — even a waterborne attack on two airmen rowing on a lake. Overall, German forces had to operate against a national backdrop that was at best lukewarm and at worst murderously antagonistic.

To make matters worse, Kesselring was hardly getting rock-solid support from his own hierarchy. Keeping his Führer in touch with reality was a full-time task, and there was no comparable buffer between Hitler and Kesselring to deflect the inconsequential or downright dangerous as there was between Allied commanders in the field and Churchill or Roosevelt. C-in-C Southwest wrote:

'On top of my far from pleasant exchanges with the Führer's headquarters together with the burden of military work, the spread of the air war to the whole of Italy, and the gloomy prospects ahead gradually frayed my nerves.'[5]

Even the boss of his own service was more hindrance than help. After its pilots had battled against overwhelming odds for weeks, Luftflotte 2 received the following telex on 25 June 1943:

'The fighter pilots who took part in the defence against the bomber raid on the Strait of Messina are guilty of dereliction of duty. One pilot from each of the participating Jagdgruppen is to be brought before a court martial on a charge of cowardice in the face of the enemy.

Signed
GÖRING
Reichsmarschall'

To crown it all, there was precious little good news coming from elsewhere. The Hamburg firestorm ignited by RAF Bomber Command at the end of July 1943 signalled the miserable way ahead for many families whose sons were serving in Italy. The V-weapons experimental site at Peenemünde was being bombed as the last Germans left Sicily, and when Kesselring heard of the consequent suicide of Hans Jeschonnek, Luftwaffe Chief of Air Staff, morale must have fallen even lower in high places — and after June 1944 Germany had to fight on French, Balkan and Eastern fronts as well as Italian.

All of which seemed in marked contrast to Allied fortunes. After the fall of Sicily, Allied commanders were a winning team on a roll, supported by predominantly welcoming Italians. Although the navy insisted on running its operations from Malta, Alexander and Tedder set an excellent example of jointery by collocating their headquarters at La Marsa on the coast northeast of Tunis. The major elements of the Mediterranean Air Command organisational tree on 1 September 1943 are shown in Table 2 (page 25).

Allied strategy in Italy had two aims — the elimination of Italy from the war, and containment of the maximum number of German divisions.[6] The mixing of a political with an indefinable military aim was not ideal, nor were recurring Anglo-US disagreements over the relative importance of the Italian Front. To Stalin, Churchill likened the effort in the Mediterranean to an attack on the 'soft underbelly' of a crocodile.[7] Victory in Sicily fired up the British to press forward around the whole eastern Mediterranean — both to suck more German troops into the region to reduce the numbers opposing the cross-Channel operation, and to entice Turkey to enter the war on the Allied side. The US chiefs on the other hand pointedly re-christened the cross-Channel invasion 'Overlord' to reinforce its pre-eminence, and they were particularly insistent on priority being given to the invasions of Normandy and the south of France in 1944. British talk of soft underbellies, and an implied reluctance to meet the Germans head-on, were seen as examples of Limey backsliding and prevarication.

None the less, inter-Allied and inter-service co-operation was tried and tested. Commanders had proved themselves in North Africa, since when they had enjoyed the fruits of Ultra intelligence. Ultra was derived from decrypting the radio traffic of the German armed forces, and it revealed timely information varying from Kesselring's strategic discussions with Hitler, right down to the movement of individual flying units to new bases.

'It is impossible to convey in words the wealth and variety of intelligence about German activities throughout the whole of the Mediterranean that poured into GHQ from [the Code and

Cypher School at] Bletchley . . . no previous commander was informed so extensively and so accurately as Alexander.' [8]

Turning to the numbers game, relative ground dispositions varied throughout the Italian campaign, but there was never any doubt about who was superior in the air. On the eve of the invasion of mainland Italy, the Allied air complement totalled 3,127, of which 1,395 were fighters and fighter-bombers, 461 heavy bombers, 162 medium night-bombers, 703 medium and light day-bombers and 406 transports. This left Mediterranean Air HQ with around 800 fewer aircraft than it had for the invasion of Sicily, and there was much wailing and gnashing of teeth over withdrawal of the heavies back to the UK to supplement the strategic bomber offensive against Germany. But the main reductions were in fighter provision, for which there seemed to be every justification.

Although von Richthofen beefed up the Luftflotte 2 command system and increased his aircraft strength by over 50% (440 aircraft) of which almost 60% were single-engined fighters,[9] none of this prevented the Luftwaffe from being driven out of Sicily at a very early stage. The reasons for this were depressingly clear. First, Axis fighter defences were just not up to the task; they were numerically inferior to the Allies, aircraft serviceability rates rarely bettered 50% compared with Allied 75%, early warning times had been much reduced with the loss of Pantelleria and Lampedusa, and Adolf Galland was no longer surrounded by pilots of comparable expertise. The Inspector of Fighters made the air defence of Sicily a personal matter, and he asked much of the fighter Gruppen in the south — demands that he himself and some

of the outstanding fighter pilots of 1940–41 might have been able to meet, but not those who were serving in Sicily in the summer of 1943. In the opinion of Luftflotte 2's Commander of Fighters, Maj-Gen Osterkamp, the 'old hands' were worn out by months of unbroken operations, the 'youngsters' lacked experience and were inadequately trained, and all were flying equipment inferior to that of the enemy.[10]

So when the Allies mounted massed bomber raids against German airfields — christened 'Reich Party Days' by their opponents — there was no stopping them. Lt Kohler, a pilot on 1/JG77, wrote:

'Towards noon (on 16 July) 105 bombers came and destroyed the Jagdgruppe Vibo Valentia, which had about 80 aircraft. Not a machine was left intact, not even the Ju which had just landed. Fuel trucks, hangars, aircraft, autos, everything was burning. The German fighters in Italy have been wiped out.'[11]

Richthofen came to the same conclusion in his diary: 'It is no longer possible to speak of orderly fighter control or relatively successful missions.'

The Luftwaffe was soon 'bombed out' of Sicily. 740 Axis aircraft were lost defending Sicilian skies, while 584 damaged or destroyed aircraft were abandoned on the ground, including 280 Bf109s, 70 FW190s and 80 Ju88s. Add to that the fact that 210 aircraft were moved from the theatre in August (mainly to the Western Front) and it is understandable why, reinforcements notwithstanding, Luftwaffe strength in the Mediterranean had

Left:
Field Marshal (*Generalfeldmarschall*) von Richthofen (centre) with Gen Buelowius (right) during a visit to Fliegerkorps II at Merate.
Author's Collection

shrunk to 880 by 3 September. Of these, only some 650 were available to Luftflotte 2, and the time in which to rebuild and recover would be even briefer than that between Tunisia and Sicily.

On 20 July, Adolf Galland returned to Germany after handing over control of fighter operations in Italy to Oberst Vick. At Vick's disposal were the remnants of eight Jagdgruppen, of which I and II/JG77 and III/JG53 were based in Calabria; II/JG53 and IV/JG3 in southern Apulia; I/JG53 and II and III/JG27 defended Naples and Foggia. Oberst Vick was on a hiding to nothing, and within nine days von Richthofen had sacked him, together with the Commander of Fighters Osterkamp. 'I have decided,' recorded the mercurial von Richthofen, 'to close the door on the entire fighter command business and subordinate the fighter units directly to II Fliegerkorps.'

On 10 August Gen Buelowius, Commanding General of II Fliegerkorps, was given 'strict orders concerning the fighters, which will finally now be sent against the enemy. At present the fighters just fly around and do not accept combat. It is Buelowius' job to get them back into combat again after the shock they received in Tunisia and Sicily.' Buelowius must have had mixed emotions about receiving such a poisoned chalice.

Once the Allies were firmly established in Sicily, Axis ground forces appeared to stand a chance only if the Luftwaffe could keep Allied air power off their backs. But this was never to be. Luftflotte 2 never had the time or opportunity to make good its losses in both machines and experienced personnel given the more pressing claims of other fronts. In the 12 months after July 1943, German front-line Mediterranean air strength shrank to 475 aircraft, while the Allies expanded their strength throughout the whole Mediterranean to some 7,000 aircraft, supported by 315,000 air and ground crews, by the end of 1943.

From mid-1943, Axis forces endured what John Terraine described as, 'the misery of trying to fight under a canopy of hostile air power; and this was to be the German soldier's hard lot for the rest of the war in the West'.[12] The Pantelleria experience implied that prolonged and continuous air attack would inevitably degrade ground force morale, especially as established air power wisdom was that, 'if we lose the war in the air, we lose the war and lose it quickly'.[13] On the face of it, therefore, the campaign against the 'soft underbelly' of the Axis should have been over by Christmas 1943. But because the crocodile had a hard skin all over, events did not work out that way.

Notes to Chapter 3

1. Macksey, K.; Kesselring; p.173.
2. Kesselring, A.; The Memoirs; p.162.
3. Deakin, F. W.; The Last Days of Mussolini; p.228.
4. The basic Luftwaffe flying unit was the Gruppe — about 30 aircraft — divided into three Staffeln (equivalent to an RAF squadron). Bomber and fighter units were organised into individual Geschwader (equivalent to an RAF Group) which normally comprised three Gruppen and represented, with its Stab (Staff) Flight, about 100 aircraft.
5. Kesselring, op. cit, p.176.
6. Combined Chiefs of Staff Memo 242/6, 25 May 1943.
7. Churchill, W. S.; The Hinge of Fate; p.393.
8. Lewin, R.; Ultra Goes To War; pp.286–87.
9. Many were FW190s transferred from harassing attacks against southern England.
10. Prien, J.; Jagdgeschwader 53; p.620.
11. Ibid, p. 642.
12. Terraine, J.; The Right of the Line; p.570.

Below:
A Kittyhawk is seen ready to taxi out from one of the network of landing grounds at Gerbini, Sicily, on 10 August 1943. *RAF Air Historical Branch*

SALERNO

'The difference between us and you is that you want to die for your Fatherland, while we want to live for America.'
American GI to German PoW

On 27 July, President Roosevelt offered the Italians honourable terms in exchange for capitulation. His words were echoed a few days later by Gen Eisenhower, who flavoured his broadcast with a sharp reminder that heavy air bombardment would follow if the Italians were slow to get off the fence.

A week passed and RAF Bomber Command mounted four heavy attacks on Milan; smaller raids also attacked Turin and Genoa. During the first of these, on 12/13 August, a No 218 Squadron Stirling from Downham Market in Norfolk was bounced by a night-fighter whose fire hit three of the four engines, shattered the windscreen, put both front and rear turrets out of action and damaged the elevator cables. The navigator was killed outright and the pilot, Flt Sgt A. L. Aaron, had his jaw smashed, part of his face

torn away, a lung perforated and his right arm broken. Arthur Aaron sat beside the bomb-aimer, who took over the controls, and showed him by writing directions with his left hand how to keep the crippled aircraft under control. For five hours, Aaron drifted in and out of consciousness until they sighted the flare path at Bone in North Africa. He summoned the last reserves of his strength to direct the bomb-aimer through the difficult task of night landing the crippled bomber with undercarriage retracted, at a strange airfield with 4,000lb of bombs still live on the racks. Nine hours after landing, Flt Sgt Aaron, a former architect who specialised in designing church interiors, died from exhaustion. He was awarded the Victoria Cross for 'an example of devotion to duty which has seldom been equalled and never surpassed'.

Below:
Southern Italy and the Salerno beachhead.

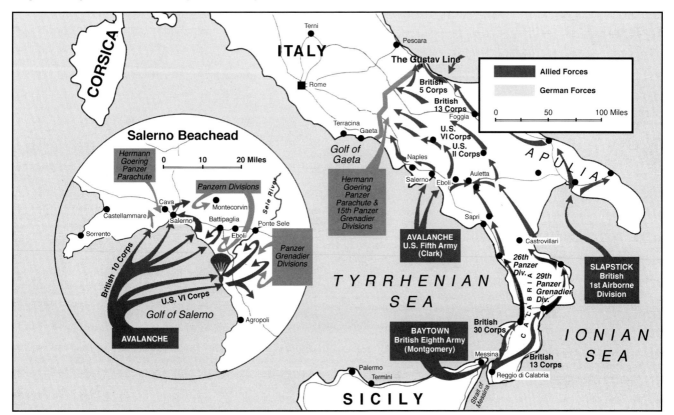

Left:
'When we were young.' Gp Capt Darwin (centre), CO of 239 Kittybomber Wing which operated out of Agnone, Sicily.
RAF Air Historical Branch

Below Left:
Lt-Gen Mark Clark, Commanding General Fifth Army (left), with Maj-Gen Matthew Ridgway, Commander 82nd US Airborne Division. For all the apparent appeal of using paratroops in the campaign for mainland Italy, most planned airborne operations after Sicily were still-born. Only a sadist would send lightly-equipped paratroops against hardened German defenders, and whenever the Germans were retreating there was either too much flak or, more often than not, any potential for successful airborne insertion was overtaken by the speed of events on the ground.
Author's Collection

Mussolini's successors hummed and hawed because they wanted a guaranteed Allied invasion force of at least 15 divisions, to arrive as if by magic north of Rome, to protect them from their former ally: it was the stuff of dreams. The entire seaboard of Italy and her islands might encompass 4,100 miles, but much of it was beyond reach. On 20 July, the chiefs of staff agreed that Italy was to be invaded immediately after Sicily had been captured, but amphibious operations were only to stretch to the limits of effective shore-based fighter cover. 'The key factor in the operation would be air protection,' wrote Eisenhower's planning staff, and the early capture of an airfield was top priority.[1]

The best that the Allies could aim for was to put three divisions ashore on the beaches around Salerno, a small port on the west coast of Italy 50 miles south of Naples: once established ashore, four fighter squadrons could fly into adjacent Monte Corvino airfield while Mark Clark's Fifth Army set about linking up with Montgomery's Eighth Army driving north from Calabria. But as only US P-38s with their huge belly tanks had the legs to reach that far north, the decision to go ahead could only be taken once five RN aircraft carriers were made available, and the British Air Ministry promised to provide drop tanks to enable its Spitfires to patrol the Salerno beaches for 30–40 minutes.

The Eighth Army crossing of the Straits of Messina — launched four years to the day after the outbreak of war between Britain and Germany — went by the book. 300 landing craft conveying the troops from Sicily were protected by menacingly-sounding Landing Craft Flak, Landing Craft Gun and Rocket Craft, while overhead the Desert Air Force flew constant Spitfire patrols. On the face of it, this effort was justified; 123 Axis fighters were

Table 2:

Higher organisation and chain of command of forces engaged in the invasion of Italy as at 3 September 1943.

MEDITERRANEAN AIR COMMAND
Commander and Air C-in-C: ACM Sir Arthur Tedder, RAF
Deputy Commander and CG NAAF: Maj-Gen Carl Spaatz, USAAF
Deputy Air C-in-C: AVM H. E. P. Wigglesworth, RAF

NORTHWEST AFRICAN AIR FORCE	MALTA AIR COMMAND	MIDDLE EAST AIR COMMAND
CG: Maj-Gen C. Spaatz, USAAF	AOC-in-C: AVM Sir K. Park, RAF	AOC-in-C: ACM Sir Sholto Douglas, RAF
Dep: AVM J. M. Robb, RAF		

NORTHWEST AFRICAN STRATEGIC AIR FORCE
CG: Maj-Gen J. H. Doolittle, USAAF

AIR DEFENCE EASTERN MEDITERRANEAN

NORTHWEST AFRICAN COASTAL AIR FORCE
AOC: AVM Sir H. P. Lloyd, RAF
Dep: Brig-Gen E. Quesada, USAAF

US NINTH AIR FORCE
CG: Maj-Gen L. H. Brereton, USAAF

NORTHWEST AFRICAN PHOTO-RECCE WING
CG: Col E. Roosevelt, USAAF
Dep: Wg Cdr E. Fuller, RAF

NORTHWEST AFRICAN TROOP CARRIER COMMAND
CG (temp): Brig-Gen R. Dunn, USAAF

NORTHWEST AFRICAN TRAINING COMMAND
CG: Col J. W. Monahan, USAAF

NORTHWEST AFRICAN TACTICAL AIR FORCE
AOC: AVM Sir A. Coningham, RAF
Dep: Maj-Gen J. K. Cannon, USAAF

Desert Air Force	XXII Air Support Command	Tactical Bomber Force
AOC: AVM H. Broadhurst, RAF	CG: Maj-Gen E. J. House, USAAF	AOC: Air Cdre L. P. Sinclair, RAF
		Dep: Col Lowe, USAAF

Left:
An FW190 of SKG10, carrying a 1,100lb bomb, being guided to the take-off point by an airman on each wing.

Below:
Bf109G-6s fitted with underwing 21cm mortars. *IWM*

scrambled to carry out freelance patrols and to escort 40 fighter-bombers, but the latter operated pretty ineffectively against the landings. But the Germans never had any intention of fighting for the strategically useless heel and toe of Italy: aerial delaying tactics were what really mattered, to allow Axis ground forces to withdraw in good order at their own pace to join the bulk of von Vietinghoff's Tenth Army contesting the Salerno landings.

Allied photographic reconnaissance soon showed large-scale enemy troop movements north, plus all enemy airfields in the neighbourhood having been abandoned; resistance was so negligible that, five days after the Eighth Army arrived on the mainland, two squadrons of Kittyhawks brought their bombs back for lack of anything worthwhile to hit. 'The day was dull in the extreme . . . there were no combats at all.'

The Germans weren't born yesterday. They knew that the beach gradients at Salerno were the most ideal on the west coast and that the moon was at its most favourable during the chosen period. They noted the progressive pattern of air attacks on radar sites and communications links in the south, and Axis air staff could calculate the limits of single-engined fighter range from Sicily as easily as their opposite numbers. Kesselring correctly judged that the invaders would land at Salerno, and 16th Panzer Division was deployed in the immediate vicinity. At the end of August, the Germans even staged an exercise simulating the repulse of a night landing on the Salerno beaches.

On 3 September, Allied intelligence estimated that Axis air forces in Italy and Sardinia consisted of 220 long-range and torpedo-bombers, 50 reconnaissance-bombers, and 266 fighters and fighter-bombers. Given known logistic problems, no more than half of these aircraft were expected to be serviceable at any one time. In response, the Allies planned to call on some 350 heavy bombers, 650 medium and light bombers, 160 fighter-bombers, 300 troop carriers, 40 tactical and fighter-reconnaissance aircraft, 352 fighters (including 32 night-fighters) and 110 carrier-borne Seafires.

The complex Allied air plan was ready by late August. Northwest African Air Forces, with some help from IX Bomber Command of the Ninth Air Force still stationed in North Africa, had primary responsibility for air superiority and interdiction. On and after the invasion itself, Coastal would protect shipping to within 40 miles of the beaches; Tactical would be responsible for the airspace after that. Desert Air Force was to continue its traditional collaboration with the Eighth Army by supporting the invasion of Calabria, while the US XII ASC would support Salerno. The Sicily-based TBF was to assist both operations.

The combined Allied air contribution to early attainment of the ground-pounders' objectives was expected to be three-fold. Before, during and after the assault, they had to 'neutralise' the enemy's air forces. Then they had to provide air cover for the convoys on their way to the beaches, the actual assaults, and the subsequent land fighting. Finally, forces not necessary for these missions, or freed by their progressive accomplishment, were to be directed against German lines of communication, which were expected to become the primary target.

Having ensured that the Salerno area was within range of Allied air cover, the next objective was to put it out of bounds to enemy fighters and bombers. Available Axis air strength may have fallen to around 650 but they were still a menace. On 17 August, upward of 90 Axis bombers had flown across the Mediterranean to attack invasion shipping at anchor in Bizerta. A week later, some 40–50 Ju88s and Do217s bombed Palermo harbour.

The Allied air plan provided for two squadrons of A-36s (the dive-bomber variant of the P-51 Mustang), 19 of Spitfires and four of Beaufighters, all from XII ASC, to provide inshore close air support for landing forces and air cover for the invasion fleet. When augmented by three Strategic Air Force groups of long-range P-38s, this gave a total of 528 day fighters and 32 night-fighters at normal rates of serviceability, which sounded impressive. However, only a small percentage could be orbiting over the beachhead at any daylight hour given the extreme distance from their Sicilian bases. It was to help offset this limitation that the British provided one fleet and four escort carriers with their 110 Seafires (the naval version of the Spitfire). Even so, there would only be an average of 54 aircraft over the Gulf of Salerno at any time during the day, and the air planners feared that this would prove inadequate if the Luftwaffe attacked resolutely.

The counter lay in hitting German airfields. Most of the He111 torpedo-bombers were based at Salon, just north of Marseilles, but it was deemed much more important to deny the Luftwaffe the use of eight important airfields within 110 miles' range of Salerno, plus three others just beyond.[2] From 18 August to 2 September, Strategic Air Force was tasked to drive the Luftwaffe out of range of Salerno by attacking central and southern Italian airfields. Of

these, Strategic went straight for the greatest threat — the Foggia complex on the eastern side of Italy. The main Foggia airfield, with its 1,250yd and 1,100yd runways plus 17 aircraft shelters, stood two miles outside Foggia town. Around it were no less than nine satellites, all growing in importance.[3]

On 3 September, a wave of Fortresses was met by a mixed swarm of some 70 Bf109s, Bf110s, FW190s, Macchi 202s and 200s, and Reggiani 2001s, all of which attacked vigorously. It was do or die to protect these crucial airfields, and it was all too often die. Wave after wave of B-17s — 130-plus at a time, escorted by P-38s — dropped nearly 15,000 fragmentation bombs in half an hour. Post-attack photographs showed a bag of 48 enemy aircraft destroyed. Not surprisingly, the German Army based its defensive plans on the premise that effective support of the army by the navy or air force could not be expected.

When German defenders achieved any success against Allied raids, it was usually down to luck. On 25 August, 136 B-17s and 140 P-38s blasted Cancello, inflicting severe damage and destroying 28 aircraft on the ground. At around 10.00hrs, some 50 P-38s passed low over what remained of Cancello heading for the Foggia complex. By chance, a JG77 fighter pair led by Maj Johannes Steinhoff was airborne nearby on a practice flight. Five P-38s were shot down, four of them by Steinhoff.

But there would be fewer such masterclasses in future because the Luftwaffe was running out of experts to lead them. III/JG53 lost all three of its veteran Staffelkapitäne (squadron leaders) in short order, and there were just not the replacements to lead and inspire during the difficult battles ahead. By mid-September, only three out of nine JG53 Staffelkapitäne had been in place for more than three months, none wore the Knight's Cross once commonly expected of a Staffelkapitän, and fewer and fewer likely young lieutenants were going to live long enough to take over from them at the right time.

Meanwhile, the energetic Col (Oberst) Peltz sent KG26 and KG100 from France down to central Italy to bolster an all-out bomber effort. Countering Axis air was not easy, even though the Allies possessed numerical superiority. The weather often prevented accurate bomb aiming, and as soon as it knew trouble was coming, the German command and control system was flexible and responsive enough to put many aircraft out of harm's way through the cunning use of dispersed landing strips. A great raid on 3 September by B-17s and P-38s against the Grazzanise fighter landing grounds managed to account for only one Fieseler Storch communications aircraft — and many a well-cratered field showed up 24 hours later on the aerial prints as having been levelled and being back in the flying business. In the end, it was not bombing which forced German airmen to withdraw their aircraft; only the imminent arrival of Allied ground troops on their doorstep was guaranteed to do that.

The last attempt to cripple Foggia before the Salerno landings came on 7 September. Bizerta had been attacked again the previous day by 79 German bombers, 11 days after 40 had gone for Algiers, and although neither effort proved fruitful, they stung the Allies into sending 147 B-17s against Satellites 1 and 2. Three of the four bomber groups ran into aggressive opposition from 50-60 Bf109s and FW190s. Some came in to 300yd range, and the interceptors fought the bomber streams for upwards of half an hour, losing 37 of their number for the loss of two Fortresses. But the mere fact that the enemy could still mount such opposition after weeks of concentrated Allied efforts to drive them from the skies, showed how difficult it was to destroy even large enemy air formations on the ground when the airfields were large, the aircraft were skilfully dispersed and the weather was bad. As if to cock a snook at the Allied efforts to date, as soon as the Salerno assault got under way, all German fighter and fighter-bomber units were concentrated at Foggia to co-ordinate striking power; throughout the Salerno landings, Foggia served as the base for all the fighter units of the German close-support forces, as well as a large number of Ju88 bombers.

To climax their work to date, 131 B-17s attacked German operational HQ in the beautiful vineyard town of Frascati, some 33 miles north of Salerno. Army and Luftflotte 2 commands were both there, and the aim was to paralyse this nerve centre just before the landing. Flak was intense and accounted for one Fortress. Battle was joined by some 40 Axis fighters, which came off second best to the B-17s' defensive armament. Damage among the HQ villas was considerable, and around 80 Luftwaffe headquarters staff were killed, though Kesselring himself escaped unscathed. The crucial signals network was disrupted — but within six hours the staffs were back in control of their forces. The only drawback with such pointed aerial activity was that it did not take the brains of a German rocket scientist to recognise that the invasion was about to begin.

*   *   *   *

Three main Allied invasion convoys left Oran, Tripoli and Bizerta. By first light on 8 September, Luftwaffe reconnaissance aircraft had a clear view of them passing Sicily. The Bizerta convoy was attacked by FW190s and Ju88s off Capri during the afternoon. At Frascati, Kesselring tried to reconcile separate reconnaissance reports. When confirmation came through that the invasion fleet was steaming through the night for Salerno, Kesselring had only nine hours to make his dispositions. It was enough. The Germans were able to take over all the coastal defences from the Italians who, as one German officer noted, 'threw their weapons away and showed their joy that the war was now over for them'. That evening, acceleration of the German withdrawal from Calabria was ordered, with the emphasis on saving flak batteries. At Hitler's Supreme HQ, Chief of Operations Staff Gen Jodl noted that 'the most urgent problem is to get Tenth Army and the Luftwaffe out of southern Italy'.[4]

At 20.15hrs on 8 September, the first flares illuminated the fleet. In swept the largest long-range German bomber effort seen in that theatre for a long time — 158 aircraft including 25 torpedo-bombers. New blood had been added from the two Geschwader from the south of France, but the controller made the fundamental error of vectoring his bombers onto the heavily-armed warships rather than the much more vulnerable troopships. Fighters and anti-aircraft gunners ensured that 18 fewer German aircraft returned to base than left it.

At 03.45hrs on 9 September 1943, the US 36th Division landed on the right of the Salerno beaches, while the British 46th and 56th Divisions landed on the left. Very little enemy air action was encountered on the first day — just five attacks by small formations of FW190s and Bf109s in the morning, and never more than four attackers at a time in the afternoon. In essence, Luftwaffe attacks on the beachhead lacked the weight of numbers to put the air defenders under any great pressure. The Allies mounted an aerial layer cake of A-36s between 5,000–7,000ft, P-38s between 10,000–14,000ft and a mixture of British and American Spitfires and Fleet Air Arm Seafires as top cover. Shore-based aircraft had come from airfields as far away as central Sicily (up to 220 miles distant) and they could only maintain 25-minute patrols over the beaches by using long-range jettisonable fuel tanks. At night, protection duties were taken over by AI (Airborne Intercept) radar-equipped Beaufighters from Sicily.

Yet although Luftwaffe efforts against the beachhead were at best half-hearted, the Germans had not lost the power to make an impact. On the eve of the Salerno landing, the Italian government finally severed its 52-month Pact of Steel with Germany. In accordance with the armistice conditions, the main body of the Italian fleet set sail from La Spezia and Genoa for Malta under the command of its new C-in-C, Adm Bergamini. Three battleships, six cruisers and eight destroyers followed a route to the west of Corsica and Sardinia laid down by the Allies, but on reaching the Straits which separate the islands, course was altered east for no definite reason.

Shortly before 16.00hrs on 9 September, Adm Bergamini swung his force back west just as 11 Do217s made their appearance. The Do217K was designed for the night-bomber role, and in December 1942 the K2 version made its debut designed specifically to carry the FX 1400 FritzX stand-off missile. 23 Do217K2s belonging to II/KG100 were dispatched that day in three formations from Istres airfield near Marseilles. Believing the Do217s to be Allied aircraft, the Italians were slow to take countermeasures. In their defence, the Do217s would have been high in the sky because the unpowered 3,000lb FritzX — it looked like a normal free-fall bomb apart from four stabilising stub-wings midway along its body — relied on simply accelerating under gravity to close on the speed of sound to penetrate large warship armour. The missile was released using the normal bombsight, after which the pilot put his Do217 into a climb to drag the speed back from 290mph to 165mph to keep the bomb-aimer lined-up with both missile and target. The Exocet of its day had a tracking flare in its tail, and the observer used this to help him radio-control the missile in its final 10–15 seconds to impact.

FritzX was very crude compared with Gulf War hardened aircraft shelter-busting, but it was no less effective for that. The Italian flagship, Roma, was hit near the forward magazine, causing a fire. The crew fought the blaze for about 20 minutes before the magazine blew, taking the 35,000-ton battleship, Adm Bergamini and most of the crew to the bottom.

*   *   *   *

Serviceable German close-support forces on the first day of the Salerno invasion totalled 98.[5] The bomb-toting FW190s of SKG10

(Schnellkampfgeschwader or fast bomber wing) relied on speed to penetrate defensive fighter screens. Mortar Staffeln were another German attempt to offset growing numerical inferiority by cunning ingenuity. During the Italian campaign, the German Army made particular use of an impressive piece of kit known as the Nebelwerfer to fire volleys of solid-fuel rockets. The Bf109G6/R2 variant was modified to carry a pair of these heavy 21cm mortars, one under each wing. On 10 September 1943, elements of II/JG53 were sent against the Allied landings first thing in the morning. 'Approaching from the south,' wrote Uffz Robert Gugelberger in his diary, 'we attacked landing boats with our rocket machines. I saw my two rockets land right between two landing craft. We engaged Mustangs, Lightnings and Spitfires. Four aircraft shot down, two losses of our own.'

Mortar-equipped Bf109s suffered from many shortcomings: the flight path of the unguided projectile was rather unpredictable because there was no aiming device, range calculation for setting the rocket's time fuses was 'purely a matter of feel', and the electrics were sufficiently rudimentary to cause many rockets to fail. Pilots such as Gugelberger had good cause to view the new 'wonder weapon' with considerable suspicion when employed in the Pulk-zerstörer, or 'formation destroyer' role, shortly before the Salerno invasion.

'09.00hrs cockpit readiness. I have a rocket machine. 13.04hrs scramble, direction Naples. Rail station south of Vesuvius under attack by strong enemy formation. We climbed to 6,000m; the enemy formation is at 4,500m. Over land about 40 Lightnings in two groups and about 60 twin-engined bombers also in two groups. Then the bombers turned towards the sea. When I heard the call "launchers clear", I switched on the special armament and released the safety. Lightnings behind us, 500m lower — I turned towards the target, aimed well in front and fired both rockets. A brief flash of fire and both of the things blasted off. They shot towards the enemy formation at great speed, but unfortunately they exploded short of the target in large clouds of black smoke. After launching our rockets we climbed and tackled the Lightnings. I got in several bursts while diving, but they were flying a perfect defensive circle which made it hard to do much. After a general dogfight well out to sea, we turned around and soon saw land. At 14.15 we landed on our last drops of fuel.'[6]

Because the mortars could be fired from outside the range of the B-17s' 50-calibre guns, the sight of 'rocket-type shells leaving a trail of white smoke' gave the bomber boys something extra to worry about, and could prove formidably effective in the right circumstances.

In the face of 796 Allied beach patrol sorties on the first day, the 98 available Luftwaffe aircraft could not cover all commitments, so, like the Argentinians in the 1982 Falklands Conflict, they concentrated on the ships offshore. Formations of 10 Ju88 or Do217 bombers, escorted by four to six Bf109s, made seven separate attacks on shipping, and on one of these in the morning of 11 September, the US cruisers Philadelphia and Savannah were each damaged by FritzX bombs, the latter seriously. In the afternoon, another radio-controlled bomb hit the British destroyer Uganda without warning.

FritzX came as a nasty surprise to the Allies, and it made a telling point about air power. In modern management parlance, what matters is 'value added'. To pit a handful of Do217s against a host of Seafires was a poor play. Far better to threaten the aircraft carriers themselves, especially as the Royal Navy was still scarred by the loss of the Prince of Wales and Repulse to Japanese air attack. And it worked. The day after the Philadelphia, Savannah and Uganda were hit, the Royal Navy withdrew all five carriers from the fray. As it happened, the carrier-based fighters had enjoyed limited success, in part because the FW190 could outrun the Seafire, but also because the Germans were able to jam the three controlling radio frequencies. But the tactics were exemplary: in forcing the carriers back to Malta and away from guided-bomb attack, the Luftwaffe drove them out of range of the beachhead. That was pretty impressive 'leverage' from a handful of radio-guided bombs.

*　　　*　　　*　　　*

In September 1943, Salerno was a minor industrial centre, a fishing port and a market for locally grown oranges, tomatoes, chestnuts, tobacco, olive oil and wine. All these were cultivated on the level plain which Allied troops moved across as they left the beaches. At the eastern edge of this plain, some three miles inland, lay Monte Corvino airfield, the capture of which was an important part of the invasion plan. From the Allied perspective, the beaches were ideally suited for an amphibious operation; the bad news was that the whole plain was dominated by surrounding hills and mountains, and the Germans held this high ground.

During the first three days of Salerno, Allied troops advanced 10 miles inland and the fight seemed to be going Alexander's way; but it was touch and go, as typified by the struggle for control of Monte Corvino airfield. It was occupied on the second day by 3202 Servicing Commando, RAF, who began stocking fuel and ammunition. It was then retaken by the Germans, and although it fell back into Allied hands late on 11 September, the airfield was unsafe to use until 20 September.

The great spanner in the Salerno works was the failure of Montgomery's Eighth Army to join up with Clark's Fifth as planned. On the very day of the Salerno landings, Monty reported that he was halting way to the south to improve his lines of communication. On 10 September, he received an anxious signal from Alexander, in effect urging Monty to disregard administrative niceties and hurry to Clark's aid. This had no effect, so Alexander sent his chief of staff to Montgomery on 12 September to re-emphasise the need for haste. That very day, the 29th Panzer Grenadier Division, and what remained of the 15th and 16th Panzer Divisions, resolutely emerged out of the foothills. Behind the advancing Panzers, gun batteries provided accurate fire support from the overlooking heights. By the end of the following day, Allied troops had been forced back and the Germans had almost achieved their aim of cutting the beachhead in half — and

Montgomery's Eighth Army would be in no position to help for at least another five days.

Back at the Allied command post near Tunis, it was clear that the situation had passed from 'causing grave anxiety' to 'critical'. Tedder, turning to Alexander, promised all the aid the air could muster, as did the navy. While Allied naval forces maintained a fierce bombardment of German positions, the whole weight of available Allied air power, including all the strategic bombers, was directed against the German counter-attacks.

Fighters and fighter-bombers sped up and down the battlefield from dawn to dusk, reaching a crescendo of more than 700 sorties flown against targets of opportunity. In parallel, heavy and medium bombers of the Northwest African Air Forces continued to attack roads, railway junctions and bridges to prevent reinforcements from reaching the battle zone from either north or south. On 13 September, 91 Wellingtons tore up a five-mile stretch of road to the east of Pompeii with 164 tons of bombs. A single Ju88 was rash enough to try and interfere but it could not stop another 23 B-25s from coming in to bomb the roads again. The old city of Pompeii received slight damage, its first since AD79: 'it was not even safe among the ruins', lamented an unhappy inhabitant.

The main thrust came the following day, when over 1,200 bomber sorties of all categories were flown. Just as importantly, apart from 37 B-24s sent to the Pescara marshalling yards, every target in the day's effort was in the battle area; certain areas received as many as 760 tons of bombs per square mile. Until then, Mark Clark's requests for direct support through his air liaison staff had seldom been accepted, and when they had, the air force response had been slow. It had taken the humiliating prospect of the Fifth Army being pushed back into the sea to persuade the USAAF to come to Clark's aid, and raise the daily mission rate from 66 to 587. It was a measure of the desperate situation that the P-38s which had been providing air cover over the beachhead were sent to strafe on or about the battlefield, even though the Luftwaffe was still flying 100 or more sorties a day against the invasion fleet.

The reason why, up to then, Clark's troops had been given what they perceived to be every assistance short of actual help, was because senior airmen thought that the best service they could give the army was to isolate the battlefield. Contemporary intelligence estimated that 96% of Italy's oil and 80% of her coal were imported by rail, and it was only by rail that large numbers of German troops could be brought quickly from points north. Consequently, the principal Strategic Air Force interdiction mission was to attack communications north of the Sapri-Trebisacce line in order to slow the movement of reserves southward to Salerno. Closer to the action, the two main road junctions through which German men and arms flooded into the fray were Battipaglia and Eboli. At 09.36hrs on 14 September, 58 B-25s — followed three hours later by 38 B-17s — bombed Battipaglia heavily. Then 77 B-26s and B-17s went for the stretch between Battipaglia and Eboli, while Eboli itself was progressively destroyed throughout the day by Mitchells and Marauders. On the night shift, the largest formation of night-bombers to date in the Mediterranean theatre was dispatched, dropping 237 tons of bombs on Battipaglia and Eboli.

The Luftwaffe responded as best it could, but as in Sicily it was overwhelmed. In the opinion of General of Bombers Werner Baumbach, those raids which did get off 'were and remained no more than pinpricks'.[7] By 15 September, the Germans had lost 221 aircraft; the Allies had lost 89. Air superiority allowed the Allies to mount 17,500 sorties and drop 10,000 tons of bombs between 1–15 September, and fly about 1,400 bomber sorties on 15 September alone. Over the most crucial three days and nights, Allied air dropped over 2,300 tons of bombs on the Salerno battlefield or its approaches, while the navy mounted 129 bombardments of land targets. It was enough. In the late afternoon of 16 September, Gen von Vietinghoff's war diary recorded sorrowfully that his attacks,

'. . . although well-equipped and carried out with spirit, had been unable to reach their objective, owing to the fire from naval guns and low flying aircraft, as well as the slow but steady approach of the Eighth Army. This caused the Army Commandant to withdraw from the battle.'

Offshore, the battleship HMS Warspite was proceeding north towards Salerno Bay when she was attacked by 10 FW190s. While Warspite's air defences were suckered into concentrating on the FW190s, three radio-controlled bombs suddenly appeared overhead at 6,000–8,000ft and then dived vertically onto the battleship. One bomb hit, penetrated No 4 boiler room, and burst. By 15.00hrs, all boiler rooms had filled with water and all steam failed. The sight of Warspite being towed sideways back to Malta underlined the fact that, although the Germans might be about to be driven out of Salerno, they were still a force to be reckoned with.

Notes to Chapter 4
1. AFHQ Planning Papers, 24 and 25 July 1943.
2. Naples/Capodichino, Naples/Pomigliano d'Arco, Monte Corvino, Grazzanise, Capua, Aquino, Foggia and Scalea; the extra trio were Frosinore, Bari and Gioia delle Colle.
3. On the first day of the Salerno invasion, Foggia housed the following units: I and II/KG1; II/KG30; III/KG54; I and II/KG100 and the Lehr (Tactical Development Unit) of II/KG1.
4. Operations Staff War Diary, 8 September 1943.
5. III/SKG10, 8 aircraft; II/SKG10, 19 aircraft; Stab JG77, 2 aircraft; I/JG77, 14 aircraft; IV/JG3, 7 aircraft; Mortar Staffel/JG3, 7 aircraft; I/JG53, 14 aircraft; II/JG53, 11 aircraft; Mortar Staffel/JG53, 4 aircraft; III/JG53, 12 aircraft.
6. Prien, op.cit, p.674.
7. Baumbach, W.; Broken Swastika; p.142.

SEE NAPLES, AND DIE

'It was a mixed day of planes, one moment Jerry, then the RAF, then Jerry. The Ack-Ack boys took no chances and fired at the lot.'
Lance-Bombardier Spike Milligan

Under Allied air cover, at a cost of around 150 aircraft plus another 99 damaged, more than 200,000 troops, 100,000 tons of supplies and 30,000 motor vehicles landed on mainland Italy. That was no mean force, and when the first elements of the Fifth and Eighth Armies met on 16 September, ruined Battipaglia and Eboli fell to the Allies shortly afterwards. Against stiff opposition, Allied troops pushed through the hills and then swept across the Vesuvius plain, enabling the King's Dragoon Guards to enter Naples at 09.30hrs on 1 October. Across on the east coast, 1st Airborne entered Bari on

14 September, and Foggia fell just under a fortnight later. The two Allied armies only halted when the Fifth reached the next German defensive line along the banks of the Volturno River and the Eighth was opposite Termoli.

In parallel, the Allies retook Sardinia and Corsica because it would have been unwise to leave the Luftwaffe free to operate out of these island bastions on the left flank. The 325th was the only single-engined US fighter group in the Northwest African Strategic Air Force, and Sardinia was the only target within range of their

Below:
Inter-Allied co-operation. Sgt C. L. L. Sherbrooke (centre), an RAF Beaufighter navigator, discusses local flying conditions with French Spitfire pilots in Corsica, 23 November 1943. *RAF Air Historical Branch*

North Africa-based P-40 Warhawks after the fall of Sicily. General Doolittle told the 325th to go to it and fly a mission every day over Sardinia, aiming to shoot down the enemy's aircraft, harass and destroy his facilities, and disrupt his communications.[1] Capt John Watkins recorded:

'Ours was strictly a gentleman's war. We set our own time and place to fight. We ranged up and down the island, staging dogfights in the best Hollywood style when we — by dropping fragmentation bombs on their aerodromes — made their fighters mad enough to come up and fight us. We dive-bombed power stations, bridges and factories, strafed air raid warning stations and enemy ships whenever one of them attempted a rare dash down the coast in daylight.'[2]

On 11 September, as all Sardinian airfields were reported demolished, some 60 Allied bombers and 20 fighters took-off for the island, hoping to find the Germans evacuating. As it happened, they intercepted and shot down seven bombers, but by 17 September the Luftwaffe had withdrawn from Sardinia to concentrate on Corsica.

Despite the odds being stacked against them, the Germans planned and carried out another tactical triumph in Corsica — the systematic evacuation by air and sea of 30,000 personnel and over 600 tons of matériel between 16 September and 3 October. There was no ground support on offer because every fighter-bomber had been pulled too far back, but Fliegerführer Corsica admirably fulfilled his remit to supervise the airlift operation, redeploy his aircraft and control the island's flak operations. To take one example, 36 B-24s were sent to render Borgo aerodrome unusable. But the close-grouped 88mm flak batteries disturbed the bomb-aimers' concentration, and the airfield was back in use again that evening.

On 23 September, a formation of Beaufighters ran into 40 lumbering Ju52s and accounted for eight. 'From my tent,' wrote Gen Frido von Senger und Etterlin, 'I saw the air transports being shot down over the sea and watched the raids on my extempore airstrips.'[3] But from 29 September, a continuous German fighter patrol was maintained over the sea on both flanks of the main Ju52 route from Corsica to Leghorn. Air and sea routes cleared 3,000 men a day.

*   *   *   *

Gen Alexander had already been told that the Mediterranean would now be secondary to the northwest European and Pacific theatres. Seven of his divisions would be withdrawn to the UK, to be progressively replaced by French divisions. His bomber strength would be reduced by some 170 aircraft by December, and there was to be a significant withdrawal of troop-carrying aircraft and assault shipping for more pressing invasions. In other words, Alexander had to 'go for it' while he could, and on 21 September he briefed his commanders that they were to press forward with the aim not only of securing Rome, its airfields and road and rail centres by 7 November, but also of taking Florence and securing the entrances to the Po Valley three weeks later.

It has been argued that it would have made much more military sense for the Germans to abandon Italy south of the defensible mountains between Pisa and Rimini, and Greece and the Aegean south of a line running east-west through Salonika. The Central Powers held this position very successfully during World War 1, and if the Germans had hunkered down here, they could have concentrated on holding the Eastern Front and Normandy in the hope that a new generation of wonder weapons would arrive to save them. But the great change since 1918 had been the development of the credible strategic bomber. Kesselring the pilot, tried repeatedly to explain to Berlin what possession of the Apulian air bases meant in the battle for Germany, arguing that 'with every step the Allies advanced towards the north the conditions for an air war on southern Germany improved'.[4] Yet such was the pace of the Eighth Army's advance after Salerno that German bomber aircraft were forced to withdraw from the Foggia complex on 19 September.

Hitler was still wavering about whether to make a stand in the north or south. In his diary entry for 10 September, Propaganda Minister Dr Göbbels wrote 'naturally we shall not be able to hold southern Italy. We must withdraw northward and . . . establish ourselves on the defence line that the Führer has always envisaged, namely the line of the Apennine Mountains.'

Consequently, the Oberkommando der Wehrmacht (OKW) — the German high command under Hitler's direct control — refused to release a single division from northern Italy for the task of defending Foggia. The 1st Parachute Division of LXXVI Panzer Corps hung on as best they could, but the area was too vast and the paratroopers too lightly equipped to cope with armour; they destroyed the important installations and left on 27 September, the same day that the Eighth arrived. The Foggia Plain — the only large mass of level ground in spiny Italy south of the Po Valley — was now set to become the Allies' terrestrial aircraft carrier. Henceforward, from Lincolnshire and Foggia, Allied bomber spokes would radiate outwards over every part of the Reich except, ironically, the ostensible cause of the war in Europe, Danzig. To Kesselring, the loss of the Apulian airfields 'was a terrible blow'.[5]

As it happened, 'all our plans were changed by the situation in the Balkans,' wrote Gen Walter Warlimont, Deputy Chief of Wehrmacht Operations Staff.[6] Hitler took to commentating on the importance of the Romanian oilfields and Balkan mineral deposits to the Reich war effort on an almost daily basis, and the more he dwelt on holding the Balkans and Aegean islands, the more he became insistent on denying Italy as an Allied springboard to attack across the Adriatic. In parallel, Hitler held to the view that if Anglo-US forces were given a bloody nose in Italy, they might think twice about mounting an invasion across the English Channel. On 1 October, Hitler finally decided that the defence of Italy should be conducted much further south than the shortest front on the Apennines.

All of which explained why, when Allied troops waded ashore at Salerno, there were 14 German divisions in Italy, and by the end of October this had risen to 25. The Führer finally opted for pooling Army Groups B and C and, given the way in which Kesselring had given the Allies a scare at Salerno, it is not surprising that Hitler formally confirmed him as C-in-C Southwest. With his two armies — von Vietinghoff's Tenth and the Fourteenth under Eberhard von Mackensen — 'Smiling Albert' ushered in almost six months of attritional warfare to the south of Rome.

*   *   *   *

From the Axis standpoint, it was a pity that Hitler's decision to stand and fight for southern Italy came just after his forces had lost the Apulian airfields: the divisions held back in northern Italy could have made a real difference. But Luftflotte 2 HQ had seen the loss of the Foggia complex coming a month before, and had ordered the beefing-up of north Italian bases to convert them into Festungen (fortresses) ready to receive the long-range bombers. Built by the Organisation Todt along the lines of the interlocking Malta system, these vast super-airfields consisted of concrete runways, interlinked with innumerable taxi tracks and sub-taxi tracks, to allow aircraft to be moved from one field to another or to be dispersed away from bomb dumps and workshops.

By 21 September, what remained of Axis fighter and fighter-bomber units had withdrawn at least as far north as Rome and Viterbo. Shortly after III/JG53 arrived at Ciampino, Capt Jürgen Harder wrote that:

'. . . we received a heavy blow . . . The English came in four columns of heavy bombers and destroyed the whole Gruppe. Saboteurs had cut the telephone lines and we received no warning. Suddenly we heard the aircraft over us and then came the bombs. It was frightful to lie on the ground with no cover while bombs rained down on the airfield.'

Eight pilots were injured, one fatally: 14 Bf109s were hit and at least seven had to be written off. 'We have been literally bombed out.'[7] JG53's II Gruppe fared little better:

'During the night the Tommies chased us from our nest with the rumble of bombs — it went on without let-up for an hour and a half . . . They blasted Littoria airfield — how did they learn of it so quickly?'

If only the Germans had known about Ultra!

Not that Allied airmen had everything their own way. During their time in support of the Italian invasion from North Africa, the 97th Bombardment Group (BG) and its B-17s were typical in having to live with sand and dust.

'Engine after engine failed to function properly . . . the job seemed never ending, for as fast as an engine was torn down for repairs, more sand and dust would find their way into the intricate mechanism . . . supply failed to keep up with demand and within a month, the 97th found its efforts in the war seriously hampered. At one time more than 25 airplanes sat on the ground lacking engines.'[8]

The greater part of US and RAF fighter units was operating from mainland airfields by 25 September, which set them up nicely for the heavy winter rains which began on 3 October. Thereafter, 'General Mud' assumed command. Bypasses round road demolitions were reduced to a gooey swamp in which vital tanks, field artillery and ammunition vehicles sank. In the Fifth Army sector, the Volturno River was 150–300ft wide and anything up to 6ft deep in mid-stream. But at the very time that the Fifth Army wanted to cross, the current was swift and the icy stream swollen by daily rains. In such circumstances, and facing battle-hardened opponents, it took 10 days' fighting of 'unparalleled ferocity' before the Allies took and held the Volturno line.

The role of Allied tactical air remained unaltered: fighters and fighter-bombers were to pave the way for the army's advance, while the bombers were to attack German reinforcement routes leading to the front. On 1/2 October, 160 US Tomahawks prepared the ground for an Eighth Army landing at Termoli on the Adriatic, by bombing and strafing troops and vehicles on roads north and west of the town. During the landing on 3 October and the day after, fighter-bombers with some help from B-25s hammered German traffic despite bad weather. Fighters and fighter-bombers then went flat out to help the Eighth hold onto the bridgehead against a series of hard German counter-attacks, and over the crucial 5/6 October, Spitfires and Warhawks of the RAF and US 57th and 79th Fighter Groups flew around 950 sorties over the battle area. They broke up the main enemy concentration, struck hard against road traffic, flew direct support missions over the battle line and protected ground troops from Luftwaffe raids. 'Without their efforts,' wrote the official history, 'it is doubtful that the bridgehead could have been saved.'[9] After the crisis had passed, Warhawks bombed the German escape route through Palata.

In general terms, light bombers operated over a belt of ground between eight and 39 miles ahead of Fifth Army, while the mediums concentrated on the stretch 13–24 miles distant. Although bad weather affected continuity, the army was grateful for whatever it got. On 6 October, 34 missions were flown against troop movements and tanks around Termoli, resulting in claims of 84 enemy vehicles destroyed and 113 damaged. 'Many thanks for the terrific effort you put up today,' signalled 78th Division enthusiastically to Desert Air Force HQ; 'jolly good show!'

On nights such as 12/13 October, 46 Wellingtons tried to hole rail bridges to hinder German reinforcements reaching the battle area; supplemented in daylight by Kittyhawks, Marauders, Baltimores and Mustangs going for anything that moved if it looked like menacing Allied river crossings.[10] About one in six bomber formations met German fighter opposition, but the wide numerical margin of Allied air strength cleared all before it. It was only when clouds and rain clamped down that effective flying stopped. Foul weather was a 'double-whammy': it made advancing even harder over difficult terrain, and it often rendered air superiority, on which so many Allied hopes rested, largely irrelevant.

By early November, Mark Clark's Fifth Army was along the Garigliano River, while Montgomery's Eighth was up against the

flooded banks of the Sangro. The weather was awful. The US 79th Fighter Group, providers of fighter-bomber and strafing services to the Eighth Army, typified what everyone was up against. As they moved on 19 November into muddy Madna (a coastal airfield hacked out of the lowlands just south of Termoli), trucks bogged down, clothes became crusted with layers of mud and the tent area was surrounded with water.

'It was a lousy place, the worst they had ever encountered. Everyone sort of came apart. By the end of December, morale was the worst since leaving for overseas; men rarely washed — it was too cold — and most of the food was canned and dreary . . . The runway, which ran uphill (take-offs were downhill, landings uphill, regardless of wind direction) had been covered with a narrow strip of PSP matting,[11] but dispersal areas were still knee-deep in a sea of sticky gumbo . . . With the almost incessant rain, it was a rare day when the 79th could get their P-40s off the ground, so when the weather broke slightly near the end of November, everything that could fly was put into the air to support Monty's attack across the Sangro.'[12]

For five days in mid-November, over 700 US Invaders and Warhawks were launched in support of the Fifth Army, protected by over 800 RAF and US Spitfire sorties. Across in the east, the Warhawks of the 79th flew a total of 277 sorties against enemy gun positions between Orsogna and Ortona, but the clearing skies brought the Luftwaffe out as well.

Six Warhawks were over the bomb-line on 30 November when they spotted 10 FW190s low on the deck strafing British motor transport. Col George Lee, CO of 87th Fighter Squadron, led the charge as four P-40s jettisoned their bombs and dived into the enemy formation. Lee got behind a 190 and chased it over the mountains halfway to Rome before he got in close enough to shoot it down into a ravine. Two other FW190s had got on Lee's tail in the meantime, but Lt Jack Wainwright took care of one of them and scared the other off. Meanwhile, two Warhawks were working over some 88mm gun positions when Lt Edwin Job's aircraft was hit by over-enthusiastic British anti-aircraft fire; he managed to bale out at 500ft. To add insult to injury, Canadian Spitfires made a pass at George Lee's flight as they wended their weary way home. Later in the day the group had another narrow escape when a flight of mediums dropped their entire bomb load through a formation of P-40s belonging to the 87th. 'Friendly fire' casualties in the heat of battle were one of the saddest aspects of the air war over Italy.

Up to October, it is not being unkind to say that 'the Eighth Army had stumbled up the comparatively open and unencumbered east coast of Italy'.[13] Montgomery's army was doing business in the way that had served it so well in North Africa, including the system for describing battlefield targets that the infantry wanted Desert Air Force to attack. This task fell to ground-based air liaison officers at all wing and group HQs and with the mobile operations room; when a target had been accepted by DAF and Army Area HQs, the air liaison officer briefed the squadrons detailed to carry out the operation.

Such an arrangement worked fine over open sandy deserts, but in the much more rugged and closer-combat Italian theatre, faster and more precise responses were needed. The answer came from David Heysham, Wg Cdr Operations at HQ DAF, who created the mobile observation post in a lorry, or jeep and trailer, situated with the forward troops at brigade HQ and in direct VHF communication with aircraft already airborne. The same photographic map with a grid superimposed upon it was used by both pilots and controllers. A 'cab rank' of 6, 12 or 18 fighter-bombers would patrol overhead, usually in line astern, for 20 minutes. If they heard nothing, the formation attacked the pre-selected target. If, however, the army called for an attack on a more worthwhile target that was giving them grief, one or more aircraft from the 'cab rank' would dive down to bomb or strafe with cannon.

This system, known as 'Rover David' after its creator, proved an instant success. Fixed or moving targets could be attacked within minutes of being chosen, and German officers complained in writing about the way in which Allied aircraft picked out individual vehicles for attack. But 'Rover David' needed a very large number of aircraft to sustain 'cab ranking', and it would have been unworkable if the Luftwaffe had been able to dispute the presence of Allied aircraft over the battlefield.

It was bad enough that the 70–80 Bf109s and 25 FW190s supporting German ground troops were based back around Rome and Viterbo, but on top of wasted transits had to be added time spent dispersing and transferring to escape Allied air attacks. Yet SG4, with its FW190s, was the only unit in the south which could boast any real success and whose fighting morale was excellent.[14] Their lively banter and aggressive fighting spirit came across clearly over on the radio, especially on those exceptional days when the German offensive fighter-bomber effort rose to 80–90 sorties.

FW190 Jabos in the over-land attack role were generally sent out in groups of four, flying 80–100yd from each other in line abreast. When more than one Schwarm was involved, the second was staggered some 150–200yd behind the first, and so on. The formation leader would take the fighter-bomber pack to an easily identifiable initial point, from where he would turn to run them in line astern towards a clearly defined target like a motor convoy. For the standard Steckrubenwerf (turnip-lob) low altitude attack profile, the leader would ease up to around 1,000ft for final alignment about one mile out, and then go into a shallow descent, holding the target in the centre of his sight throughout. One second before bomb release, the nose would be eased up to ensure that the bomb cleared the propeller, and then it was time to make an evasive turn and getaway while the remaining FW190s followed suit.

The impact of German Jabos was never forgotten by those on the receiving end. 'I was sitting on alert over in front of the 58th on 15 January 1943,' recalled Jeep Crowder, a P-40 pilot with the 33rd Fighter Group, 'when three FW190s came over and dropped bombs about 100yd to the left of the nose of the plane. Then they and two Bf109s ground strafed us. It took 10 years off my life.'[15]

Ditto on the British side. Lance-Bombardier Spike Milligan of the 56th Heavy Regiment, RA, wrote:

'I had my head under the tap enjoying the refreshing cascade of cold water, at which time 12 109s are enjoying roaring out of the sun, guns hammering. There's a God-awful scramble, we all meet under a lorry. I caught a glimpse of the planes as they launched their bombs on the 25-pounder regiment behind us . . . On another occasion, a great ragged mob of Hun fighter planes surged over the nearest crest, bellying down right over our tree tops, cannons going. The evidence of this was a six-foot-deep trench at the bottom of which looking up white-faced and saying "Tell Hitler I'm sorry" was Lance-Bombardier Milligan.' [16]

A young South African pilot, Lt A. Sachs of No 92 Squadron, RAF, was flying his Spitfire when he came across a dozen FW190s attacking Allied forward positions. Sachs dived into the fray, shooting down two FW190s pretty quickly. When the second blew up, it damaged Sachs' Spitfire, which was further assaulted by the remaining Focke-Wulfs. Half Sachs' tail was shot away, both wings were damaged and his Merlin engine set on fire before he collided head-on with an FW190. As his Spitfire fell burning to the ground, Sachs felt it prudent to bale out. His parachute opened at the last possible moment and, on landing, he was surrounded by a number of local Italians who rushed forward to kiss his hands.

Once it became clear from aerial reconnaissance that the enemy was withdrawing from the Volturno, German forces fell back at their own pace on the 'Gustav Line', which stretched from hardened positions north of the Sangro in the east and along the rugged Abruzzi mountains to the River Garigliano in the west. It was a pretty awesome stretch of natural defences in its own right, but forward delaying positions were held to gain time for Italian workers (conscripted by the thousand) to add concrete and mines out to a depth of 20 miles in places, and for the inevitable further deterioration in the weather.

On top of terrain and weather, the Allies were up against the motivation of a hardened German enemy blessed with scientific and engineering expertise. On 18 September, von Vietinghoff issued an order of the day in which he congratulated the men of the Tenth Army on their victorious failure to reach the sea and destroy the bridgehead at Salerno, and on their splendid evacuation of Corsica. That may sound risible today, and most German veterans saw through the 'bullshit', but like Napoleon's Imperial Guard after the retreat from Moscow, their morale remained high and their discipline and traditions transcended personal hardship.

Perversely, German morale seemed to improve once they dug in, and the lack of air cover only added to their self-esteem in adversity. Take the Hermann Göring Panzer Division, which had lost most of its men at the fall of Tunisia, re-formed and then, along with the 15th Panzer Grenadiers, 'had known nothing but dispiriting retreat since action was joined in Sicily'.[17] Despite always being on the back foot, and the often unrealistic expectations of their own hierarchy,[18] the Hermann Göring initially threw the British back across the river at Capua when they assaulted the Volturno positions. The unexpected sight of 64 Luftwaffe fighter-bombers in action against various targets near Capua and along the middle Volturno raised morale, but even when air support was non-existent, German troops became masters of the 'victorious retreat'. The German rearguard would defend their position for as long as they could, then they blew up the bridges and approach roads, laid minefields and created roadblocks before retiring to the next suitable defensive position. This delaying tactic, according to the Hermann Göring Division, 'was always enough to allow all the artillery to be in the new position and ready to fire by evening to keep the enemy at a distance. That this tactic worked was due to the cautiousness of the enemy, who were slow in following the withdrawing Germans.'[19]

Notwithstanding the capture of the great port of Naples and an Allied air effort amounting to 27,500 sorties and 10,000 tons of bombs dropped in December alone, Gen Alexander's vision of a quick victory in Italy soon faded. By the end of 1943 the Allies had advanced only 70 miles beyond Salerno, with precious little to look forward to other than more hard slog. On the Adriatic coast, Eighth Army casualties throughout December numbered 6,453, while the mean rate of advance of a mile a day had halved. With no prospect of bringing the superior weight of his armour to bear in such country and weather, Montgomery called a halt.

On the other side of Italy, the Fifth Army had lost just under 22,000 officers and men [20] since landing at Salerno, yet Rome was still 80 miles distant. 'Were I as young as you,' remarked Oliver Cromwell to one of his generals, 'I should not doubt, before I died, to knock at the gates of Rome.' 290 years later, Allied troops were not so sure. As one commentator observed, 'The three services were tired and disappointed in the deferment of their hopes.' To a man they looked to the precise use of massive air power to swing the odds back in their favour.

Top Left:
FW190 of 2/SG4, sporting a 'desert' camouflage on a central Italian airfield. *Author's Collection*

Below:
An FW190 in a dive attack. *Author's Collection*

Notes to Chapter 5

1. Luftwaffe strength in Sardinia was fairly constant at 5 Ju88 reconnaissance aircraft, 60 Bf109/FW190 fighters and fighter-bombers, and 10 tactical reconnaissance Bf109s.
2. McDowell, E. R. and Hess, W. N.; Checkertail Clan, pp.30–31.
3. Senger und Etterlin, F.; Neither Fear Nor Hope; p.166.
4. Kesselring, op.cit, p.191.
5. Warlimont, W.; Inside Hitler's Headquarters; p.383.
6. Ibid, p.383.
7. Prien, op.cit, p.690.
8. Hicks W. E.; 97th Bombardment Group; pp.142–43.
9. Craven, W. H. and Cate, J. L.; The Army Air Forces in World War II; vol 2, p.551.
10. Such destructive efforts were a mixed blessing. The Germans demolished about 600 bridges in their own right as they were beaten back, which, when combined with Allied bombing successes, meant that the Fifth and Eighth Armies were at a great disadvantage when they were in a position to move forward. The order eventually went out for all inessential bridges in North Africa, Sicily and southern Italy to be dismantled and sent to the forward area.
11. With Pierced Steel Plate (PSP), airfields could be built wherever there was a stretch of flat land. Bulldozers flattened fields and ditches, gravel was smoothed in their wake, the PSP was clipped together and, hey presto, a new airfield was ready for use! PSP freed the army from making the capture of permanent aerodromes part of the tactical plan, and permitted flying operations irrespective of the weather.
12. Wörpel, D.; A Hostile Sky; p.119.
13. Richards and Saunders, op.cit, p.351.
14. Report by Prof Dr Robert Skawran, Luftwaffe psychologist and contemporary eyewitness, October 1943.
15. Ethell, J. L.; Wings of War; p.45.
16. Milligan, S.; Mussolini, His Part in My Downfall; pp.26, 32.
17. Molony, C. J. C.; The Mediterranean and Middle East; vol V, p.447.
18. Even von Vietinghoff was moved to remark on 1 November, 'One cannot fight and build defences at the same time; they don't fully understand that at the top.'
19. Kurowski, F.; History of the Fallschirm Panzerkorps Hermann Göring; p.211.
20. Nearly 12,000 were American and over 10,000 British Commonwealth.

FAR AND NEAR

'We had this sort of Tactical headquarters overlooking the Sangro. One day an Australian fighter pilot was shot down quite near us. Monty saw the parachute going down, so he said, "Send somebody out, bring him back to lunch." . . . Now Monty had decided to rewrite the Principles of War — at least to introduce his new principle of war, the first and greatest principle of war, which was: "Win the air battle first." He was very proud of this and about halfway through lunch he turned to this Australian and said, "Now, do you know what the first and greatest Principle of War is?"

"Well, I don't know much about principles of war, but I should say it's stop frigging about!"'

Sir William Mather

The capture of air bases on the Italian mainland opened up a whole new ball game. Once Foggia-based bombers were added to the weight of offensive effort being mounted from the UK, assault from both north and south would place an increased strain on German manpower and material capacity, and help pave the way for a successful outcome to 'Overlord'. Jimmy Doolittle pointed out that the plain of Apulia was better protected from winter weather than East Anglian bases, while RAF Chief of Air Staff Charles Portal argued that, from Italian bases, all southern Germany would be within comfortable range, two of the largest German aircraft factories could be reached, half the German fighters currently facing the UK would have to be moved down south, and bombers flying from Italy would enjoy an Alpine shield against the German warning system.

As a result, Twelfth Air Force was split into two. Its six heavy bomb groups, three P-38 groups, the 352nd Fighter Group and the 68th Recon Group went into a new Fifteenth Air Force which, after it became operational on 1 November, took over the strategic part of the spectrum. The Twelfth and its remaining groups assumed responsibility for tactical operations. Its commanding general was Coningham's former deputy, Maj-Gen John K. Cannon, and under 'Uncle Joe' came the US 42nd and 57th Medium Bombardment Wings, the US Twelfth Air Support Command and Harry Broadhurst's Desert Air Force.

American preponderance was to become most marked in the Strategic Air Force, comprising the Fifteenth Air Force day-bomber element and the night-bombers of 205 Group RAF. To the six heavy bomb groups from the Twelfth — four B-17 and two B-24 — were added others thick and fast: the 449th, 450th, 451st, 454th, 455th and 456th Bombardment Groups (H), each with 62 B-24H aircraft, were scheduled to leave the US for the Mediterranean before the end of December. A B-24 Liberator came off the converted Ford production line at Willow Run, Michigan, every 52 minutes, while across in Seattle, an average of 12 B-17 Flying Fortresses a day rolled out of Bill Boeing's facility. Such awesome manufacturing capacity soon enabled the Fifteenth Air Force to reach its total of 21 bomber groups. Back in May 1943, the British Prime Minister was proud that he had 'almost as many aeroplanes available for actual operations (in the Mediterranean) as the Americans'.[1] Thereafter, the disparity between the two allies steadily widened until, by 1945, the Fifteenth possessed no fewer than 85 bomber and 22 fighter squadrons, compared with 205 Group's total of nine.

As only a few Italian airfields initially captured were capable of handling four-engined bombers, on 29 September 1943 it was decided to construct six all-weather bomber airfields at Foggia, two in the Salerno area, three around Naples and to extend Pomigliano. This was a huge logistic task; a 2,000yd all-weather, heavy bomber runway had to be laid at all 12 airfields, each of which consumed 5,000 tons of honeycombed PSP. 71,800 tons of PSP was brought in between October 1943 and March 1944 — together with the fact that the air forces' domestic stores had increased to 6,300 tons a day by April 1944, this took up a lot of shipping space; it was calculated that necessary transport, materials and equipment to establish the Strategic Force approximated to the lift of two divisions. Fifth and Eighth Armies had to forgo a great deal to get Mediterranean Strategic Air up and running.

Back in the spring of 1943, there were roughly as many German single- and twin-engined fighters escorting supply traffic between Sicily and Tunisia as there were defending the entire Reich. What is more, every third Bf109 coming off the production line went to the Mediterranean theatre to offset front-line attrition. That all changed in response to the threat mounted by RAF Bomber Command and the US Eighth Air Force from England. During 1943, the German fighter force in the West grew from 1,045 to 1,650, and by the end of the year three-quarters of them were based inside Germany. This was very pleasing for Allied aircrews operating over peripheral Italy but was bad news for the UK-based bomber crews. The Luftwaffe threw everything into the fight for air superiority over the Reich, and in the darkest months of the winter of 1943–44, it was touch and go as to whether USAAF and RAF strategic bombers would end up victors or vanquished.

Thus, while the experts could argue till the cows came home over the respective importance of ballbearings or oil to the German war machine, these options were all dependent, in Ira Eaker's

Twelfth and Fifteen Air Forces,
1 November 1943.

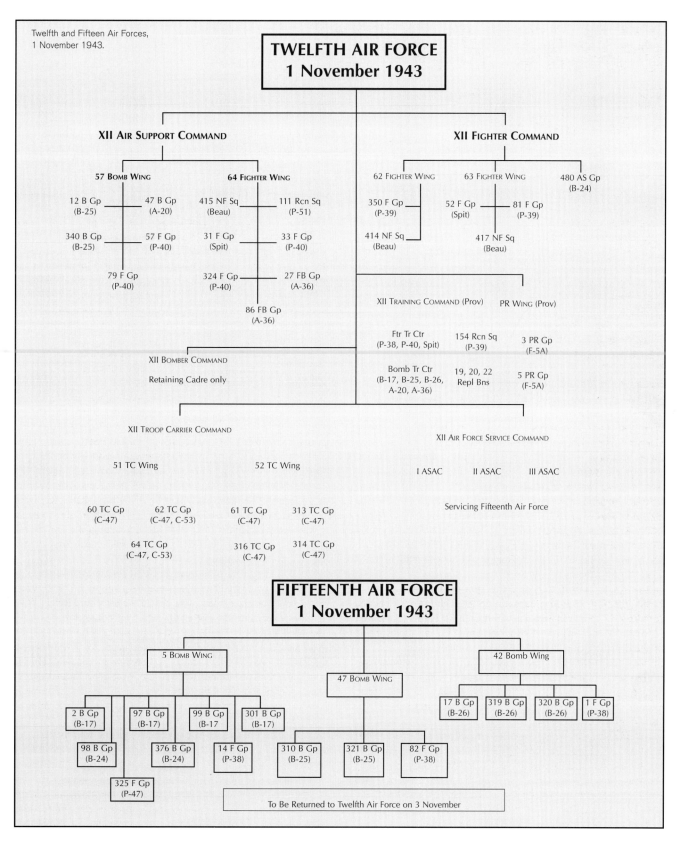

**TWELFTH AIR FORCE
1 November 1943**

XII AIR SUPPORT COMMAND

57 BOMB WING

12 B Gp
(B-25)

47 B Gp
(A-20)

340 B Gp
(B-25)

57 F Gp
(P-40)

79 F Gp
(P-40)

64 FIGHTER WING

415 NF Sq
(Beau)

111 Rcn Sq
(P-51)

31 F Gp
(Spit)

33 F Gp
(P-40)

324 F Gp
(P-40)

27 FB Gp
(A-36)

86 FB Gp
(A-36)

XII FIGHTER COMMAND

62 FIGHTER WING

350 F Gp
(P-39)

414 NF Sq
(Beau)

63 FIGHTER WING

52 F Gp
(Spit)

81 F Gp
(P-39)

417 NF Sq
(Beau)

480 AS Gp
(B-24)

XII TRAINING COMMAND (Prov)   PR WING (Prov)

Ftr Tr Ctr
(P-38, P-40, Spit)

154 Rcn Sq
(P-39)

3 PR Gp
(F-5A)

Bomb Tr Ctr
(B-17, B-25, B-26,
A-20, A-36)

19, 20, 22
Repl Bns

5 PR Gp
(F-5A)

XII BOMBER COMMAND

Retaining Cadre only

XII TROOP CARRIER COMMAND

51 TC Wing

60 TC Gp
(C-47)

62 TC Gp
(C-47, C-53)

64 TC Gp
(C-47, C-53)

52 TC Wing

61 TC Gp
(C-47)

316 TC Gp
(C-47)

313 TC Gp
(C-47)

314 TC Gp
(C-47)

XII AIR FORCE SERVICE COMMAND

I ASAC   II ASAC   III ASAC

Servicing Fifteenth Air Force

**FIFTEENTH AIR FORCE
1 November 1943**

5 BOMB WING

2 B Gp
(B-17)

97 B Gp
(B-17)

99 B Gp
(B-17)

301 B Gp
(B-17)

98 B Gp
(B-24)

376 B Gp
(B-24)

325 F Gp
(P-47)

14 F Gp
(P-38)

47 BOMB WING

310 B Gp
(B-25)

321 B Gp
(B-25)

82 F Gp
(P-38)

42 Bomb Wing

17 B Gp
(B-26)

319 B Gp
(B-26)

320 B Gp
(B-26)

1 F Gp
(P-38)

To Be Returned to Twelfth Air Force on 3 November

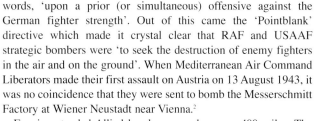

words, 'upon a prior (or simultaneous) offensive against the German fighter strength'. Out of this came the 'Pointblank' directive which made it crystal clear that RAF and USAAF strategic bombers were 'to seek the destruction of enemy fighters in the air and on the ground'. When Mediterranean Air Command Liberators made their first assault on Austria on 13 August 1943, it was no coincidence that they were sent to bomb the Messerschmitt Factory at Wiener Neustadt near Vienna.[2]

Foggia extended Allied bomber range by some 400 miles. The inaugural Foggia-mounted operation on 1 October was a re-run against the aircraft factories of Wiener Neustadt, but from now on it would be possible to bomb not only southern Germany, but also all the Balkan peninsula, the industrial areas of Silesia, the factories of Czechoslovakia and the oilfields of Romania. Thirty one plants, producing around 44% of German crude and synthetic oil, were less than 600 miles from Foggia, which was just one reason why the Intelligence staffs now considered that, 'qualitatively', more of the important targets were now closer to Italian bases than the UK.

Disorganisation caused by the wholesale evacuation of Luftwaffe operational flying units northwards in September not only brought the German bomber effort to a standstill for a month, but also allowed the Allies to acquire 832 German and Italian aircraft in various states of serviceability. When surviving fighter aircraft were rationalised, only three Jagdgruppen remained in action at the beginning of October: I/JG53 and I and III/JG77 with a total of just 75 serviceable Bf109s between them, compared with 10 Jagdgruppen deployed in Tunisia and Sicily nine months earlier. Richthofen played what few cards he had left as best he could. III/JG77 became the 'heavy Gruppe' with specific responsibility for using its 21cm mortars to attack Allied strategic bombers. I/JG53 and I/JG77, on the other hand, were expected to operate from just behind the Tenth Army's front, their primary roles being to provide air support for the ground forces and top cover for the only FW190 ground-attack outfit left in theatre, II/SG4.[3] The two 'front-line Bf109 Gruppen' were also able to take on Allied heavy bombers seen coming from afar while they continued to be based in North Africa.

German air defenders lost this precious early warning time once the heavies moved in to Italy. The fighter Gruppen still had their successes — during a B-17 raid on Bologna on 25 September, a dozen Bf109s joined the fray and ten Fortresses went missing. But bad weather probably played a big part in that outcome, and thereafter Luftflotte 2's defensive track record became pretty unimpressive. On 17 November, Field Marshal von Richthofen took advantage of a weather-induced pause in flying to hold a conference of front-line fighter leaders to determine why 'nothing was being shot down' despite continuous operations. The fighter leaders were unanimous in blaming the poor level of training of the new fighter pilots,[4] the overworked and tired state of the veterans, and the technical inferiority of the Bf109G6. One attendee, Flg Off (Oberleutnant) Kohler of I/JG77, later wrote in his diary:

'The enemy vastly outnumbers us, he has the better machines. Is it a surprise that all the new ones, who with their brief training cannot even master their own aircraft, fail to return from their

Left:
Flak bursts in the sky as Baltimores near their target over the Sangro in December 1943.
RAF Air Historical Branch

Above:
Col Günther Freiherr von Maltzahn (left), *Jafu Oberitalien* until August 1944 with Maj Franz Gotz, *Gruppekommandeur* III/JG53. A pretty impressive staff car sits in the background. *Author's Collection*

Top Right:
S/Sgt Alvin J. Dietz, Cpl John E. Bussolini and S/Sgt Louis J. Nichols gaze fondly at the millionth pound of bombs about to be dropped on German positions in Italy by a P-40 Warhawk Fighter Bomber Group that had been in service since North Africa. *IWM*

Right:
After getting safely back to base in December 1943, the crew of an RAF Baltimore examine flak damage to one of their engine cowlings.
RAF Air Historical Branch

first sorties? They should give us the FW190, here where the fighting is hardest! But it will never change: those up above will never understand the conditions at the front.' [5]

But the German hierarchy did understand the threat posed to the Reich war effort by the Fifteenth Air Force, and by the end of the year Allied heavies passing in and out of Italian airspace crossed the control area of Jagdfliegerführer Norditalien (Jafu Norditalien — Fighter Controller North Italy). This newly created position was formally given to Col Günther von Maltzahn on 4 December. He immediately set about building up a fighter control and reporting system, and for defence of the Po Valley von Maltzahn soon had four fighter control stations — West, at Pinerolo near Milan, covering the western industrial zone; Süd at Bologna; Ost at Triscesino near Udine, for control against Allied formations flying into Germany; and Mitte at Verona to cover the Brenner.

Around 11.15hrs on 28 December, Jafu Norditalien succeeded in bringing his three fighter Gruppen into action against a formation of unescorted B-24s attacking Vicenza airfield. A running air battle resulted between Padua and Vicenza, with the Germans claiming 20 Liberators shot down and the Americans admitting to 11. But this isolated success could not mask the magnitude of what the German defenders were up against. In December 1943, they could only mount 511 air defence sorties over northern Italy, as against at least 3,500 by heavy bombers and their escorts. The consequent total claims of 29 shot down throughout December — an Allied loss rate of 0.87% — was pretty meagre, and a true reflection of the numerical and qualitative inferiority under which the defenders were working.

For the mass of Allied tactical aircraft operating at low level, life was much more challenging. Take the experiences of the US 79th Fighter Group. Lt Ernest Kellerman, a native of Weehawken,

NJ, was strafing the Ancona coast road on 2 December when his Warhawk was hit by flak and exploded 75ft off the ground. Six days later, Lt Charles Kehr, another native of New Jersey, was killed after his Warhawk took a direct flak hit, and Lt William Glasgow had to bale out after being hit by anti-aircraft fire. The next day, another pilot was slightly wounded when a 20mm cannon shell tore through his cockpit. Two more pilots were shot down on 12 December, and six days later, Lt Ralph Scott 'mushed into the ground during his bomb run, Lt Wendell Simmons' Warhawk was seen to explode before he could bale out, and Lt William Marshall baled out over the water after taking a fatal hit.'[6]

Flak in the southern operational zone was controlled by 22 Flak Brigade with its HQ near Rome. As more and more Allied aircraft operated at low level over Italy, losses increased. November saw 150 Allied aircraft destroyed or missing, and 277 damaged. The following month, 209 were lost (61% of which were US) and 544 damaged (85% US). In part, the increase was caused by more aggressive tactics being flown by German fighters, but in the main they resulted from enhanced flak reaction, or from flying into the ground while trying to evade it.

At the end of December, the Fifteenth Air Force had 4,872 officers and 32,867 men, to whom Gen Henry 'Hap' Arnold, Commanding General of the USAAF, sent an unequivocal New Year's greeting: 'My personal message to you — this is a MUST — is to Destroy the Enemy Air Force wherever you find them, in the air, on the ground and in the factories.' Otherwise, Arnold declared, neither 'Overlord' nor the invasion of southern France would be possible.[7]

On 3 January 1944, Maj-Gen Nathan F. Twining, former Thirteenth Air Force commander in the South Pacific, became Commanding General of Fifteenth Air Force, a post he would hold until after the war. Twining's crews were to be employed primarily against Combined Bomber Offensive targets determined by the chiefs of staff. As Washington felt that there should be a single commander of the forces engaged (whether operating from the UK or Italy), a commander of European bomber forces was appointed. In the event, it became so difficult to mesh the necessarily elaborate convergence criteria that on only 10 occasions was it possible for co-ordinated strategic attacks to be carried out successfully. In practice, control of Fifteenth Air Force operations reverted almost entirely to the local operations centre, leaving European bomber co-ordination to broad target directives and close personal relationships between the senior commanders themselves.

In extremis, C-in-C Mediterranean could use the Fifteenth in a strategic or tactical emergency as he saw fit. This sounded pragmatic, but the devil was in the detail. While 'Pointblank' made perfect sense to the strategic bomber fraternity, others saw things differently. As far as the MAC was concerned, it had three main tasks in descending order of priority besides the perennial objective of keeping enemy aircraft out of the air. The first was to assist the armies, mainly by close support and interrupting enemy lines of communication. The second was to assist the strategic air offensive against the German war system, and the third was to weaken the German hold on the Balkans and Aegean.[8] So, while strategic bomber commanders were convinced that their activities

had priority, MAC placed them second to support of the land campaign. It was fortunate that, for most of the air war over Italy, Allied air resources were up to doing both.

There was an element of 'chicken and egg' about all this. In the words of the next Deputy Air C-in-C Sir John Slessor:

'The job for which it (the Strategic Force) existed was participation in the combined bomber offensive . . . In fact, so far from the Strategic Force being in Italy to assist the land forces, the object of the earlier operations of the land forces in that theatre was largely to seize and cover the Foggia complex of airfields for the use of the Strategic Air Force.'[9]

It is doubtful if the average infantryman was sustained in his hard slog by an overwhelming desire to provide a risk-free operating base for the bomber boys. As Hilary Saunders remarked:

'From the point of view of Gen Alexander, the presence at Foggia of the Strategic Force was more a liability than an asset. They were engaged in carrying out the strategic bombing programme which had no direct relation to the military operation for which he was responsible. Yet they were based in Italy . . . The problem of supplying the heavy bombardment groups stationed at Foggia put a severe strain on the supply service and on shipping, while their maintenance requirements were nearly as great as those of the Eighth Army.'[10]

*   *   *   *

By November, the German long-range bomber force had settled into its new bases in northern Italy. In concert with anti-shipping units based in southern France, and supplemented by a brief appearance of the latest German bomber — the 'heavy' twin-engined He177 with its wing span of over 103ft — von Richthofen was ready to resume the offensive.[11]

Col Peltz returned to Brussels at the end of August to take up his old job of Angriffsführer England, whereupon the post of Fernkampffliegerführer Luftflotte 2 (Long-range Bomber Controller of Luftflotte 2) was disbanded. There being no longer a separate bomber command, the bomber staff was absorbed by Fliegerführer Luftflotte 2, and Col Hubertus Hitschold was made responsible for all bomber, fighter and tactical air recce units operating in support of von Vietinghoff's Tenth Army. In place of Peltz's doctrine of concentrating all available bombers on a single target within a short space of time, Hitschold's team went for simultaneous or close-succession attacks by smaller formations. Best results were achieved by the Do217 force with torpedoes and the new Henschel Hs293 glider-bomb against Allied supply convoys, but it was only at the cost of appreciable losses, amounting on occasion to 20%. This probably helped explain why the long-range bombers in Italy only operated eight times between 15 October and 5 December — this averaged out at 55–60 sorties per week by a force of 145–185 bombers. He177s and their stand-off missiles notwithstanding, just over one sortie every fortnight per serviceable bomber was an uninspiring utilisation rate.

For some time, Luftflotte 2 staff had been wrestling with how best to help delay the advance of the Allied armies. Attacking widely dispersed troops or airfields was too hit and miss; the only practical option was to blitz a busy bottleneck in the hope that this would bring the already over-extended Fifth and Eighth Armies to an abrupt halt through lack of supplies. So while the anti-shipping forces went for convoys, Luftwaffe bombers concentrated on ports.

Bari, an important east coast port of 250,000 inhabitants, was crowded with more than 30 Allied vessels. Most were merchant ships, full to overflowing with all manner of stores for the Allied armies and aviation fuel bound for the Foggia complex to the north. A former Italian Air Force headquarters building in Bari was even in the process of being set up to serve as command post for the new Fifteenth Air Force.[12]

Above Bari at 23,000ft in the late afternoon sunlight of 2 December, recce pilot Flg Off Werner Hahn could both see and count all the ships from his Me210. Richthofen had sent a Me210 over Bari every day for a week, and post-flight photo-interpretation showed more and more ships mooring at the port. The order went out for all available bombers to stand by, and when Hahn landed with his update, around 100 Ju88s set off. At 19.25hrs, two or three circled Bari harbour at 10,000ft, dropping bundles of aluminium tinfoil strips to confuse air defence radars, as these produced echoes equal in magnitude to those of aircraft.[13] The pathfinders also dropped illuminating flares, though these were hardly necessary because, as darkness fell that Thursday evening, all harbour lights were on to speed the docking of ships and the discharging of their vital cargoes.

Flg Off Gustav Tauber was at 1,000ft over the sea 50 miles northeast. His flight leader lowered the nose of his Ju88 and Tauber followed with Hans Feich, a former Stuka pilot with hundreds of Eastern Front missions under his belt, on his left wing. All bomber units remaining in Italy — KGs 26, 30, 54, 76, and 100 — were represented. Out of Milan/Cameri and Bergamo, Ghedi and Villafranca, Villaorba and Aviano they came, running in well below whatever low level radar cover remained unaffected by Duppel. They were to use the 'Swedish turnip' approach —

Luftwaffe attack profile designators seemed to have a thing about root vegetables — which involved attacking vessels beam-on at a constant height of 150ft while maintaining 200mph.

The plan worked and the Ju88 crews achieved complete surprise, allowing them free rein from 19.30–20.30hrs to drop bombs and parachute mines. Fourteen merchant ships laden with 34,330 tons of cargo were destroyed, three more were submerged with 7,500 tons but were salvaged and six others were damaged. The bulk fuel pipe was severed and serious fires started — Bari did not return to its former operating capacity for three weeks. Worst of all, the SS John Harvey, which was bringing 100 tons of 100lb mustard gas bombs into theatre just in case Hitler resorted to gas warfare, was hit and exploded. That only added to the horrific deaths and ensured that the Bari raid went down, in Eisenhower's words, as 'the greatest single loss from air action inflicted upon us during the entire period of Allied campaigning in Europe'.[14]

The subsequent inquiry into the worst Allied shipping disaster since Pearl Harbor found that, besides the dropping of 'Window', the air defence of Bari suffered from the bare minimum of anti-aircraft guns, poor telephone communications and the best-sited air defence radar being unserviceable. One US Beaufighter was patrolling at the opening of the attack, and three more were scrambled, but no interceptions resulted. With hindsight, it was foolhardy to keep the harbour lights on, and it is hard not to conclude that the Allies, after enjoying a lengthy period of air supremacy, had grown complacent. AM Coningham, in his last month before returning to the UK, held a press conference in Bari on the afternoon of 2 December in which he assured his listeners that the Germans had been defeated in the air. 'I would regard it as a personal affront and insult,' he said, 'if the Luftwaffe should attempt any significant action in this area.'[15] He must have rued that remark when he visited the injured in hospital only a few hours later.

Below:
A bombed-up Junkers Ju88 taxies out wearing toned-down camouflage for night operations. *Author's Collection*

Yet although there was much to admire in German planning for the Bari operation, Gp Capt P. Hugo, a very operationally experienced observer on the ground, counted just 50 Ju88s overhead. Local radar, though degraded, only picked up 30. This meant that, although there was no Allied defence activity worth the name, no more than half the Ju88s that took-off managed to make it over Bari. In potency terms, the Luftwaffe bomber force was a mere shadow of its former self.

Bari was the last hurrah. Hitler was insistent that the Luftwaffe should pay the British back for what RAF Bomber Command was handing out to German cities, and in early December all six bomber Gruppen — the entire north Italian bomber force of around 180 aircraft — were withdrawn to Germany to prepare for large-scale raids on the United Kingdom in mid-January. At the end of December, the German bomber force in the Mediterranean was down to 29 serviceable aircraft, as against 214 on 30 November.

Luftwaffe strength in the Mediterranean, which by October had already declined by 40% from the peak figure of 1,280 aircraft in July, fell to 575 aircraft by January 1944, of which only 370 were available in the central and western Mediterranean. It was indicative of changed priorities that Luftflotte 2 was assigned just 35 new Bf109s during the whole of November. In Kesselring's words, his air arm was now fighting a 'poor man's war'. With their potential reduced to between 50–100 sorties per day, the best Luftflotte 2 could do was conserve its strength in order to give battle only when vitally necessary or the odds were most favourable.

*   *   *   *

As the invasions of northern and southern France assumed priority, Eisenhower, Montgomery, Tedder, Doolittle and Coningham were moved on to prepare for greater things. On 1 January 1944, Gen Sir Henry 'Jumbo' Maitland Wilson became Allied C-in-C, Mediterranean Theatre while, at the same time, Mediterranean Allied Air Forces (MAAF) replaced Mediterranean Air Command.

Up to then, Northwest African Air Forces had been an almost exclusively tactical organisation whose mission was to assist land and sea operations. That co-operation might be direct or indirect, it might be delivered by the relatively short-range aircraft of the Tactical Air Force or against enemy transportation in Italy by the longer-ranging Strategic Air Force, but it was all in the cause of furthering the advance of men and ships. To illustrate the point, the attack on Wiener Neustadt on 13 August 1943 was one of only four occasions when NAAF aircraft were sent to strike directly against the enemy's capacity to wage war. As a sign of changing times, Northwest African Tactical, Strategic and Coastal Air Forces were now renamed Mediterranean Allied Tactical, Strategic and Coastal Air Forces respectively — each a combined RAF–AAF command with its own distinct mission, but each obligated to work closely with the others.

'Jumbo' Wilson was not noted for his grasp of air power, but that did not matter. The supreme commander could be likened to the conductor of an orchestra; he was told what to play via directives from above, and as MRAF Portal pointed out, it was not 'necessary for him to be able personally to play the bassoon'. Such matters

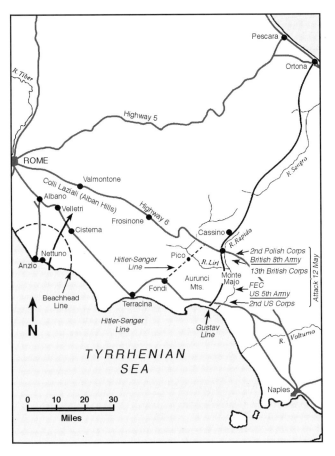

Above:
The road to Rome.

were best left to the respective service commanders-in-chief, and on the air side Wilson was fortunate in being given Lt-Gen Ira Eaker, the forceful proponent of daylight precision bombing who had led the first USAAF bombing raid on Europe back in August 1942, to replace Tedder as Air C-in-C. Giving overall command to a respected airman like Eaker made perfect sense. Notwithstanding the US chiefs' reluctance to become embroiled in Italy, after just a month on the mainland the USAAF was flying two-thirds of the total sorties, dropping more than 70% of the bombs and, perhaps not surprisingly, claiming two-thirds of all enemy aircraft destroyed in aerial combat.

Eaker's deputy was AM Sir John Slessor, one of the RAF's foremost thinkers, who had commanded RAF Coastal Command at the most critical phase of the Battle of the Atlantic. MAAF HQ was on the fifth floor of the former Bourbon palace at Caserta near Naples, enabling Eaker and Slessor to work alongside Gen Alexander who had mastered 'the difficult art of managing Americans' and was now known as C-in-C Allied Armies in Italy. His Fifteenth Army Group was as before — the American Fifth Army on the western side of Italy under Lt-Gen Mark Clark, and the British Eighth on the east under Lt-Gen Sir Oliver Leese after Monty left.

From dusk on 19 November to dawn on 1 January 1944, Mediterranean Air Command flew the equivalent of 917 sorties every 24 hours. Excluding attacks on shipping, total sorties amounted to 38,512, of which the fighters flew 21,905, the bombers and fighter-bombers 14,852 and the recce boys 1,755. The Allies lost 209 aircraft over the same period, compared to 71 German aircraft destroyed in the air or by ground action and 76 which did not return from operations owing to unknown causes. As five of these German casualties were transport aircraft, the remaining 142 lost from a total of 740 available operational aircraft gave a 19% attrition rate. Given that Allied air commanders regarded 10% as the greatest sustained rate of attrition a fighter force could suffer and remain effective, and RAF Bomber Command put its greatest endurable rate at 5%, the Luftwaffe was going down fast.

On the other hand, Allied air appeared to have enjoyed a very successful four months over Italy. It was beholden to nothing and no one apart from the weather, and its air-to-ground potency was demonstrated most emphatically on 2 December when Tactical Air Force flew over 1,200 sorties in support of Fifth Army operations; there was even spare capacity to mount some 70 Desert Air Force Warhawk sorties against Jugoslav objectives. This was the highest aerial turn-out since Tunisia, and when mated with the heaviest concentration of artillery fire to date in the campaign, its effect was awesome.

Yet despite 'a tale full of sound and fury', between the Allied's 11 divisions and the Italian capital were nine divisions of stubborn and resolute Germans dug-in across the 'waist' of Italy on the Gustav Line. This formidable obstacle ran from the Garigliano and Rapido river courses, backing onto the Aurunci Mountains in the west, across the central mountain spine of Italy and down to Ortona behind the Sangro in the east. The classic path from Naples to Rome — now known as Route 6 — ran through the only gap in the line, down the Liri Valley. It passed by the central bastion of the Gustav Line at Cassino, dominated by the towering intensity of Monastery Hill rising 1,700ft behind the town.

Hitler told Kesselring that the Gustav Line was to 'mark the end of withdrawals', so it is perhaps not surprising that the Fifth Army failed in its attempts to rush the line head-on. Having, as he admitted, 'no great numerical superiority', Gen Alexander played the amphibious card again. A successful landing at the two small ports of Anzio and Nettuno on the west coast within easy distance of Rome, followed by the immediate seizure of the Alban Hills, would surely outflank the stalled situation around Monte Cassino. Anzio would obviate the need for a frontal assault on a seemingly impregnable position, and it would either isolate the Germans holding the Gustav Line, or at least bustle them back in confusion to Rome.

On 17 January a new Allied offensive was launched to force the Germans from their positions on the Garigliano and Rapido. The sting in the tail of this cunning plan was that as soon as German reserves had been drawn south, the landing craft would go in to land one British and one American division either side of Anzio. As at Sicily and Salerno, the primary task of Allied air forces over the beachhead was to eliminate all enemy aircraft from the skies.

The next priority task was disruption of the enemy's supply lines, then protection from the air for the assault convoys, and bottom of the list, close air support by attacking suitable targets on or around the battlefield.

So effective were the hard-struck bomber raids on all the central Italian airfields — particularly against Ciampino, Centocelle, Guidonia, Rieti and Viterbo — that the Luftwaffe was unable to get even one reconnaissance aircraft airborne. Consequently, when the invasion was launched on 22 January, it achieved complete surprise and the convoy of 243 vessels reached the Anzio beaches unobserved. By evening, 36,000 troops and 3,000 vehicles were ashore within 30 miles of Rome and 60 miles behind the German lines on the Rapido. It was not until 08.20hrs, six hours after the landings had been carried out, that a Bf109 succeeded in getting through the air defences to bring back proof-positive to Kesselring of what was going on.

Ever since 1915, Winston Churchill had favoured such 'indirect' manoeuvres. Yet although there was no danger of the landing failing for lack of air support, Anzio became more Gallipoli than Inchon in the face of Allied over-caution and consequently inspired German resistance.

Notes to Chapter 6

1. Churchill, op.cit, p.656.
2. The single-engined fighter plants at Wiener Neustadt and Regensburg together produced around 500 of the German total of 650 Bf109s a month.
3. II/SKG10 was redesignated II/SG4 in October. SG stands for Schlacht (ground-attack) Geschwader.
4. In 1943, the Germans managed to double the number of new fighter pilots coming out of training schools from 1,662 to 3,276. But that was still barely enough to cover wastage at the front (2,870), so there was little opportunity to build up a reserve. More dangerous in the long term, German pilots received less than half the flying time of their US and British equivalents. Murray, W.; Strategy for Defeat, The Luftwaffe 1933-1945; p.254.
5. Prien, op.cit, p.706.
6. Wörpel, op.cit, pp.115–16.
7. Copp, D. S.; Forged In Fire; pp.455–56.
8. ACMT.69 31 October 1943, D/Cas Operations from Italian Bases — Priority of Tasks.
9. Slessor, J.; The Central Blue; p.567.
10. Richards and Saunders, op.cit, p.348.
11. Luftflotte 2 HQ was now at Abano, near Padua, where it remained until May 1944.
12. At that stage, Foggia was still described as a 'shambles'.
13. Known as Duppel in German, 'Chaff' in the USA and 'Window' to the RAF, these strips had first been used in anger by RAF Bomber Command over Hamburg the previous summer.
14. Butcher, H.; My Three Years With Eisenhower; p.224.
15. Infield, G. B.; Disaster at Bari; p.35.

A LONG, HARD WINTER

Why should we crawl up the leg like a harvest bug, from the ankle upwards? Let us rather strike at the knee.'
Winston Churchill

All fighter aircraft working for the Desert Air Force were controlled from one central operations room. 'Daylight found the site an indescribable scene of desolation,' recorded the Mobile Operations Room Unit diary for 1 January 1944. 'In the small hours the abominable gale returned accompanied by very heavy rain. One and all suffered. The orderly room was flattened and draped half across the road.' The airmen at Penna Point found shelter in neighbouring houses, while seven officers took refuge in a nearby chapel where the verger made them all toast Capo d'Anno from a vast bottle of Vino Rosso. There was no such comfort for the three squadrons of Spitfires of the 7th South African Air Force Wing on the nearby beach at Trigno; they were washed out by high waves driven on to the shore by the strong northerly gale.

It was against such a foul-weather backdrop that the battle for Anzio unfurled. As Sir Oliver Leese's Eighth Army looked after the eastern side of Italy, Mark Clark's Fifth Army on the west had responsibility for the Anzio invasion, code-named 'Shingle'. The task was given to VI (US) Corps under Maj-Gen John P. Lucas, a stolid, methodical Southerner nicknamed 'Corncob Charlie' from the pipe he smoked. The invasion beaches, though poor, were the best available south of the Tiber, but more importantly they led straight out to the Alban Hills. Rising just south of Rome, this large massif dominated both Highway 6 and Highway 7 from Rome to the Gustav Line. Highway 7, the coastal Appian Way, could have been cut with ease by a landing almost anywhere on the west coast, but the Alban Hills marked the first point where the inland Route 6 was not protected by the almost trackless Aurunci Mountains. Allied thinking was that if the Alban Hills were seized, the enemy's communications would be cut and Rome would be within their grasp.

Unfortunately, the resources and timetable for the invasion plan were inextricably tied to those being shaped for an amphibious thrust (Operation 'Anvil') into southern France that would coincide closely with 'Overlord' in Normandy. Despite Churchill's

Left:
The impact of Italian winter rains and blown roads on modern warfare.
Author's Collection

Top Right:
Desert Air Force reconnaissance photo taken on 26 January 1944 of hits on roads and railway bridges spanning the River Jordino at Guilianova. The Germans had been using both road and railway to transport supplies.
RAF Air Historical Branch

wholehearted support for the Anzio enterprise, it was only by pleading with President Roosevelt that the Prime Minister managed to retain as much logistic support for Alexander as he did. On the other hand, Kesselring had plenty of reserves around Rome and if they were able to come down in force upon the vulnerable Anglo-US divisions straggling out from the beachhead to the Alban Hills, the Germans might well succeed in driving them back into the sea.

To make matters worse, Fifth Army hopes of quickly breaking through the Gustav Line and into the Liri Valley were soon dashed. The German line was initially broken in force at Castelforte, supported in no small measure by XII ASC's air defenders and close-support aircraft.[1] But in the face of terrible weather and appallingly difficult country, the British could not extend their bridgehead over the upper Garigliano, while American attempts to cross the Rapido in darkness and fog were repulsed with heavy losses. 'Shingle' was launched knowing that a rapid link-up with the rest of the Fifth Army was no longer possible.

One of the biggest factors sustaining the Allies throughout all this was their bombing programme which, like Roman Gaul, was divided into three parts. The preparatory phase, covering the first two weeks of January, saw the disruption of central Italian rail communications combined with feint operations designed to make the Germans think that the landing would be made at Civitavecchia, north of Rome. It gave the number-crunchers great

pleasure to calculate that, during these Anzio preparations, MAAF flew a total of 12,974 sorties, dropping 5,777 tons of bombs and destroying 91 enemy aircraft, for the loss of 27 Allied bombers and 55 fighters.

The second phase (15–21 January) involved an all-out effort to isolate the battle area by increasing attacks on railways and roads north of Rome and those leading to Anzio from the Fifth and Eighth Army fronts. The third phase — whereby Tactical Bomber Force went for railways in central Italy while Strategic concentrated on those in the north — was designed to isolate the battle area further. It is interesting to note that, at this stage, there were no plans to bomb the battlefield.

The reason why Kesselring's staff did not see the invasion fleet coming was straightforward. A standing force of 20 long-range reconnaissance Ju88s and Me410s was based at Perugia in central Italy. 48 B-25s attacked this field as part of the opening blitz on Luftwaffe assets, while Wellingtons attacked 52 fighters sitting at Viterbo. Four nights later Perugia was revisited, this time by Wellingtons. Bad weather limited the effectiveness of these attacks but on 19 January, 28 US B-24s found Perugia in the clear. Up to then, the German routine had been to fly two or three sorties daily and nightly up and down the Tyrrhenian and Adriatic coasts. The 19 January raid was so successful that for four days the Luftwaffe was unable to resume any long-range reconnaissance. 'There are no indications that any major undertaking in the Mediterranean

Left:
Allied bombers flying over an Italian town en route to bomb Axis positions, 9 February 1944.
RAF Air Historical Branch

Right:
An Me410 reconnaissance aircraft belonging to 2.(F)/122 after being shot down on 11 November 1943 on the banks of the Sangro River. RAF Regiment troops are helping an intelligence officer to salvage the important bits. *IWM*

Below:
A tactical reconnaissance Bf109G belonging to NAGr11 sweeps over the Italian battle front in early 1944. The aircraft's range was extended by the underwing droptanks.
Author's Collection

area is imminent,' declared the OKW Intelligence Section in Berlin on 20 January.[2] German High Command was to remain blind because, as luck would have it, fog prevented any last-minute reconnaissance once Perugia was back on line, and the German radar warning system broke down on the night of 21/22 January.

To meet the overriding remit to eliminate all opposition from the air, the Allied airfield attack plan was to send the heavies in first to hole the runways and operating surfaces with demolition bombs, thereby preventing aircraft from taking off. An hour later, the mediums would attack with fragmentation clusters to destroy and damage the aircraft stranded in the dispersal areas. Such all-out attacks goaded enemy fighters into opposition: of the 50–60 German fighters encountered on 13 January, seven were destroyed for the loss of two B-25s, two P-38s and one P-47.

The Allies could afford such loss ratios; the Germans could not. German fighter strength in Italy on 22 January 1944 was estimated at 200 Bf109s and 25–30 FW190s, with no night-fighters in-theatre. More than a third of the 109s and all the FW190s were based around Rome, immediately behind and in support of the Tenth Army front. This left the remaining 109s in northern Italy for the defence of industrial and communication targets north of the Apennines and to intercept Allied bomber formations bound for central Europe. Once Allied bombers were based on mainland Italy, there was precious little warning time for the 109s of III/JG53, based in the middle of northern Italy on the Reggiane aircraft company's airfield at Reggio Emilia, to react. This air defence base was vulnerable on two counts: first for its own sake, and second as a 'Pointblank' target because the Reggiane factory was then producing 30 fighters a month for the Luftwaffe.

Mediterranean Allied Air Forces had a grand total of 4,658 aircraft on 21 January 1944, of which 2,567 were available in direct support at the start of the Anzio invasion, increasing to 2,903 by the end. Just over half of these were based around Bari, Foggia and Termoli. US B-24 groups, defensive fighters and Coastal aircraft were at Bari. US B-17s, RAF Wellingtons, some US B-25s, RAF and South African light bombers and South African fighters, and RAF Photo-Reconnaissance Spitfires and Mosquitos, were all around Foggia. In the Termoli area, DAF Kittyhawk, US Warhawk and Spitfire squadrons stood ready to support the Eighth Army.

Remaining aircraft were based at Naples, Corsica and Sardinia. Around Naples were concentrated nearly 850 bomber, fighter, coastal and reconnaissance aircraft, predominantly belonging to XII ASC but also including a large US B-25 force and Coastal's defensive squadrons. The US B-26 bomber force was based on Sardinia, alongside strong US P-38, Beaufighter and Mosquito contingents. There was a sizeable B-25 detachment on Corsica, together with a strong fighter element operating from fields dotted along the east coast. In the rear areas a force of defensive fighters and Coastal aircraft were based on Sicily and Malta, as well as along the North African seaboard; between them they covered the central Mediterranean.

Given such aerial preponderance, it is perhaps not surprising that the initial Anzio invasion went very well. With the withdrawal of the long-range Ju88s to Germany during December for reprisal raids on England, the only striking force available to von

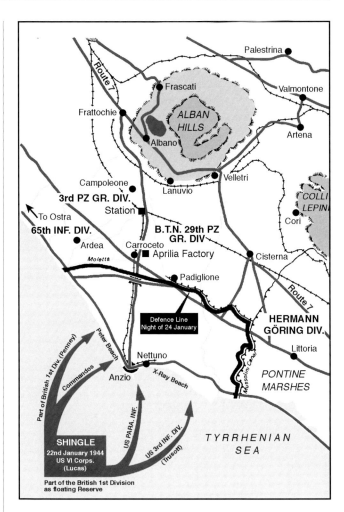

Above:
The Anzio landings.

Richthofen to meet an amphibious landing were 50 Ju88s in Greece and Crete and two Gruppen of torpedo-bombers (about 60 Ju88s and He111s) in the south of France. Allied aircraft attacked the northern bases of Osoppo and Villaorba, in part because they now housed a number of Bf109s, but also in case they were used to launch attacks on shipping off Anzio and Nettuno. What airfields were still serviceable around Rome were bombed on 19 and 20 January, forcing Luftwaffe tactical squadrons back to the Rieti and Viterbo fields — which were then visited by 163 B-25s and B-26s. That left only the French long-range bomber bases at Istres and Salon; as a precautionary measure, 32 B-17s bombed Istres and 36 bombed Salon on 21 January.

Then came the great day and three layers of fighter cover were over the invasion fleet and Anzio from dawn to dusk. Four Spitfire patrols were flown at 20–25,000ft, while at 1618,000ft eight Spitfires were constantly over the beachhead and four over the convoy. Finally, at 8,000ft came 16 US Warhawks (eight over the beachhead and eight over the convoy). In the course of some 500 patrols over the beaches and 135 over the convoy lanes, XII

ASC's fighters intercepted six fighter-bomber waves and shot down at least seven aircraft for the loss of three of their own. 'We are being made to fly too high for effective interception,' lamented the Spitfire pilots stooging around up high. 'We will never have any joy.'[3]

The Curtiss P-40 Warhawks of the US 33rd, 79th and 324th Fighter Groups, fitted with both wing bomb racks and six .50 calibre guns, did sterling service throughout the invasion. During the Gulf War nearly 50 years later, the US Navy was justifiably proud of its pair of F/A18s which, on approaching to bomb an airfield in western Iraq with 8,000lb of bombs apiece, received a warning that two MiG21s were coming head-on. With hardly a pause, the Hornet drivers switched from air-to-ground to air-to-air radar mode, locked up the MiGs, shot them down, then switched back to air-to-ground before proceeding to bomb their target successfully. 'That,' said the USAF's senior historian, 'would have been unthinkable in any previous air war.'[4] Not so. Warhawk pilots operating over Anzio were known as 'triple threat' men — to get maximum value from their time in the air, they dropped bombs on their way to their beachhead patrols, did their time providing air defence cover and strafed the enemy on the way back.

Behind the beachhead, US P-47 strategic fighters swept the Rome area and claimed five Bf109s, while other fighters and fighter-bombers assisted the heavies and mediums in their efforts to isolate the battlefield by cutting and harrying railways and roads. It was all to good effect, except perhaps for the two million warning leaflets dropped over German lines which probably ended up being used for purposes other than their designers intended. In all, over 1,200 MAAF sorties were flown that day in co-operation with the landings. From the Pope's summer residence at Castel Gandolfo in the Alban Hills, the villa's director saw hundreds of vessels through his binoculars, 'with aeroplanes circling overhead like protective birds, sometimes darting inland to blast or machine-gun German vehicles and troops arriving from all directions'.[5]

Apart from some largely ineffectual long-range shelling from the Alban Hills, a quickly-silenced resistance from some coastal artillery and flak units, and a brief raid on the harbour by six Bf109 dive-bombers that managed to penetrate the air defence screen protecting the fleet, there was virtually no opposition to the Anzio landing. The 2nd North Staffordshires went ashore at 02.25hrs, followed by the 6th Gordons. The only German unit in the area, and for 25 miles on either side of it, was a battalion of the 29th Panzer Grenadier Division, which was resting after having been severely mauled in recent fighting.

In the opinion of Kesselring's very able chief of staff, Gen Siegfried Westphal, 'the road to Rome was open, and an audacious flying column could certainly have penetrated to the city'. His boss was just as sure that here was 'a uniquely favourable chance of capturing Rome and of opening the door on the Garigliano front'.[6] But to Westphal's amazement — and Kesselring's profound relief — the Allies made no attempt to move out of the beachhead. While they undertook a painstaking consolidation, the Germans reacted with characteristic speed and verve. Fourteenth Army commander Gen von Mackensen was given the task of throwing out the invaders, and Kesselring ordered all available troops to take up positions without delay to hold the Alban Hills and prevent the Allies from reaching Highway 6.

Men were summoned from far and wide. They came from the Gustav Line and from Rimini, Genoa, Perugia and Leghorn, from base camps and rest areas — even the VD hospital in Rome was emptied — while men prepared to leave from Yugoslavia and southern France and Germany. Notwithstanding the deposition of over 5,400 tons of bombs on the Italian rail and road system between 1 and 22 January, the Germans assembled the equivalent of about two divisions to resist the troops coming ashore. Bad flying weather after 24 January seriously reduced the effectiveness of heavy and medium bomber raids, and by then the Germans had grown accustomed to moving by night and speedily repairing damaged bridges. Certainly they were developing the repair of broken track into a fine art.

The initial German air response to the major strategic threat posed by Anzio was equally prompt and energetic, the aim being to strike against shipping and hinder the Allied build-up. Between 22 and 31 January, 135 long-range bombers were rapidly moved to Italy from northwest Germany, France and Greece.[7] Included among them were aircraft which as recently as 21/22 January had been part of the force of 447 aircraft led by Col Peltz to bomb London. No naval fleet or army could have readjusted its sights so quickly, and when He111 crews swapped charts of the Thames Estuary for the Tyrrhenian coast, they underlined the inherent flexibility of air power.

Simultaneously, the anti-shipping force in southern France was reinforced by 50–60 Do217s and He177s, operating from as far away as Bordeaux, with the Hs293 stand-off weapon. More than 20 attacks were carried out against shipping off Anzio, opening with a total effort of 145 sorties over the nights of 23/24 and 24/25 January. In among those operating on 23 January were seven He177s of II/KG40, each with two Hs293 missiles and 16 110lb flares; they mounted a dusk attack on invasion shipping off Nettuno, but without any success. The following day, 11 aircraft from the Gruppe had an equally abortive experience, though fighter-bombers managed to sink one Allied hospital ship and damage two others.

Back in late 1940, the Bristol Beaufighter had made its name as the first British night-fighter with the speed and firepower to take advantage of the new airborne interception radar. By 1943 the Beaufighter had been largely replaced by the Mosquito as the standard night-fighter over Britain, but it was still a formidable opponent, and Coastal Beaufighter night-fighters of No 255 Squadron were put under the operational control of XII ASC for operations seaward of the assault area. In concert with tactical fighters, their claims for the night of 23/24 January were six Ju88s, four He177s, four Do217s and one He111 — even allowing for standard aircrew exaggeration and double-claiming, that was quite an achievement.

The German anti-shipping effort remained high until 26/27 January, but although it gradually fell off after that, the Luftwaffe scored a major success on 29 January when radio-guided bombs sank the cruiser HMS Spartan and the cargo ship Samuel Huntington with heavy loss of life. Between 23 January and

19 February, the Luftwaffe sank three naval vessels and damaged five more, plus one merchantman sunk and seven damaged. Maj Denis Healey, future British Chancellor of the Exchequer, was beachmaster to the British Assault Brigade at Anzio. This veteran of Sicily and Salerno recalled that 'the effect of German air power came most strongly to me when we were dive-bombed at Porto Santo Venere in September 1943, and when I saw a British naval vessel sunk by a German dive-bomber off Anzio'.[8]

After 30 January, bad weather prevented bomber operations over Italy for a week — not that the hiatus did German airmen much good. On 30 January, 215 B-17s and B-24s from the 97th, 99th, 301st, 449th and 450th Bombardment Groups, well escorted by P-38s from the 1st, 14th and 82nd Fighter Groups, dropped some 29,000 20lb fragmentation bombs on four German bomber bases in the Po Valley. Warned by radar of their approach, the local German aircraft got airborne for safety. At that moment, a force of Thunderbolts from the 325th Fighter Group swept in below radar cover at tree-top height, 15 minutes ahead of the main bomber force. They caught the Germans at their most vulnerable — taking-off, with neither height nor speed in reserve — and shot down 36 German aircraft for the loss of two P-47s. It was one of the cleverest tricks of the air war.

Apart from a move of some 50 single-engined fighters from north to central Italy towards the end of January, there was no strengthening of Luftwaffe close-support forces from outside Italy until February.[9] Ever adaptable, Kesselring rushed one light and

eight heavy anti-aircraft battalions from around the Rome area under Luftwaffe Gen Maximilian Ritter von Pohl.[10] Covering the whole of Anzio from the Alban Hills, these flak guns powerfully reinforced German Army artillery. 4,000 tons of road transport managed to ply between the railheads at Florence and Bologna to sustain the flak gunners in their expenditure of some 20,000 shells a day. When supported by newly arrived troops, the flak-cum-siege artillery proved sufficient to prevent an enemy breakout. Had it not been for Allied air strikes on their communications, within a week of the first landing the Germans might have advanced on the beachhead, rather than the other way around.

Lt-Gen Mark Clark came to chivvy up his forces and after he left, the commander of VI (US) Corps wrote sadly in his diary that 'apparently some of the higher levels think I have not advanced with maximum speed'. Lucas had no wish to take on the Germans before he was good and ready, but advocacy of his understandable caution was not helped by his Eeyore personality. Eventually the corps, with its 70,000 men, 27,000 tons of stores and over 500 guns, was ready to go. Lucas' hopes rested on the American tanks of the 1st Armored Division swinging round British positions and up towards the Alban Hills. The tank crews' hopes, in turn, rested on the ground being as the aerial photographs said it would be.

'Knowledge comes before power,' wrote the British historian Sir Walter Raleigh after World War 1, 'and the air is first of all a place to see from.' The Allies understood this from the outset, and their aerial photographic reconnaissance organisation was one of the great success stories of the Italian campaign. To quote one example, the Northwest African Photographic Reconnaissance Wing mapped the entire 10,000 square miles of Sicily before the invasion of the island, from which maps were made for distribution down to company level.

No 336 PR Wing was established to co-ordinate the efforts of one South African and three RAF squadrons,[11] and to work in harmony with the USAAF 3rd and 5th Photo Groups. Once Allied forces passed Naples, No 336 PR Wing moved to San Severo in the Foggia complex. This sleepy township, supposedly founded by refugees from Troy, found itself transformed overnight: schools, inns, palazzi, the opera house and even the prison were converted into laboratories, workshops, cookhouses and messes to accommodate the host of pilots, mechanics, photo-interpreters, wireless operators, clerks, dispatch riders and police that descended upon it. Seven hundred years earlier, the British astrologer to Frederick II of Hohenstaufen had rested there awhile. His requirements of space for determining intelligence for his master must have been considerably less than those of No 336 PR Wing. His equipment was probably limited to a grimoire with a few alembics and, perhaps, a stuffed crocodile for subsidiary researches — nothing to compare with the aircraft, cameras and automatic processing machines which were then flooding in.

PR Spitfires and Mosquitos ranged alongside US F-4 and F-5 PR Lightnings over everything of strategic interest from Munich to Ploesti, while closer to home German communications and troop positions came under close and regular scrutiny from No 285 Wing, the only tactical reconnaissance asset available to the Fifth and Eighth Armies.[12] Taskings arrived every day by signal to be divided among the PR squadrons, depending on the range involved, the type of cover required and the availability of crews and aircraft. From the aerial photographs brought back from Anzio, the country through which 1st Armored was to move seemed to be almost ideal tank terrain, open and free of obstacles, the kind of country that tank commanders had rarely been able to find in Italy.

At first all went well on 29 January. American tanks and half-tracks rumbled up a track for about two miles but as soon as they moved off it and began to fan out, they were in trouble. Not only was the ground soft and waterlogged, but also the little streams and ditches that meandered through the valleys made far more formidable obstacles than had appeared from the aerial photographs. They were much deeper than had been imagined, with banks covered by tangles of undergrowth and brambles which in places reached a height of 20 or 30 feet. Tanks could not operate effectively in country like that.

So the poor bloody infantry, like the Sherwood Foresters, were on their own. Each time they attacked they were held by the ferocity of German fire. Casualties mounted until, in one company, there were no officers left at all. Maj-Gen Ernest Harmon, commander of 1st Armored, came up to see what was holding the British up. He said afterwards:

'I have never seen so many dead men in one place. They lay so close I had to step with care. I shouted for the commanding officer. From a fox hole there arose a mud-covered corporal with

Top Left:
The Fritz-X armour-piercing radio-guided bomb under a He177. The control surfaces were recessed into the fins at the rear of the missile.
Price

Right:
Foggia airfields.

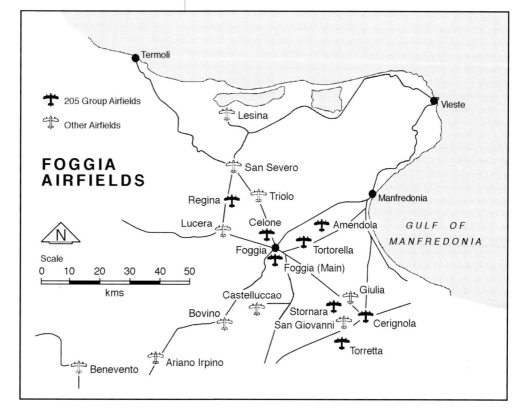

FOGGIA AIRFIELDS

a handle-bar moustache. He was the highest ranking officer still alive. He stood stiffly to attention.

"How's it going?" I asked. (The answer was all around me.)

"Well sir," the corporal said, "there were 116 of us when we first came up, and there are 16 of us left."'

By the end of the day, the Sherwood Foresters had all but been destroyed. Massive air superiority had nothing to offer 1st Armored which was ordered to fall back. For the first time since Salerno, the Fifth Army was on the defensive. Churchill spoke for many at the beginning of February when he lamented with characteristic fervour, 'We hoped to land a wildcat that would tear out the bowels of the Boche. Instead we have stranded a vast whale with its tail flapping about in the water.'[13]

*   *   *   *

After the Allies bombed his villa at Frascati in September, Field Marshal Kesselring moved his headquarters to Monte Soratte, a mountain outcrop likened by Byron to a huge wave about to break near the Sabine Hills to the northwest of Rome. The German C-in-C would usually fly from Soratte to the front at dawn, returning at dusk to minimise the chances of running into any Allied aircraft.

Hitler had ordered the elimination of what he described as the 'abscess' south of Rome, and German efforts to lance the boil or drive the Allied whale back into the sea (depending on your metaphor) began on 3 February when Mackensen had enough forces for a limited attack against the US 3rd Division before switching to the base of the British salient. The Germans timed their attack to take advantage of the bad weather, but Kesselring's plans for considerable fighter and fighter-bomber support for his attacking troops and to silence Allied batteries were also ruined.

Bad weather constantly undermined the continuity of round-the-clock air support, while handicapping armoured movements and severely limiting aerial reconnaissance efforts by both sides. In the event, neither guns nor aeroplanes could dislodge the German infantry, while the Fourteenth Army built up ample supplies of stores and ammunition. Eventually Mackensen amassed a formidable force of over 125,000 men. 'I was convinced,' wrote Kesselring later, 'even taking their powerful naval guns and overwhelming air superiority into consideration, that with the means available we must succeed in throwing the Allies back into the sea.'[14]

Not that the German C-in-C was totally devoid of air support; in fact, he paid tribute to Luftflotte 2 which, 'did all it could, with an imposing concentration of flak and an operational strength reminiscent of past glories'.[15] For three days prior to the main counter-attack, the German close-support air effort was kept down to conserve aircraft for what was seen as the decisive operation. Only 65 combined fighter and fighter-bomber sorties were flown in the battle area on 13 and 14 February. All fighter-bombers were rested the following day, while only a few harassing fighters appeared over the beachhead. Aircrew and ground personnel were briefed on the decisive importance of the coming attack and the necessity of supporting it from the air with all available resources.

The German ground plan, scheduled to start in the early hours of 16 February, was to attack on a narrow front of about 4,000yd straight down the Albano–Anzio road to Anzio itself, a mere eight miles from the starting point. Once Anzio was reached, the Allies would be deprived of their port; the beachhead would be split in two and, with beaches of such poor value, Allied troop evacuation may well have been out of the question.

The Germans held a good start line, on which had been mustered the equivalent of over 10 divisions, as against rather less than half that Allied number. Four German infantry divisions were to launch the assault; they were promised massive air support and the privilege of operating for the first time with the newest secret weapon — the miniature Goliath remote-controlled explosive tank.

During the night of 15/16 February, a force of about 40 long-range bombers — mainly Ju88s, but including a few Do217s from southern France — bombed beachhead positions, but only one landing craft was burnt out and two more damaged. Then at 06.00hrs on 16 February, German artillery opened up a barrage lasting half an hour to herald an attack by infantry and tanks. Fighter-bombers, escorted by fighters, supported these ground operations by strafing Allied troops and installations in unaccustomed strength and with considerable aggressiveness. Luftwaffe efforts that day totalled around 95 fighter-bombers and 150 fighters on escort, armed sweep and patrols. Gp Capt Brian Kingcome, CO of 244 Fighter Wing, said:

'Maintaining the standing patrol over Anzio called for good organisation, with squadrons starting up at exact times, taking off in pairs, forming up into two or three flights of four aircraft in box formation, climbing out over the coast and heading to Anzio. No patrol could leave the bridgehead area until it was relieved . . . The squadron which finished its patrol at dusk did not return home, but stayed at Nettuno for the night and went up again at dawn. The Jerries shelled Nettuno most of the time, so the pilots spent their nights in dug-outs and hoped to wake up and find that their aircraft had not been hit.'[16]

But then the Nettuno air strip was heavily bombed and rendered unusable; for the remainder of the crisis, all Allied fighter support had to come from bases in the Naples area.

Coincidentally, this was a historic period in the Monte Cassino sector. The Allies intended to start a major assault which included heavy air support, but arrangements had to be radically altered as the German attack towards Anzio assumed menacing proportions. Warhawks, Invaders and Baltimores were brought into the battle area in increasing numbers, while plans were hurriedly drawn up for full-scale air support the next day by the Strategic Air Force, Tactical Bomber Force and XII ASC, leaving the Desert Air Force, whenever it was not grounded by weather, to continue the reduction of the Cassino redoubt on its own.

Inside the 'Shingle' beachhead, the constriction was appalling. Penned in on the low-lying, notoriously unhealthy coast, Allied troops found life becoming very unpleasant. Technology was a mixed blessing; no fewer than 21,940 vehicles, including 380

Camouflaged dug-out at a Luftwaffe air base in Italy with a Ju88 in the background. *IWM*

The landing strip at Anzio in May 1944. *RAF Air Historical Branch*

tanks, had been delivered, representing one vehicle for every four men.[17] 'We must have great superiority of chauffeurs,' commented Churchill wryly, but they had little opportunity to drive anywhere as Allied echelons fell back. Nowhere was safe from the shelling. The American hospital area was known as 'Hell's Half Acre' and some men of the 1st Armored Division actually declined to report their wounds for fear that they would be taken to it and killed there.

A few Do217s were over the beachhead during the night and, come 17 February, the Germans strove to exploit their success by pressing through the gap they had created. Some 35 mixed FW190s and Bf109s were sent over at 07.40hrs to bomb and strafe 45th Division's front line. A few minutes later, a powerful force of German infantry followed up with tank support. Once again, they had air support as around 70 fighter-bombers, escorted by some 135 fighters, hit Allied positions: this was one of the few instances during the long Italian campaign when the Luftwaffe really came to the aid of German ground troops. But although some 50 single-engined fighters came down from northern Italy to lend a hand after 19 February, thereby denuding fighter defences up there, this represented the best that the Luftwaffe was capable of doing to support what Hitler had decreed to be a crucial land operation.

Allied intelligence had correctly surmised that the main attack would come down the Albano Road. During the night of the 16/17, many Wellingtons carrying either 18 250lb bombs, or 48 40lb anti-personnel bombs and six 250lb bombs, made two sorties up to the

beachhead from Foggia. It was a 320-mile round trip and, whereas in the past the crews had been given specific targets, that night the order was to hit 'anything that was lit up'.

As the weather on 17 February (for the first time in ages) was good all day, Allied air forces went flat out against the German offensive. A-20s, A-36s and P-40s attacked guns, tanks, troops, vehicles, dumps, communications and buildings along the battle lines, while DAF Baltimores worked over the Carroceto Factory area where both troops and armour were taking cover. US mediums bombed towns, dumps and refuelling points behind the lines, while Bostons visited supply dumps and road traffic south of Rome.[18] An estimated 813 aircraft of all types dropped almost 1,000 tons of bombs on front-line positions — the greatest weight ever before recorded in direct support on a single day. More than a third of these sorties were by heavies which, as at the most critical phase of Salerno, operated in a strictly tactical role, often to within 400yd of the Allied troops they were trying to assist.

The 288 heavy bombers employed in direct support of Anzio ground troops on 17 February was a record to date.[19] Such force was impressive, and in the words of Lt-Gen Jake Devers, Deputy

Below:
A B-17 of the 341st Bomb Squadron, 97th Bomb Group, in action. The 'Y' on the tail was sported by all six B-17 groups in Fifteenth Air Force's 5th Heavy Bombardment Wing. The geometric shape on which the 'Y' was superimposed designated the group: 97th Bomb Group used a triangle. *Author's Collection*

Allied C-in-C Mediterranean Theatre, its blistering impact 'contributed greatly to the morale of our own troops, giving confidence in defensive effort'.[20] Yet the massive air effort, coupled with naval bombardment and ground resistance, did not stop the Germans with their apparently never-ending large infantry reserves from driving a wedge two and a half miles wide and over a mile deep into the invaders' territory. By nightfall, the Germans were in a position to make a direct attack on VI (US) Corps' final defence line. Notwithstanding the efforts of 63 Wellingtons against the main stream of reinforcements and supplies that night, 18 February dawned as a day of supreme crisis for the Allies.

Plans for full Allied air support broke down in the face of the weather on 18 February which was cold, with overcast skies and gusty winds. It was so bad all day that all tactical bomber sorties were either cancelled or rendered abortive. XII ASC managed to launch 35 reconnaissance missions, but most suffered the same fate as the South African fighters which took-off for an armed recce of the roads, only to have to turn back. The bulk of the offensive effort was achieved by the fighter-bombers, with 127 Warhawks and Invaders supporting Allied troops opposing the main German thrust which began at dawn. The odd tank was hit and fires were started on local railway tracks, but although the army reported that fighter-bomber attacks near the bomb-line were very effective on the whole, the rapidly deteriorating weather increasingly affected their accuracy.

The one outstanding air contribution that day was made not by whizz kids hurtling in and out of danger but rather by men like Capt William H. McKay, a US artillery spotter in a little Piper L-4 Cub that was nimble enough to operate when its heavier brethren could not. McKay was observing for the US 45th Division artillery and at 11.10hrs he spotted a force of tanks and around 2,500 Germans moving south from Carroceto along the Albano road. Within 12 minutes of receiving his signal, the Corps Fire Control Centre had massed the fire of 224 guns — including some British — on to the advance, which became disorganised and broke up. Over the next 50 minutes, Capt McKay directed the fire of the guns on to four further German concentrations. The small force of US observation aircraft evaded all attempts by the Luftwaffe and artillery to liquidate them, but it must have been no fun sitting there wondering if your luck would hold.

The Germans made their third attack of 18 February at 17.00hrs. Allied artillery and ground troops took the brunt of the push, and they received diminishing air support because of the worsening weather. The Luftwaffe's support programme suffered similarly, but although only 44 fighter-bombers and 60 fighters got airborne, they were reported as being lively in action. But 1st Armored Division launched an effective counter-attack and the infantry stood their ground.

The final German attempt to break through began at 04.00hrs on 19 February. It just so happened that Saturday 19 February saw the start of the 'Big Week', when 1,000 heavy bombers of RAF Bomber Command and 900 escort fighters of the Eighth Air Force launched a devastatingly co-ordinated attack against leading German aircraft and aero-engine plants. During six February days, 13 major strikes were carried out against 15 centres and, as had

been foreseen, the Luftwaffe came up to fight. At the end of Big Week, 600 Germans were claimed shot down by Allied crews for around 200 of their own. The true figures were academic; it was the trend that mattered. The Allies had won air supremacy and from then on they ranged almost at will over Germany.[21]

Ira Eaker, C-in-C of all Allied Air Forces in the Mediterranean, received operational directives for the US Twelfth Air Force from Allied C-in-C Mediterranean Theatre, General Wilson. For Fifteenth Air Force operations, Eaker's directives came from General Spaatz, Commanding General of US Strategic Air Forces, except in the event of an emergency proclaimed by Wilson. Given the desperate battle being fought at Anzio, not to mention a little local difficulty around Cassino, strategic bomber men feared that 'Jumbo' Wilson might be forced to proclaim an emergency in the middle of Big Week. But, by agreement, Eaker managed to meet both his obligations: he split his heavy bombers to send 105 against the Germans at the beachhead and 126 against Regensburg. This compromise not only illustrated the awesome weight of air power available to him over Italy but it also set a pattern for the future.[22]

Given the seriousness of the situation, it was planned to divert the strategic and tactical air forces from a big effort planned against marshalling yards in the Rome area, and the railways further north, to VI (US) Corps' battle area. Yet 19 February saw another day of the worst sort of winter weather, and almost the whole effort had to be cancelled. The entire Desert Air Force was grounded by gales, so no help was forthcoming from the other side of the snow-covered Apennines. It was left to two groups of B-25s, and around 160 Warhawks supported by 56 A-26s, to keep the Allied aerial end up by flying throughout the day to bomb troops and tanks.

The Luftwaffe equalled its fighter-bomber effort of the previous day, sprinkling anti-personnel butterfly-bombs over the unappreciative Irish Guards, but a total effort around the 100 mark paled against an Allied effort of over 1,700 sorties two days earlier. The Germans did not lack flak batteries, which proved to be ubiquitous, intense and accurate both in the ground and anti-aircraft roles; yet in the end, although the Germans committed their best reserves and gained ground, they could not break the Allied line. In five days of fighting between 16 and 20 February, the Allies lost another 5,000 men to add to the loss of 14,000 already suffered before the attack began. But they derived a new confidence from the experience, and although Allied positions were being held by fewer and more tired men, they inflicted equal casualties on their opponents. By the afternoon of 20 February, German forces were exhausted and Mackensen had to withdraw them to reorganise. Two days later, Eaker felt safe to release the Fifteenth to join Big Week for the first joint attack on Regensburg.

More than 10,000 fragmentation bombs were dropped on German concentrations near Carroceto on 20 February, and the US Army subsequently awarded an appreciable share of the glory for breaking down the German communication and supply chain to air bombardment along the road from Carroceto back to the Alban Hills. The German Army attributed the majority of its casualties to Allied artillery fire, though they felt they would have been more successful if their armour had not got frequently bogged down.

Both sides agreed that the Goliath explosive tank, which easily got mud-bound, had been a ludicrous failure.

Having sustained heavy casualties in their failed attempt to destroy the Allied salient, the Germans were left in a state of some confusion which Allied air forces were quick to exploit. The Carroceto area seemed to offer particularly profitable targets, and 75 US B-24s plus around 100 B-26s broke through the intense flak cordon to drop high explosive, general purpose and fragmentation bombs on troop concentrations along a two-mile stretch of railway line five miles north of the Carroceto front line. Other German positions and armour were bombed by nearly 200 Mitchells, Bostons, Warhawks and Invaders.

While Mackensen pulled his ground forces together for a third counter-attack, the Luftwaffe tried to restore a modicum of strength and serviceability. A Gruppe of some 50 single-engined fighters moved down from northern Italy by 23 February, but there was no help from outside the theatre until the end of the month when 40 mixed FW190s and Bf109s were moved down from west of the Seine to central Italy. By 1 March the overall strength of Luftflotte 2 had increased by nearly 35% since the Allied landing, and there were now approximately 475 German aircraft available directly for operations in the Anzio area.

But although Allied counter-air operations against an obvious German build-up were thwarted by bad weather and bad luck, it did not really matter. When the German Army attacked for a third time on 28 February, it was not on the Albano–Anzio road but from the opposite corner of the bridgehead, from the Cisterna road against the US 3rd Division. Checked by minefields, accurate American small-arms fire and artillery, and by the spirited resistance of US troops, the German attack faltered after gaining little ground. When the weather improved from 13.00hrs on 29 February, a fairly large Allied air effort was switched to what seemed to be the most dangerous area north of Cisterna. Apart from a B-26 attack on Viterbo main airfield with its preponderance of bombers and fighters, 14 missions were flown by Allied fighter-bombers and by light and medium bombers in direct response to calls from VI (US) Corps and 3rd Division, against troops working their way along a river bed, tanks, motor transport and guns. Other aircraft undertook armed reconnaissance and strafing against anything German that moved.

By 1 March, Kesselring realised that his attempts to liquidate the beachhead would be impossible without an injection of fresh troops, which were not forthcoming. The following day, the skies cleared and the pent-up air forces had a field day. Close on 800 aircraft operated within 4,000yd of the bomb-line in direct support of VI (US) Corps. Escorted by 176 P-38s and P-47s, 10 groups of heavy bombers, four groups of light bombers and 360 fighter-bombers went into action, dropping over 600 tons of bombs on forward assembly areas and artillery positions in particular.

BBC correspondent Wynford Vaughan-Thomas thought that 'the great flight of aircraft looked strangely beautiful, remote and efficient, as they came in from the south in an endless stream, jettisoning their load of death with a clinical detachment and swung back for more'.

'Christ, General,' said a US aide, 'that's hitting a guy when he's

down,' but such a sentiment found little echo at the sharp end. VI (US) Corps' reports were full of enthusiastic comments on the extent to which bombing had raised troops' morale. 3rd Brigade described a formation of 96 bombers passing overhead as 'the best sight seen for days', while 3rd Division said that its forward troops were 'elated' with the bombing of the railway northwest of Cisterna.

Moreover, the level of enthusiastic support was not one-way. A force of 24 A-20 Bostons was on the receiving end of the most enthusiastic flak of the day while bombing a gun area. After 20 aircraft returned badly holed, the AAF asked the army to attack the same target heavily on the morrow. This plea was accepted by the chief of staff of Fifth Army.

Between 22 January and 4 March, when German troops switched from offence to defence, total American 'Shingle' casualties were officially reckoned at 10,775, British at 10,168 and German 10,306. Hitler was displeased that the Allies had not been thrown back into the sea, and he demanded that 20 officers of all ranks be sent forthwith from the front to account personally for this lamentable outcome. This group of unfortunates was led by Gen Walter Fries of the 29th Panzer Grenadiers, and as Hitler grilled them for two days, the men on the ground gave the decisive causes of failure in descending order of importance as complete Allied air superiority, Allied artillery and naval fire superiority, and the impossibility of committing heavy armoured forces at the critical time because of the soft swampy ground.

Overall, co-operation between Allied artillery air observers and their batteries had been excellent, with disastrous implications for German gun positions. Fries vigorously rejected the suggestion that German morale had been low. The most superior infantry force, he said, could not advance if it was being smashed by massed artillery fire and air attacks. Only 10% of German losses had been due to infantry weapons; 15% had been caused by Allied bombing and a massive 75% were down to artillery. The Germans could not respond in kind because, as Westphal advised Hitler in person, 'it was impossible to bring the necessary artillery allocations to the front owing to the daily severance of rail communications in Italy by bombing attacks'.

As the Germans started to dig in, ushering in a new phase of the Italian campaign, Allied Air C-in-C Ira Eaker crafted a letter to Hap Arnold in Washington outlining his thoughts on air power and the Anzio operation.

'Shortly after I came here the "Shingle" operation was launched. The landing was successful and I was personally critical of the slow progress made in extending the bridgehead, the failure to move rapidly to the high ground from the north and take the then lightly-held village of Cisterna, thus to ensure a sufficiently deep penetration to guarantee that no artillery fire would fall on the harbour of Anzio or on our landing strip.[23] After walking and driving over the terrain, I now feel that Alexander and Clark have a good case. If they had pushed the two divisions in the first landing on to these points, there is little doubt in my mind that the Germans would have gotten between them and Anzio and that, with their supplies cut off, they would

Above:
The Luftflotte 2 forward command post overlooking the Anzio beachhead. (L-R) Flg Off Kluge, Field Marshal von Richthofen, Gen von Pohl and Col Christ.
Author's Collection

have eventually been overcome . . . When Gen Spaatz came down here two weeks ago he felt exactly as I had . . . I think you know what ardent airmen Tooey and I are and that we both have the aggressive spirit. When you find the two if us in agreement on this point, you should be less critical of the Ground Forces . . . They might have brought on a full-scale enemy retreat as happened at El Alamein. However, we must remember that the terrain and the weather conspired to bring about an entirely different situation than that which pertained in the desert. In the desert, flanking movements were always possible. Here, both weather and terrain have forced any advances to be made through mined defiles with heavy artillery concentrations on the high ground on either side. That makes a very different picture of it entirely.

'There seems to have been a feeling on the part of some distant strategists and critics that, in some way, the air let the ground and sea forces down in this operation. Actually there have been continual messages coming back from Alexander and from Clark lauding and complimenting the air effort . . . The military critics have not appreciated what air forces can and cannot do and the true influence of the weather in placing a ceiling on their capabilities. When the navy announces that it cannot inload supplies with a wind of more than force four or with a high tide and rough seas, nobody criticises the navy! That is an accepted limitation in naval operations. The same is true

of the ground forces. When they come to a swollen steam flowing at such a strength that it prevents their laying their pontoon bridges, or when they come to a mined defile, it is well understood that they are halted for the moment. You have not, I am sure, appreciated completely the limitations which the weather has imposed on the air effort here during the last six weeks. We have had almost daily heavy rains. On many days it has rained steadily for 12 to 24 hours. There have been, generally, low icing levels, the clouds have rested on the mountain tops and generally the visibility has been greatly reduced. Despite this weather condition, we have averaged 600–1,000 thousand sorties a day: we have maintained constant patrols, by day and night, over the bridgehead: our medium bombers have worked on enemy flying fields to the point where the enemy's air effort has averaged less than 100 sorties a day. We have also made two of our most successful long-range attacks into Germany with the Strategic Air Force and they have been used most successfully in cutting communications, in attacks on airfields on southern France and, on two critical occasions, on the battlefield.

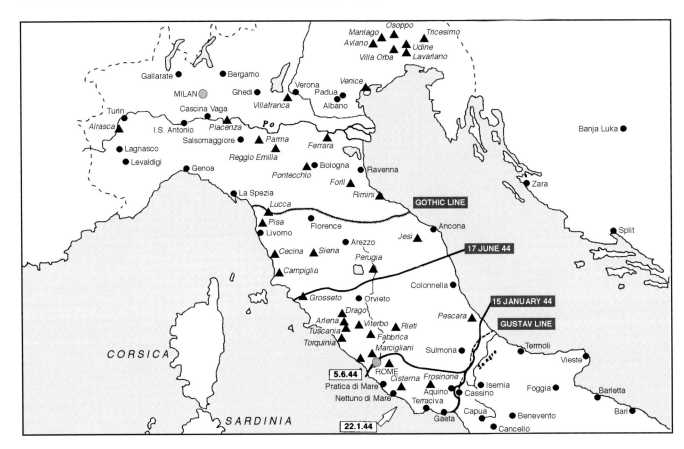

Above:
Main military airfields in Italy, January–June 1944.

'The big lesson I have gained from participating in the "Shingle" operation is this: amphibious operations are the most difficult form of military movement. They should never be undertaken except as a last resort for the very good reason that you deliberately hand every advantage to the enemy. Amphibious operations will be a failure if opposed by an enemy of the character of the Germans in strength unless they are within the reach of an overwhelming friendly air force.'[24]

* * * *

The debate over whether or not Gen Lucas was too cautious was really a smokescreen. Lucas may have been old before his time, but the great fault with the Anzio operation lay in sending a corps to do an army's job. Salerno should have made it clear to every military brain that Kesselring and his hardened subordinates, adept in exploiting Italian terrain and weather, were no pushover. To expect the Germans to cut and run in the face of a couple of amphibious divisions, handing over Rome with its attendant propaganda value in the process, was the reasoning of planners who needed to get out more often.

'I am not happy about our relative strength in Italy,' wrote British Army Chief Sir Alan Brooke on 25 January. 'We have not got sufficient margin to be able to guarantee making a success of our attacks.'[25] The strength of the Anzio venture, once envisioned as requiring only 24,000 troops, eventually expanded to over 110,000. And once the Allies were faced with having to build up the wherewithal to resume the offensive on a large scale, they lost the element of surprise, allowed the more adaptable Germans to fortify and reinforce, and handed over the initiative. As the Americans were to learn 30 years later in Vietnam, massive air power can only do so much to retrieve a strategy based on wishful thinking.

In the back of Kesselring's mind throughout Anzio was the fear that the Allies might launch a second invasion on the Adriatic coast of Italy; the field marshal felt it would have shortened the Italian campaign if the Allies had landed in his army's rear. For that reason, his air reconnaissance assets in Italy and the Balkans were particularly active. Yet despite the spreading of his meagre aerial resources, Kesselring felt that the air support given to the German Army round the Anzio bridgehead 'was by no means despicable, while the flak support was extraordinarily helpful'.[26] A Luftwaffe battle headquarters, set up in the Alban Hills under von Pohl, had a direct view over the whole battlefield and far out to sea. From there, aided by liaison officers with the divisions, Pohl's staff were able to follow the tide of battle and promptly send in close-support formations.

Why, with a 10:1 superiority in aircraft, did the Allies not swat the Luftwaffe out of the sky? As it happened, the very smallness of

German aircraft numbers, combined with highly developed expertise in dispersal, made Luftflotte 2 a far more difficult target to cripple than a much larger air force. Then there was the perennial foul weather, which grounded too many missions too often. Finally, the critical ground situation took first call on tactical and even strategic air support. Given that Allied forces at Anzio were nearly 50% fewer than the Germans massing against them, the calls for the bombing of military installations of all types immediately ahead of Allied troops were continuous, insistent and justified. Because air power was intimately linked with the fate of the troops around Cassino and Anzio, there was little let-up and certainly little air power left over for other than immediate targets. Despite reasonably regular photo-reconnaissance coverage of airfields likely to be involved in any German counter-offensive, there is no evidence of any consistent series of Allied attacks in sufficient force seriously to cripple the Luftwaffe.

One lesson learnt from this phase was that if German troop and supply movements were to be effectively limited, the bombing had to continue around the clock to keep the pressure on. The Allies needed a more meaningful night-bomber force than that provided by the elderly Wellingtons.[27] As it was, the inability to operate at night and in bad weather meant that Allied capacity to damage railways was never decisively greater than the ability of the Germans to repair them. Not for the first or last time in the Italian campaign, the cloak of darkness saved German forces from destruction.

Notes to Chapter 7

1. Over 1,000 US A-26 and 900 P-40 Warhawk sorties were flown in the first fortnight, supported by 1,400 RAF and US Spitfire patrols and sweeps.
2. Warlimont, op.cit, p.410.
3. Owen, R.; The Desert Air Force; p.209.
4. Hallion, R. P.; Storm Over Iraq; p.194.
5. Trevelyan, R.; Rome 44; p.25.
6. Kesselring, op.cit, p.194.
7. They came from the following eight units: I and III/Lehr I (45 aircraft) in Greece, II and III/KG30 and I/KG76 (55) on the Western Front, II/KG100 (5) in southern France, and 30 aircraft from I/KG30 and II/KG76 then refitting.
8. Letter to author, 10 June 1998.
9. Although a sufficient flow of replacement aircraft was maintained.
10. Pohl was Air Attaché Rome until July 1943, when he assumed command of anti-aircraft artillery in southern Italy,
11. Nos 680, 682, 683 and 60 SAAF Squadrons.
12. In early 1944, 285 Wing comprised Nos 40 (SAAF) and 225 Squadrons supporting Fifth Army and XII ASC on the west coast, and Nos 208 and 318 (Polish) Squadrons plus a flight of No 682 Squadron on the east.
13. Bryant, A.; Triumph in the West; p.130.
14. Kesselring, op.cit, p.195.
15. Ibid.
16. Duke, N.; Test Pilot; p.112.
17. 'The Allies' strength,' commented Kesselring wryly, 'lay in the vast amount of material they could squander.' Memoirs; p.165.
18. Craven and Cate, vol 3, p.356.
19. 248 fighter-bombers, 60 light bombers and 152 medium bombers supported the heavies.
20. Devers to Arnold, 10 March 1944.
21. Gen (General der Jagdflieger) Adolf Galland reported that the German day-fighter force lost over 1,000 pilots between January and April, including some of the best commanders. 'The time has come when our weapon is in sight of collapse.' Bekker, The Luftwaffe War Diaries; p.351.
22. In fact, Wilson was at no time to proclaim a formal tactical emergency, although he broached the subject on two occasions to Eaker.
23. For which poor old John Lucas was made the scapegoat when, on 22 February, he was abruptly replaced as commander of VI Corps by his deputy, Gen Lucian K. Truscott.
24. Eaker to Arnold, 6 March 1944.
25. Bryant, op.cit, p.113.
26. Kesselring, op.cit, p.197.
27. Some indication of the Wimpey's obsolescence may be gained from the fact that the last UK-based Wellington long-range bomber operation took place back on 8/9 October 1943.

THE MONASTERY

'It is the nature of war not to be a game played to the whistle between white lines.'
N. C. Phillips

The Fifth Army's main axis of advance to Rome lay along Highway 6. After crossing the Rapido River, Highway 6 passed through the small country town of Cassino and then turned south for a mile before curving round the base of the spur known as Monte Cassino. From there, the road ran northwestward along the northern edge of the Liri Valley until it reached Rome.

Methods of attacking the Monte Cassino spur had been regularly studied at the Italian Staff College before the war. Every directing staff solution assessed the position as almost impregnable, and that was without any artificial assistance. Over the four months prior to

January 1944, the Germans developed and fortified the spur, constructing steel and concrete pill boxes, and drilling and blasting emplacements in the rock.

All 1,700ft of Monte Cassino dominated Cassino town and Highway 6. Its northern, eastern and southern sides were exceedingly steep, and the southeastern tip of the mountain was crowned, if not adorned, by an enormous abbey. The Abbey of Monte Cassino, or the 'Monastery' as it was known to Allied troops, was founded in AD529 by St Benedict on the site of an ancient Roman temple to Apollo. Over succeeding centuries, the abbey developed as both a fortress and a treasure-house of Christian art and scholarship.

This mass of cream-coloured stone, shaped as an irregular quadrilateral whose longest side extended 660ft, dominated the entire eastern end of the Liri Valley. But the abbey was by no means

the only vantage point, nor even the most important; extensive German field works covered the steep eastern slope of the spur as well as a wide area of the summit. Further to the west, two other dominant features, known as Point 593 and Point 575, had also been converted into strongpoints. The whole constituted an intricate system of interlocking defences from which accurate and intense cross fire could be brought to bear on any line of Allied approach to the head of the Liri Valley, which was only four to six miles wide.

The Fifth Army planned turning movements either side of a frontal thrust into the valley. X Corps aimed to drive up from the south, while II (US) Corps assaulted across the Rapido River and the French attacked in the mountains, but the offensive did not go to plan. Little direct air support could be given while the Anzio beachhead was being consolidated, and although II (US) Corps continued to try to take Cassino, after two weeks it occupied only a few houses on the outskirts of the town. Leading troops were within 300yd of Monastery Hill by 6 February, but five days later the last attack ran out of steam. An exhausted II (US) Corps passed command of the sector to the New Zealand Corps.

New Zealand Corps, comprising the 2nd NZ and 4th Indian Divisions, was commanded by Lt-Gen Sir Bernard Freyberg. Freyberg was a trained dentist before he joined the army and won the VC in World War 1. He was responsible for the defence of Crete in 1941, and his gentle handling plus inspired leadership of the New Zealanders produced one of the toughest and hardest-

hitting combat formations of World War 2. Now he was tasked with pulling the teeth of the Gustav Line.

As early as 9 February, Freyberg had resolved to capture Monastery Hill and Cassino should II (US) Corps fail to do so, but his instructions made no mention of the abbey; it was not given as an objective and no reference was made to air support. While 2nd NZ Division was ordered to attack Cassino railway station, 4th Indian Division was expected to cut Highway 6 and capture the town of Cassino. As their engineers foresaw that they might have to enter the abbey, a subaltern was dispatched to Naples to buy whatever books and maps he could find on the structure. 4th Indian Division prepared its plans, issuing its divisional operation instruction at 22.45hrs on 11 February. No reference was made therein to the abbey, except in the air paragraph which read: 'Requests have been made for all buildings and suspected enemy strongpoints on or in the vicinity of objectives, including the monastery, to be subjected to intense bombing from now onward.'[1]

The bombing of the Abbey of Monte Cassino came into the frame because of the firm views held by Maj-Gen Francis Tuker, General Officer Commanding 4th Indian Division, on the value of air support. Tuker strongly advocated an attack to turn Monastery Hill and isolate it, and he told Freyberg that nothing would induce him to attack Monte Cassino head-on unless 'the garrison was reduced to helpless lunacy by sheer unending pounding for days and nights by air and artillery'.[2] GOC 4th Indian Division expanded his argument when he wrote:

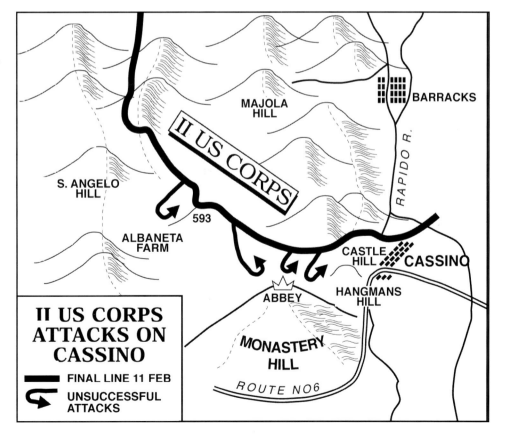

Left:
Aerial view of Cassino. Cassino town and the flat Rapido Valley with Route 6 running through are in the foreground. Route 6 curves round the Cassino massif before swinging round into the Liri Valley (top left) and heading towards Rome. In the centre, bombs are bursting on the slopes of Monte Cassino. *Author's Collection*

Right:
US II Corps attacks on Cassino up to 11 February 1944.

'. . . that the enemy are in concrete and steel emplacements on "Monastery" Hill. From a wide experience in attacks in mountain areas I know that infantry cannot "jump" strong defences of this sort. These defences have to be "softened up", either by being cut off on all sides and starved out, or else by continuous and heavy bombardment over a period of days. Even with the latter, success will only be achieved in my opinion if a thorough and prolonged air bombardment is undertaken with really heavy bombs a good deal larger than Kittybomber missiles.

'We have complete air superiority in this theatre but the "softening" of Monastery Hill has not been started . . . Already three attacks have been put in and have failed — at some considerable cost, I am told. Another attack without air "softening" will only lead to a similar result.'[3]

Tuker's forceful arguments failed to deflect Freyberg from planning a frontal attack on Monte Cassino — the big New Zealander lacked the manpower to do more than maintain II (US) Corps' drive — but they played a part in changing attitudes towards the bombing of the monastery. The abbey was no threat in itself: Tuker's rationale stood or fell on whether or not it was being used for military purposes; and the moral high ground implicit in that question was to be fought over as much as the real estate itself.

Monte Cassino Abbey came within the sector of the front covered by XIV Panzer Corps, whose commander was the former defender of Corsica, Gen Frido von Senger und Etterlin. The devoutly Catholic Senger later affirmed that there were 'no Germans in the monastery grounds, for Field Marshal Kesselring had given express orders that troops should not be permitted to enter the sanctuary, in order to avoid giving the Allies any excuse for destroying it'.[4] A German guard was posted on the abbey gate to ensure that the C-in-C's orders were carried out, and Senger visited the abbey for Christmas mass in 1943 'to confirm that no German soldiers were visiting the place once fighting had broken out in the general area'.[5]

Col Schlegel of the Hermann Göring Panzers had already persuaded the abbey's elderly abbot, Mgr Gregorio Diamare, to allow treasures including the reliquary of St Benedict and the famous library to be moved to safety. Senger was only too pleased to endorse Kesselring's order that the abbey should be spared from military operations.

'Nobody would want to sponsor the destruction of a cultural monument of this kind merely to gain a tactical advantage . . . True, Monte Cassino commanded a view of the entire district . . . But on our side it was the considered tactical opinion that so conspicuous a landmark would be quite unsuitable as an observation post, since we could expect it to be put out of action by heavy fire very soon after the big battle had started. It was the German practice to place the artillery observers half way up the hills in a concealed position with a camouflaged background.'[6]

The Germans stoutly maintained that they respected the neutrality of the abbey throughout, whereas the Allies suspected that it was being used as an observation post. But such hair-splitting cut little ice with practical soldiers such as Gen Tuker. Once the enemy included Monte Cassino in his defensive line, and according to NZ Corps records it was 'known to be the hub of the defensive system on Monte Cassino', then the building on the summit became a legitimate target. Tuker wrote:

'Whether the monastery is now occupied by a German garrison or not, it is certain that it will be held as a keep by the last remnants of the garrison of the position. It is therefore essential that the building be so demolished as to prevent its effective occupation at that time.'[7]

On 13 February Lt-Col the Hon J. Hare, an artilleryman in command of No 7 Army Air Support Control at HQ Fifth Army, visited NZ Corps to discuss co-ordination of the large-scale bombing of Cassino Abbey with 4th Indian Division's attack on the same objective. That same day, a meeting of all affected commanders and heads of services decided that the 'Monastery feature should first be subjected to intensive bombing from the air'.

From all this, it would seem that the impetus for the bombing of Monte Cassino Abbey came from the bottom up rather than from the top down. Certainly, the request at this stage had not been sanctioned by the Commanding General of the New Zealand Corps, though from now on Gen Freyberg gave it his full support. This affable man who encouraged camaraderie and self-respect — 'You cannot treat a man like a butler,' he would say, 'and expect him to fight like a lion' — probably wanted to give his boys every bit of support that he could, and if they decided that their load would be eased by bombing the abbey, then so be it.

Every day in the baroque palace at Caserta, there was a Fifteenth Army Group G3 (Air) meeting attended by Generals Alexander and Cannon. Joe Cannon, the excellent and very popular commander of the Tactical Air Force, was not going to raise any objection to Freyberg's request to bomb the abbey; he had previously told Alexander 'If you let me use the whole of our bomber force against Cassino, we will whip it out like a dead tooth.'[8] But authority for this course of action could not be given lightly. Back on the first day of the invasion of Sicily, President Roosevelt had written to the Pope, reassuring His Holiness that 'churches and religious institutions will, to the extent that is within our power, be spared the devastations of war during the struggle ahead'. Eisenhower also issued a special order at the beginning of the campaign on the mainland, reminding all commanders that Italy was rich in cultural heritage 'and that, in so far as military necessity permitted, these monuments should be spared from all damage'. On 5 November, Ike told Fifteenth Army Group that Monte Cassino Abbey was to be added to the list of monuments to be protected. Under pressure from the Holy See, Fifteenth Army Group signalled Fifth and Eighth Armies, instructing that the papal domain at Castel Gandolfo and the Abbey of Monte Cassino be preserved if possible, but that 'consideration for the safety of such areas will not be allowed to interfere with military necessity'.

There the matter rested until 29 December, when Eisenhower signalled all commanders reinforcing the significance of Italian monuments while at the same time reiterating the military realities involved:

'If we have to choose between destroying a famous building and sacrificing our own men, then our men's lives count infinitely more and the building must go . . . Nothing can stand against the argument of military necessity. That is an accepted principle.'

The military found this ruling to be very helpful when dealing with the Pope's summer residence at Castel Gandolfo.

Castel Gandolfo was not far removed from Anzio, lying as it did on the outskirts of the town of Albano. The religious colony included colleges and a cathedral, and there were nuns in the convent just outside the estate walls, yet this spiritual estate lay close to roads that sustained a mighty temporal battlefield. Eventually, Ira Eaker dispatched the following signal to the Supreme Commander Mediterranean:

'Certain areas in Italy pertaining to the Vatican have been on a restricted basis as far as air operations are concerned . . . The exception has been in case a tactical emergency should arise which would necessitate such operation in our own protection or in support of our vital ground operations. This situation has now developed in the Albano–Castel Gandolfo area wherein is located the Vatican farm and summer residence. This area is now in the midst of the battle area and contains essential road communications. I have discussed this with Alexander, who feels that we cannot prejudice the success of the Rome operations by providing in the middle of the battle a sanctuary for the opposing Germans. I have instructed Cannon to attack targets in this restricted zone only when in his opinion and in that of Alexander it is absolutely necessary, but have given him freedom to operate when this condition is met.'[9]

In response, 23 B-25s from the 321st Bombardment Group were sent to drop 82 1,000lb bombs on the Albano road junction on 1 February. Another 36 B-25s repeated the medicine on the morning of 2 February, this time dropping 127 1,000lb bombs. The impact was described most vividly by Raleigh Trevelyan:

'A huge dust cloud hung over poor, ruined Albano. Bombs and more bombs. Germans everywhere. Their mighty war machine was truly getting into gear. Lorries full of parachutists in camouflage uniform. Tanks groaning, rumbling; Panzer Grenadiers in grey, the spread eagle on their lapels. Scores of civilians were killed in an air raid. There were bodies everywhere, but the tanks went forward, crushing them.'[10]

In such circumstances, it is not surprising that 5,000 civilian refugees sought shelter in the nearby papal estate.

The Vatican subsequently reported that one bomb from the first raid hit Castel Gandolfo convent, killing 17 nuns. The apse of the cathedral was also damaged, and five bombs from the second attack fell on the domain, killing one and injuring five. On 8 February, the British Foreign Office, to whom the Castel Gandolfo affair had been referred, gave the following ruling to the chiefs of staff based on the previously laid-down policy that diplomatic immunity should not interfere with military necessity:

'It follows that if the C-in-C is allowed this latitude in the treatment of Vatican properties during the assault on Rome, he should be allowed a similar latitude in regard to those similar properties during the assault on the localities in which they are situated. In other words, the C-in-C was not only within his rights but within his instructions in permitting such action to be taken as resulted in bombs falling on properties at Castel Gandolfo.'[11]

On 10 February, Allied heavies were diverted to give tactical support to the Anzio beachhead. Among them, 36 B-17s attacked Albano, after which papal authorities claimed that as many as 500 civilian refugees sheltering at Castel Gandolfo had been killed. His Holiness was greatly distressed by the unfortunate end to so many homeless who had accepted his hospitality, but they could not 'stand against the argument of military necessity'. Castel Gandolfo set a precedent which was fresh in the minds of senior commanders when the idea of bombing Cassino Abbey was first mooted.

By February 1944, with everyone demanding a speedy resolution of the Italian campaign to clear the decks for 'Overlord', there was really no bombing Rubicon left to cross. As Allied positions at Anzio became ever more threatened, the roads and railways that flowed through Rome were hammered as never before. On 13 February, Mother Mary St Luke, an American nun working for the Vatican off Via Veneto, wrote in her diary that, 'last night British planes flew over the city. German planes rose to meet them, and there was a duel in the air. One bomb fell in Via Mecenate, not far from the Coliseum, and hit a private nursing home, wrecking a large part of it and killing the surgeon who directed it.'[12]

'A dreadful time,' wrote Mrs Whitaker, a wealthy English widow who lived to the north of the Borghese Gardens. 'Bombardments and sirens constantly. We hear they are still digging out the dead at Castel Gandolfo.' The British ambassador to the Holy See reported to London that 30 people had been killed and 600 injured in Rome from air raids on 15 February, and 80 killed and 150 injured the following day. In vain, the apostolic delegate in Washington wrote to President Roosevelt imploring 'Your Excellency's intervention that Rome may be spared from the horror and destruction of further aerial attacks'.[13] Someone in the State Department may have felt moved to exclaim, 'Christ, doesn't he know there's a war on!'

*　　　*　　　*　　　*

The 4th Indian Division made two bids for air support at Monte Cassino. The first was for the heaviest possible weight of demolition bombs for late afternoon of 16 February, with the aim of reducing the abbey to ruins. The second was for incendiary and smoke bombs on the abbey and adjacent woods, to prevent the enemy from reorganising his defences before dark. At the foot of this planning note were the following words: 'The success of this operation depends entirely on the strength of the air.'[14]

There is no doubt that 4th Indian Division's request was supported by Freyberg and Alexander, but not the Fifth Army commander. According to Mark Clark's memoirs, he was away at the Anzio Front on 12 February when Freyberg telephoned Gen Alfred Gruenther, Fifth Army chief of staff, to ask for air support to soften the enemy position in the Cassino area. Freyberg's argument was 'the divisional commander making the attack, feels that it is an essential target, and I thoroughly agree with him'.

Although Clark was preoccupied at this time 'with a big pile of administrative papers and studying reports from Anzio', both he and Gruenther considered bombing of the abbey to be unnecessary. But then he was told that 'General Alexander has decided that the monastery should be bombed if General Freyberg considers it a military necessity.' Clark was still not convinced, whereupon Freyberg played his trump card: 'He stated that any higher commander who refused to authorise the bombing would have to be prepared to take the responsibility for failure of the attack.'[15] Subsequently, Senger took great comfort from Clark's statement that, 'I say that the bombing of the abbey . . . was a mistake.'[16] It is easy to be wise with hindsight. Clark was in a difficult position, being an American general responsible for a New Zealand and Indian corps under a British army group commander. But, given the myriad political sensitivities, it is arguable that he was remiss in not going forward to see the situation on the ground for himself, and to hear the New Zealanders' and Indians' concerns first-hand, so that he would have been wise before the event.

Yet, whatever the disagreements between army men, the final decision rested with Gen Eaker, who alone was empowered to order the Commanding General of the Fifteenth Air Force to use his heavy bombers in support of the land battle; and he took his responsibilities seriously. Together with Gen Devers, Deputy Supreme Allied Commander, Eaker flew over the abbey on 13 February in a Piper Cub at a height of less than 200ft. The Germans ignored small aircraft for fear of drawing attacks by fighter-bombers, so Eaker and Devers came back safely to report seeing not only a military radio mast but enemy solders moving in and out. This was very convenient because on 10 February, Eaker had received two rather pointed signals from the Commanding General of the USAAF on the level of air support being given to ground forces. In the first, Hap Arnold noted that 'considering difficulties being encountered in the Italian campaign despite our overwhelming air superiority, it would appear that perhaps our organisation, tactics or equipment may be faulty in certain respects'. The second was blunter.

'Combat Allied airplanes operational in the Mediterranean Theatre total 4,542. A serious crisis appears to be imminent in the beachhead south of Rome and for our Fifth and for the British Eighth Army. In view of this, information is requested as to why every airplane that is flyable and has a crew is not used against German personnel, equipment and installations. Your comments desired.'

Perhaps Eaker decided that it would be politic to meet Freyberg's request, just as he had shown willing with the heavies over Anzio on 17 February. But here comes the slightly farcical twist. At some time on 14 February it was decided to bomb the abbey the next day, rather than on 16 February as 4th Indian Division requested, because the forecast flying weather was better. Unfortunately, there was no way by which the main ground-attack could have been brought forward by a day at that late stage.

Events moved quickly on the night of 14/15 February. At 21.50hrs, MAAF issued all Air HQs with the information that the abbey was now a special target and the objective was the maximum destruction of its walls and buildings. Ten per cent of the bomb load was to be delay-fused up to 24 hours, and a special bombline[17] was to be furnished. At 23.45hrs, Tactical Bomber Force HQ briefed down to wing level that the medium bombers were to cross the coast between Ischia Island and the Volturno River, and attack in three waves at 13.00, 13.15 and 13.30hrs. Before that, the heavy bombers were to start Gen Tuker's 'softening' process. Their orders, signed by Gen Twining and issued at 01.14hrs on 15 February, detailed four groups of B-17s to attack between 09.30 and 10.15hrs.

During the night of 14/15 February, leaflets were air-dropped into the monastery warning Amici italiani that it had been decided, with regret, to attack the sacred precincts. Signed 'Fifth Army', the meaning of the leaflets was clear. 'Our warning is urgent: leave the monastery. Abandon it at once.' Four Italian women inside the abbey recounted the sequence of events thereafter. The leaflets were picked up and Abbot Diamare read one. He asked for advice and two Germans were sent up to the abbey. Seeing that the refugees sheltering in the abbey were becoming frightened, the abbot sent monks to calm them with the assurance that the Germans had promised to send a message to US Headquarters to prevent the bombing of the abbey. There is no record of any such message ever being received by any Allied unit.

At 06.00hrs on 15 February, the monks told the refugees to prepare to leave. A few minutes later, two German officers and an interpreter came to inform the abbot that no civilian was to leave, under pain of being shot. Later that morning, 142 B-17s were launched against the abbey.[18] Of these, one returned early and six brought their bombs back, but the main force experienced no problem in dropping 287 tons of 500lb general purpose bombs and 66 tons of 100lb incendiary bombs on abbey buildings and courtyards between 09.25 and 10.05hrs from heights between 15,000ft and 18,000ft. 'While assigned to the 2nd Bombardment Group,' wrote Harold Kronenberg, 'I flew 21 missions, mostly as a ball turret gunner. A real "milk run" was the much publicised bombing of the monastery at Monte Cassino.'[19] Shortly afterwards, a force of 87 B-25s (from the 321st and 340th Bombardment Groups) and B-26s (319th) added their contribution of 283 1,000lb bombs. Eight mediums were holed by flak and, although three German aircraft were sighted, they made no attempt to interfere.

By the evening of 15 February, 224 bombers had unloaded 446 tons of ordnance with remarkable accuracy.[20] Owing to a lack of co-ordination between ground and air commanders, some forward Indian troops were not warned in time to adjust their positions to

Above:
The ruins of Monte Cassino Monastery after the bombing. *Author's Collection*

accord with the bomb safety line. Denied even the courtesy of a warning leaflet, one Punjabi company dug-in 300yd from the abbey suffered 24 casualties when 12 bombs from the first group of B-17s fell among them.

The heavy bombing looked spectacular: it was 'as if the mountain had disintegrated, shaken by a giant hand' according to Lt Daiber, a troop leader with 115th Panzer Battalion around the base of Monte Cassino. But there was an element of smoke and mirrors about it all. Although post-attack aerial photographs showed the monastery roof to have gone, buildings to be wrecked and some bombs to have penetrated through to the cellars, the breaches in the 150ft-high by 10ft-thick walls did not reach down to ground level. As soon as US bombers hit the abbey, the battle-hardened veterans of the crack German 1st Parachute Division, up to then 'hanging on by their eyebrows', had no scruples about moving into the rubble. 'The incorporation of the ruins into the German defensive system,' wrote Kesselring, 'followed as a matter of military course.' If there was doubt about whether German forces were in the abbey before 15 February, there was none after.

Inside the ruins, the 82-year-old abbot, who was found pinned under wreckage, was eventually released from custody along with those refugees who had not made a break for it. It was just as well because the abbey was subjected to more air raids. As Anzio took priority on 16 February, Desert Air Force responded to the Fifth

Army's urgent call for support by crossing the Apennines in bad weather to bomb the abbey. Of the 72 Kittyhawks that got airborne, 40 got through to drop 14.5 tons of 500 and 1,000lb bombs, claiming 43 direct hits. The next day, 35 Kittyhawks and 16 Warhawks bombed the abbey, with what they thought were good results. Five groups of Kittyhawks and Mustangs bombed the place again between 16.00hrs and 17.00hrs on 17 February, but the weight of bombs dropped by DAF aircraft on both days totalled only 23.5 tons.

A report by Gen Freyberg to the New Zealand Government stated: 'On February 15 the Benedictine monastery was destroyed by heavy bombardment, a step which was forced upon us because despite enemy protests to the contrary, it was being used as an observatory for military purposes.' The New Zealanders produced a corroborating statement from a German sergeant taken prisoner, and the battalion commander of the 133rd US Infantry Regiment reported a telescope in the middle row of windows on the east face of the abbey.

'I give testimony to the truth,' stated Abbot Diamare on his arrival in Rome, 'that in the boundaries (recinto) of this holy monastery of Monte Cassino, there have never been German

soldiers.' After much criticism of the bombing of Monte Cassino Abbey in the world's press, the British Foreign Office leant on the chiefs of staff who sent a signal to the Supreme Commander, Mediterranean, on 4 March asking him to furnish proof of the military use to which the Germans had put the abbey. After much scouring and delving in concert with the Americans, Wilson was forced to signal back on 15 March, admitting the failure at that point to obtain definite proof of German military occupation before 15 February.

But all the heart-searching was academic. In mid-February 1944, the fighting men at risk agreed that heavy preliminary bombardment of the abbey was necessary. To commanders like Tuker, strategic bombing was merely an alternative to the engineering problem of destroying any hopes the enemy may entertain of holding onto the Monastery Hill position. As for the soldier on the ground, he had no doubts about the wisdom of blowing the abbey to kingdom come. It is hard today to appreciate the demoralising effect of the awesome bastion on those who fought in its almost malevolent shadow. Lt Harold Bond of the Texan Division, the 36th Infantry, wrote that, 'all of us were convinced that the abbey was a German strongpoint, and that it

was being used by them for the excellent observation it gave of all our positions . . . The tired infantrymen, fighting for their lives near its slopes, were to cry for joy as bomb after bomb crumbled it into dust.'[21] But it was even more visceral than that. Lt Bruce Foster of the 60th Rifles said:

'Since you ask me what I felt about the monastery, I'll ask you something. Can you imagine what it is like to see a person's head explode in a great splash of grey brains and red hair, and have the blood and muck all over you, in your mouth, eyes, ears? And can you imagine what it is like when that head belonged to your sister's fiancé? I knew why it happened, it was because some bloody fucking Jerry was up there in that bloody fucking monastery directing the fire that killed Dickie, and I know that still.'[22]

*   *   *   *

It was arguable that the bombing of the abbey was not heavy enough. When he talked about reducing the German garrison to 'helpless lunacy', Tuker had in mind an air attack 'ten or twenty times as heavy' as that delivered. Yet bombing of itself was never

Left:
A German mortar crew using the ruins of Monte Cassino Monastery after the bombing. Author's Collection

to be enough. One parallel lesson from both Anzio and Cassino was that large-scale air support must be followed up immediately by ground troops, who must be ready to take quick and full advantage of any rupture of the enemy's defences. After the abbey was blasted, the infantry follow-up was so delayed that the German defenders on Monte Cassino were able to recover from the psychological shock of bombing, emerge from their shelters and become even more alert behind their machine guns and mortar emplacements. There was a crucial lack of procedures and a dedicated communications network to co-ordinate effective action by heavy bombers and ground forces, as had been developed between the armies and tactical air forces.

The NZ Corps finally attacked in considerable strength on the night of 17/18 February, yet notwithstanding all the bombing co-ordinated with heavy artillery fire, when morning broke, those units that had progressed were clinging precariously to their small gains. 2nd NZ Division crossed the Rapido and took the railway station, but Monastery Hill remained more firmly in German hands than before the bombing. Worse than that, the Germans were able to exploit their new commanding strongpoint in the ruined abbey to mount a counter-attack, and by 19 February they had driven the Kiwis back across the Rapido. After four days of fighting it became obvious that the key position on the Gustav Line could not then be taken, and the battle that had raged along the Fifth Army front for more than a month died down. At Cassino and Anzio, both sides had fought themselves to a standstill.

*   *   *   *

On the face of it, no competent soldier would have assaulted one of the strongest fortresses in Europe head-on in mid-winter, using a single corps without any serious diversion. But air power had delivered so much to date that there was apparently no denying soldiers who looked to it as a panacea for their ills. As Tedder predicted in 1943, 'Pantelleria is becoming a perfect curse.' The irony was that the Allies felt they had to go for Cassino to relieve the pressure on Anzio, notwithstanding that the Anzio landing had only been conceived in the first place to break the impasse around Cassino.

'When soldiers are fighting for a just cause and are prepared to suffer death and mutilation in the process,' wrote Gen Alexander, 'bricks and mortar, no matter how venerable, cannot be allowed to weigh against human lives.'[23] In a subsequent debate in the House of Lords on the bombing of Monte Cassino Abbey, Lord Latham put it more forcefully: 'I do not wish to see Europe stocked with cultural monuments to be venerated by mankind in chains and on its knees.' Over half a century later, if an enemy were to place a crucial military asset close to a famous heritage or environmental site, would the diplomatic and military response be as similarly robust?

Notes to Chapter 8

1. 4th Indian Division Op Instn No 3, 11 February 1944.
2. Prasad; Official Indian Armed Forces History, Campaign in Italy; p.98.
3. Ibid, pp.98–99.
4. 'Reflections on the Cassino Battle'; Irish Defence Journal, February 1949; p.64.
5. Senger, op.cit, p.202.
6. Ibid.
7. 4th Indian Division Op Instn, op.cit.
8. North, J.; The Alexander Memoirs; p.120.
9. MEDCOS 27, 2 February 1944.
10. Trevelyan, op.cit, p.69.
11. MEDCOS 27, 12 February 1944.
12. Scrivener, J.; Inside Rome with the Germans.
13. Trevelyan, op.cit, pp.123–24.
14. HQ 4th Indian Division GS Planning Note No 6, 14 February 1944.
15. Clark, M.; Calculated Risk; pp.299–301.
16. Senger, op.cit, p.204.
17. A line, projected forwards of friendly troops and where possible based on physical features easily identifiable from the air, beyond which aircraft were permitted to attack targets.
18. 37 from 2nd Bomb Group, 35 from 97th Bomb Group, 38 from 99th Bomb Group and 32 from 310th Bomb Group.
19. The 390th Bomb Group Anthology; Vol II, Tucson, Az, 1985.
20. Even if an unexploded bomb remained lodged in the pavement before St Benedict's tomb until long after the war ended.
21. Return to Cassino; London, 1964.
22. Trevelyan, op.cit, p.134.
23. North, op.cit, p.121.

BOMBING THE BATTLEFIELD

'German armies had learned to fight without air support, and our ground forces should be ready to do the same when flying was impracticable.'
AM Sir Arthur Coningham

One Allied theme throughout World War 2 was the importance of minimising casualties. This was not just a matter of good leadership. Senior generals and politicians never forgot how many of their contemporaries had died in the hideously expensive World War 1 stalemate on the Western Front, and they were especially anxious not to have their names associated with another national blood bath. As for more junior officers, raised on their fathers' tales of relentless slaughter at the Somme and Passchendaele, saving as many of their men's lives as possible was a matter of faith.

By 1944 it had become clear that, owing to the defensive system and calibre of those who manned it, Allied ground forces alone could not capture Cassino direct without suffering heavy casualties. Furthermore, German intentions were made crystal-clear from an order intercepted by the Allies on 24 January: 'The Gustav Line must be held at all costs for the sake of the political consequences which would follow a completely successful defence. The Führer expects the bitterest struggle for every yard.'[1] It was against this backdrop that Gen Alexander and his chief of staff, Gen John Harding, wrote to Sir Henry Wilson on 22 February arguing that greater emphasis be placed on Allied air superiority as a battle-winning factor, and land operations be framed to take full advantage of it. It was hoped that intense and concentrated air bombardment, followed by heavy artillery concentration, would so abruptly demoralise German defenders that Allied ground forces could attack with minimum losses in spite of the enemy's superior observation system. There may have been an element of naïveté about it all, but the motives were honourable and understandable.

Alexander had discussed the situation with Freyberg on 20 February and decided that the next major offensive would involve the capture of Cassino town, the seizing of Monte Cassino by simultaneous attacks from east and west, and finally the

Left:
Gen Alexander (left) and his chief of staff, Gen Harding. *Author's Collection*

Above:
B-26 Marauders dropping on Cassino. *Author's Collection*

establishment of a limited bridgehead across the Rapido to allow sufficient tank and artillery forces to be assembled for the final breakthrough into the Liri Valley. All this would follow the heaviest possible air and artillery activity, which would serve as both siege artillery and casualty-minimiser. Those who highlighted the drawbacks were not thanked; when Gen Eaker pointed out that bomb craters would make it impossible for tanks to operate, Freyberg replied that bulldozers would quickly clear a path. There seemed little willingness to accept that tanks would have a long and difficult path to follow before they were ready to take to Highway 6, and marshy land to either side would prevent any advance thereafter except along the road itself.

Airmen are often berated by their navy and army colleagues for over-selling air power, and Joe Cannon was confident that Cassino town and its defences could 'be blown out of the path of the land forces'.[2] But around the Gustav Line in the vile winter of 1944, other senior airmen were more cautious. Ira Eaker wrote to Hap Arnold on 6 March warning that:

'Little useful purpose is served by our blasting the opposition unless the army do follow through. I am anxious that you do not set your heart on a great victory as a result of this operation. Personally, I do not feel it will throw the German out of his present position completely or entirely, or compel him to abandon the defensive role, if he decides and determines to hold on to the last man as he now has orders to do.'[3]

*　　　*　　　*　　　*

As tanks needed three dry days in succession before they could operate over generally marshy ground, the first factor in planning for the next assault on Cassino was the weather. Once the weather and terrain were right, Allied troops would withdraw about 1,000yd before dawn. The bombers would hit first; when the aerial onslaught ceased just after noon, the troops would advance into Cassino under cover of an intense rolling artillery barrage.

The Air Plan — code-named 'Bradman', possibly because some staff officer mixed up his New Zealanders and Australians — specified attacks at 10 or 15-minute intervals between 08.30hrs and 12.00hrs by 11 heavy and five medium groups, with the aim of completely flattening all buildings within Cassino town. The heavies were to bomb from 14,000–22,000ft and the mediums from 7,000ft–9,000ft. Intelligence anticipated opposition from over 80 88mm and 137mm guns in the area, and from up to 80 German fighters within range.

The Allied intention was to drop around 700 tons of bombs in as short a period as possible, whereupon it was hoped that the heavy artillery barrage would paralyse the defences long enough to allow 6th New Zealand Infantry Brigade, supported by armour and anti-tank guns, to capture the town centre. The assigned target area, contained within a 1,250ft radius of the centre of the town, was divided in two: the northern half was designated principally for the medium groups, and the southern for the heavies. Mediums bombed in small formations, usually of six aircraft, while the heavies bombed in greater numbers and looser formation, creating greater bomb patterns. The northern and southern halves were to be attacked alternatively, allowing attacking formations room to manoeuvre on their run-in to target; only in this fashion could the defences be saturated. No specific aiming points were assigned.

As most bomber pilots were not familiar with the Cassino area, XII ASC asked Fifth Army if they could provide a distinctive alignment aid. XII ASC was thinking of something like smoke at the mouth of the Garigliano River, which pilots could identify before following the river to its confluence with the Rapido, and then turn to approach Cassino from the south. Fifth Army was most willing to help, though Gen Twining was quite dismissive of the idea, saying that his Strategic Air Force could identify Cassino town without any special navigation assistance.[4] In the end, Fifth Army did not provide smoke for fear that it would mark their front-line troops. Nor did the plan make any provision for bombline marking, or establish a radio link on the spot between Fifteenth Air Force and its formations.

It took until 15 March before the right conjunction of weather allowed tanks and aircraft to operate to best effect. 'Bradman will be batting tomorrow,' warned the radio announcer beforehand, which must have bemused any German signal intercept listeners, and the first Mitchells, belonging to the 340th Bombardment Group, 57th Wing, were over the target at 08.32hrs. The second wave followed 12 minutes later. Both achieved good and accurate concentrations in the eastern part of the town. Then, for 147 minutes, Fifteenth Air Force B-17s and B-24s bombed in succession. The time intervals between each bomb group went awry from the very beginning, destroying the harmony of the plan.

There was a significant difference between the Allied heavy bombing techniques. The RAF aircraft bombed in succession, with each crew aiming individually, often into a target indicator previously laid by a specialist 'Pathfinder' aircraft. The USAAF bombed in fixed groups, with only the formation leader aiming his bombs: the rest of the box released simultaneously with their leader. The RAF method placed more bombs on the centre of an objective, whereas the US bomber box achieved a more even density across an area.

The crews of the first heavy group — the 301st — reported bombing short and left of the target from 22,000ft. Ground observers were less critical, noting that bombs fell into the town as well as to the south of it. When the second group — the 2nd — arrived, 35 minutes late, they found the entire area covered in smoke. By the end of the heavy phase, the last B-24 group — the 98th — was running 20 minutes late, and 13 out of its 23 B-24s dropped on friendly territory. To redress the balance, 101 B-26s from 42 Wing flew over from 11.30–12.00hrs, pretty much dead on time, and bombing with great precision.[5]

In all, 164 B-24s, 114 B-17s, 105 B-25s and 72 B-26s, a total of 455 aircraft, dropped 2,223 1,000lb bombs (992 tons) that morning. 'I remember no spectacle in war so gigantically one-sided,' wrote a war correspondent. 'Above, the beautiful, arrogant, silver-grey monsters performing their mission with what looked from below like a spirit of utter detachment: below, a silent town, suffering all this in complete passivity.'[6]

The bomb plot confirmed that 47% of the bombs aimed at Cassino hit within one mile of the town centre, but only 8% fell within 1,000ft of that. Outside the one-mile circle, the story was of much more erratic bombing. No fewer than 25 heavies brought their bombs back or jettisoned them over the sea because they failed to find the target; yet the weather was clear and there was no wind. In the crews' defence, there was much dust and smoke over Cassino after the first groups had flown over, but the mediums coped. Better than that, the B-26s of the 17th, 319th and 320th Bombardment Groups put close to 90% of their bombs on target and 'stole the show at Cassino'.[7]

No fewer than four B-17s and 39 B-24s went badly astray. One formation, mistaking Venafro 15 miles away for Cassino, caused 140 civilian casualties. Even worse were the 40 bombs dropped by 13 B-24s on their own lines; 50 casualties were caused to 4th Indian Division's B Echelon, while another 40 were killed or wounded in a Moroccan military hospital. Overall, 96 Allied soldiers died by mistake, and as if to prove that the heavies showed no favouritism, a stick of bombs straddled Eighth Army HQ, wrecking the caravan of the army commander. Fortunately, Gen Leese was not in residence at the time.

These sad outcomes were caused by a mixture of bomb rack failure on a group leader's aircraft and the poor forward vision from B-24s of the time, plus poor aerial discipline by two new groups. Unlike the mediums, which always maintained close formation when approaching the target, some heavy bombers were all over the sky on the run-in to Cassino, which meant that they stood next to no chance of bombing accurately. One group commander was fired to encourage the others to train their crews better, and measures were put in hand to improve B-24 visibility for both bombardier and navigator.

The heavy and medium bomber effort was followed by an eight-hour artillery onslaught during which 890 guns of all calibres put down 195,969 rounds on pre-selected targets on Monte Cassino, the town and intervening hill features. It all added up to the heaviest concentration of air and artillery power yet seen in Italy, and it enabled two NZ battalions — the 25th, followed by the 26th — to enter Cassino, and for the 26th to advance to within 150yd of Highway 6 by 17.00hrs.

Although the weather became dull during the afternoon, this did not stop an eight-ship formation of P-51, P-47 or Warhawk fighter-bombers from getting airborne every 10 minutes between 13.00hrs and 17.00hrs and, flying below the overcast, attacking German targets around Cassino. These 188 aircraft dropped 69 tons of bombs, and they were supported by 24 Boston light bombers and 48 B-25s which added 83 tons. In addition, 59 DAF Kittyhawks dropped 41 tons on Aquino in the Liri Valley. Although the Luftwaffe had not been much in evidence of late, 200 P-38s and

The town of Cassino and Monastery Hill. The smokescreen in the foreground has been laid by the Allies to hide ground troop movements from German observers on the heights. *RAF Air Historical Branch*

16 Spitfires were detailed to provide top cover for the bombers of Cassino, while a further 100 Thunderbolts swept the sky between Viterbo and Cassino.

One man who was in the thick of this very complex day of air operations was Sqn Ldr Neville Duke, CO of No 145 Squadron (Spitfires) since 3 March. Duke went on to achieve fame as a postwar test pilot, and in March 1944 he had 22 'kills' under his belt — one for every year of his age. His diary entry for 15 March gave a clear air picture:

'Led a patrol over the Cassino area covering bombing by everything our bomber force has got in Italy. All day long bombers — Forts, Libs, B-25s, B-26s, Lightnings, Kittys — have been bombing the area for the attack at 12.00hrs today. The weather closed down to 6,000ft on our patrol, so sat over Cassino and watched the terrific artillery barrage and the Kittys bombing. Saw my first enemy aircraft on this tour — two Me109s — but they ducked into cloud. Cassino is one mass of bomb craters and shell holes, and covered in smoke.'[8]

In spite of all this unstinting assistance from Strategic, Tactical, XII ASC and DAF, the ground-attack ultimately failed for two reasons. First, New Zealand Corps was pitted against some of the best German troops in Italy. Cassino was held by 950 members of the 1st Parachute Division on 15 March. Their 2nd Battalion, in the northern part of the town, caught the full weight of the bombing, losing at least 160 men out of 300. Yet others sheltered securely in cellars, steel and concrete pill boxes, caves and tunnels. A subsequent Allied Air Force appreciation reported that, 'bombs falling 3–4yd from a pill-box lifted it out of its position without seriously harming the men inside'.[9] As experience to date showed that approximately three tons of bombs were needed to kill one paratrooper, it was all so crudely inefficient. Although many ammunition dumps were blown up, the heavy weapons and artillery did not suffer serious damage.

Worst of all from the Allied standpoint, the heavy bombing and shelling did not lower the morale of the German fighting men, who emerged into the light dazed but undaunted, to offer dogged resistance to the Allied advance. In fact, far from being stunned by the bombing, the Germans came forth highly enraged; the first hours of fighting were as vicious as any experienced throughout the Italian campaign. Gen Alexander admitted:

'The tenacity of these German paratroops is quite remarkable, considering that they were subjected to the whole Mediterranean Air Force plus the better part of 800 guns under the greatest concentration of firepower which has ever been put

Top Left:
Camouflaged German flak guns around Cassino. *Author's Collection*

Centre Left:
German flak guns during the Cassino battle. *Author's Collection*

Bottom Left:
The wreckage of an American fighter brought down during the battle for Cassino. *Author's Collection*

down, and lasting for six hours. I doubt if there are any other troops in the world who could have stood up to it and then gone on fighting with the ferocity they have.' [10]

That said, some people were slow on the uptake. When the Mitchells of 57th Wing went in first, whistling devices were attached to some bombs in the hope that the noise as they fell would scare the Germans. Given the track record of the hard men down below, it is not surprising that a subsequent report noted that 'the screamers attached to the bombs from the mediums were wasted on the Germans'.[11]

The other reason why the attack failed was more complex. In the immediate aftermath of the bombing, there was no real opposition — Gen Eaker's photographer walked through many of the Cassino streets taking post-attack pictures for his boss without drawing so much as a rifle shot. But just as Ira Eaker had predicted, bombing debris blocked the narrow streets and obstructed Freyberg's tanks. Instead of the planned advance rate of 100yd in ten minutes, 25th NZ Battalion barely managed 100yd in an hour as it tried to advance round craters or over masses of debris. This gave the Germans ample time to gather their wits, while the rubble provided good defensive cover. The defenders' task was further eased when heavy rains began to fall, filling the huge 40–50ft-wide bomb craters and making them into even more efficient anti-tank obstacles. Most craters needed bridging, and overnight rains reduced the debris to the consistency of dough, making its removal practically impossible. The extent of the problem led a brigadier to estimate that even without German interference, it would have taken 48 hours for bulldozers to clear a single route through the town.

Deprived of their tank support, the New Zealand infantry was soon compelled to crawl over the debris in a continuous battle with snipers and machine gun posts. Although the Kiwis managed to penetrate a greater part of Cassino town by the close of the day, the laboriously slow advance enabled the Germans to develop new strongpoints and reinforce others. The bombing may have enabled the New Zealanders to break into Cassino with fewer casualties than may otherwise have been the case — the 41 sustained by the 25th Battalion were not excessive — but the random destruction it caused prevented the Allies from exploiting the one important advantage that mass bombing could offer — shock disruption of the German defences.

*   *   *   *

From 16 March onwards, air missions were linked to the difficult but vain struggle to unseat the Germans at the head of the Liri Valley. On 16 March, 325 sorties — fighter-bombers against German positions, and light and medium bombers against reserve areas and supply dumps — were flown, and there was a slight increase in air effort the following day as Allied tanks attacked at dawn. Kittyhawk and Warhawk fighter-bombers attacked daily in variable weather, assisted on occasion by a few Invaders, while air supply was crucial in sustaining troops of the 5th Indian Brigade who were making repeated attempts to capture key features on Monastery Hill. But despite 500 fighter-bomber sorties mounted

against German gun positions on the heights above the battlefield, the defender's knowledge of the terrain and his still superior observation positions allowed him to respond with heavy and accurate mortar fire.

The Luftwaffe tried to make its presence felt, as Neville Duke noted:

'Friday, 24 March 1944. A big day. Led a patrol over Cassino and engaged 30+ Bf109s and FW190s, who were on a sweep of Cassino at about 16,000ft. Fired at one who rolled over and went down vertically — chased him but no luck. The rest of the patrol got three. Led another patrol over Cassino in the afternoon, and again engaged 109s and 190s. The Huns going pretty fast but again we shot down another two. Not a bad day's work. Big party in the Mess.' [12]

In general the strong opposition feared from German flak and fighters did not materialise. Any Bf109 brave enough to venture forth soon found at least six opponents on his tail. The sky was usually so thick with Allied aircraft that, in Duke's words, 'I think we chased ourselves quite a lot.' As if to show that Italy was not to be trifled with, on 21 March, ash and cinders from Vesuvius put Monte Corvino airfield out of action for six days and burnt every scrap of fabric off 80 aircraft.

By 23 March, both sides were thoroughly exhausted, and with no possibility of a breakthrough, the latest round in the battle for Cassino was called off. Having suffered 2,106 casualties in the last phase of the battle, New Zealand Corps was dissolved the following day. The Fifth Army had worn itself out in fruitless, costly frontal attacks on Cassino, and air support had not even given them a moral victory.

Fifth Army casualties on this front from 16 January to 31 March numbered 52,150, of which over 30,000 were incurred against the Gustav Line. Notwithstanding all the aerial support on offer, Rome seemed as far away as ever. Shrewd observers drew some telling conclusions:

'The bombing and shelling of Cassino, although a surprise to the enemy, did not greatly overcome his resistance or considerably reduce his morale. It undoubtedly reduced many German strongpoints and caused some casualties, but it did not destroy his skilfully deployed observation system. His machine guns, mortars (particularly the fearsome, multi-barrelled Nebelwerfer) and artillery were only partially neutralised and the heavily fortified area of the defending infantry, well dug in, was not cleared. All routes for vehicular traffic were destroyed, blocked and cratered . . . This resistance at Cassino . . . was a model of mastery in military exploitation of terrain, and of offensive and defensive warfare.' [13]

If anything the bombing was too successful. Compared to the 40 bombs per acre and 400 aircraft needed to have any meaningful impact on open country and outlying suburbs, Cassino proved that five bombs per acre sufficed in a heavily built-up area. After the cessation of such bombing, Allied ground commanders seem to

have expected little more than a mopping-up operation. Yet experience over Italy was to show that the effect on morale of bombardment, either by air or artillery, was of short duration. If that 'window' was to be exploited, it was imperative to attack immediately after the air or artillery onslaught ceased. A sergeant (Unteroffizier) of the 578th Grenadier Regiment, taken prisoner at Il Casone later that year, told his British captors that artillery bombardments were terrifying while they lasted but that they lost their impact within about three minutes of ceasing.[14] Operational data from the Italian campaign showed that air attack affected morale quicker, and its effects lasted longer, but not so much that ground forces could afford to hang about.

The failure of Allied infantry to take Cassino after the great air assault proved two things. One was that mass air attack was a double-edged weapon — it flattened buildings and temporarily disorientated defenders, but in so doing it created obstacles that made the speedy use of armour impossible and handicapped the infantry. The other was that any ground-attack designed to follow a massed air onslaught must be launched immediately, vigorously and on a large scale. The assault by the New Zealanders on 15 March was characterised by none of these. To use nearly 1,000 tons of bombs and 200,000 shells to launch a couple of battalions was ludicrous, and to illustrate the degree of wishful thinking, total New Zealand casualties for the day were just four officers and 13 men. After so much wasted effort around Cassino, Sir John Slessor hoped 'we shall have learnt by the time we attack again that 500 casualties today often saves 5,000 in the next week'.[15]

Pantelleria had a lot to answer for. After the island surrendered so easily, 'it became the new army conviction that tons and tons of bombs only had to be rained down on strongpoints ahead to make land movements a matter of flitting from one dazed body of enemy troops to another'.[16] But Eaker and Slessor did not buy into this.

The latter wrote to his Chief of Air Staff, on 16 April:

'Another lesson which I think has been confirmed in recent fighting in Italy is that . . . the bomber is not a battlefield weapon. I believe that to be as true today as it was in 1918 . . . As a general rule I am convinced that bombers of any class should be used on the battlefield only as a last resort in defence. Except in those conditions, even your fighters and light bombers will contribute far more effectively to the army's battle by paralysing the movement of enemy supply and reserves behind the battlefield than by attacking strongpoints, battery positions etc on the battlefield — that is the job of artillery.

'We were never [at Cassino between 15–26 March] entitled to expect that a few hundred tons of bombs and a couple of hours' artillery bombardment would do in 1944 what far more heavy, prolonged and intensive bombardments failed to do 28 years ago, namely, blot out all resistance in a strongly fortified defensive position . . . As far as I can remember, the only occasion in the last war when a preliminary bombardment came anywhere near to blotting out all opposition was Messines — and I think I am right in saying that we fired 250 trainloads of ammunition in that bombardment in addition to blowing half of Messines ridge sky-high with mines. Even so, we did not capture Messines ridge without casualties . . .

'On the battlefield itself when we are attacking, as at Cassino, it is not a question of stopping enemy movements, it is a question of moving ourselves. If we imagine we are going to enable ourselves to move forward without casualties by blotting out all enemy defences, we are in for another sad disillusionment . . .'[17]

Slessor's boss, Ira Eaker, was equally blunt when he wrote to 'Jumbo' Wilson stating that the bombing of an enemy stronghold like Cassino must be followed by a determined, vigorous ground-attack in the shortest possible time after the last bomb was dropped. It went without saying that the army would be foolish to insist on any degree of bombing that would, by its very success, inhibit such rapid movement. As for the 'glitches', if heavy bombers were to be used in a similar operation again, Eaker believed that bomb leaders and leading navigators should fly over the target the day before to become familiar with the terrain and select the best bomb run. Precise release heights and aiming points should be specified, clearly visible bomb-line markers should be provided, and the intervals between groups should be decreased to compress the attack, thereby inflicting greater enemy losses. Eaker was emphatic that '. . . everything possible must be done to bring about a thorough understanding on the part of ground forces of the powers and limitations of air forces'. But his great plea to Wilson was that 'the heavy bomber's normal use should be on targets remote from the battlefield . . . So long as adequate Tactical Air Forces were available, heavy bombers should not be used in close-support operations.'[18]

*   *   *   *

In 1944 the RAF defined the term 'close air support' as the immediate availability of aircraft to attack and destroy, in response to army requests, targets engaging or being engaged by the forward troops, thereby improving the tactical situation of the moment. It has to be said that pilots were never overly fond of that activity. To find and hit well-camouflaged and relatively small tanks or guns was far from easy while hurtling along, jinking to keep clear of solid ground and ever mindful that a thousand and one guns of all calibres were about to let loose, many of which were on your side. Air planners preferred 'general air support', which was defined as the attacking of targets not in close proximity to friendly troops but immediately behind the battlefront, in order to hamper the fighting capabilities of the enemy's front-line troops. Such attacks included the blocking of road and rail links, the demolition of bridges and tunnels, and transport supplying the front line.[19]

Back in October 1943, Professor Solly Zuckerman, Scientific Adviser to MAC and then MAAF, submitted a report on the effects of Allied bombing of land communications during the Sicilian and initial Italian campaigns. In his analysis, Zuckerman stated that 'railway and road bridges are uneconomical and difficult targets, and in general do not appear to be worth attacking except where special considerations demand it in the tactical area'. Zuckerman concluded that the most effective strategic means of crippling an enemy's rail communications was by 'attacks on large railway centres which contain important repair facilities and large concentrations of locomotives and rolling stock'.[20]

Unfortunately, there were not many marshalling yards in Italy which satisfied both these conditions, yet somehow or other Zuckerman's advice was misinterpreted to justify air attack on marshalling yards in general. Those air planners who favoured the 'Marshalling Yards Plan' soon discovered its limitations in Italy. At the end of February 1944, MAAF's Intelligence Section was reporting that the Germans were building locomotives in such numbers throughout occupied Europe that they could 'afford to send into Italy each day the numbers of locomotives required to haul the 15 trains of military supplies to the front, and discard each locomotive at the end of the haul.' More discouraging, the intelligence officers noted that 'in the 19 weeks since the capture of Naples, Allied bombers (all types) have dropped a total of 8,258 tons of bombs on 47 marshalling yards without critically weakening the enemy supply position'. In conclusion, Intelligence called for 'a policy of bombing designed to sever all rail lines to the front and thus interdict completely the flow of necessary military equipment by this means of transportation'.[21]

The 'Interdiction' school argued for attacks on sections of railway track, bridges or viaducts. Zuckerman was of the opinion that 'Interdiction' might achieve more immediate and worthwhile results in the immediate battle area, but that it would cost far more air effort. On 11 February, AM Slessor tried to reconcile what was becoming an increasingly heated debate by ordering a review of bombing policy in general and an investigation of 'Interdiction'.

HQ MAAF's desire to strangle Kesselring's armies 'emerged from the frustration of Anzio and the stalemate before Cassino'.[22] From distant Washington in early March, Hap Arnold wrote to Ira Eaker that 'we are all very greatly disturbed here at the apparent bogging down of the Italian campaign'. It was becoming a matter of high air politics. Ground commanders wanted the Army Air Force to be at their beck and call, whereas airmen like Arnold were loath to lose the relative independence of action that the AAF had acquired in North Africa. If Eaker's wings did not make a demonstrable difference, Arnold feared that it would furnish 'ammunition to the advocates who decry the use of air power except as artillery'.[23]

Eaker knew that massed bombers could not break the German front at Cassino but he was more confident of another scheme:

'The air phase of the plan which will win Rome for us and eventually force the enemy back to the Pisa–Rimini line has been carefully worked out. It calls for cutting lines of communication, road and rail, and the destruction of enemy coastal shipping to the point where he cannot possibly supply his 17–20 divisions south of that line. We have sufficient air force to carry out this plan in good weather. It is not a novel or original idea. It is the same old plan which pushed Rommel out of Africa.'[24]

The justification for this enthusiasm was contained in a long memorandum from Slessor to the director of operations, Brig Lauris Norstad.

'There are now some 17 German divisions south of Rome. I do not believe the army — even with our support — will move them. But I think it is more than possible that the Hun, by concentrating all his forces so far south has given us — the Air Forces — an opportunity. I find it hard to believe, that by increasing those forces, he has not put a load on his communications which they will not be able to stand if we really sustain a scientifically planned offensive against the right places in his lines of communication.'[25]

The upshot was Bombing Directive No 2, which aimed 'to reduce the enemy's flow of supplies to a level which will make it impossible for him to maintain and operate his forces in central Italy'. This operation became known as 'Strangle', designed to force the Germans to retreat by attacking their railways 'at about 100 miles from the front so as to increase the strain on the enemy's already inadequate motor transport'. Given the hope that, 'German resources would wither below the tourniquet applied by Mediterranean Allied Air Forces', 'Strangle' was nothing less than an attempt to break the Italian stalemate through an aerial siege of the Gustav Line.

*   *   *   *

Gen von Senger und Etterlin was justifiably proud of 'the tough German resistance on the Cassino front, which cost the Allies three whole months for an advance of 15km'.[26] This grim struggle epitomised the Allied slog up Italy. First, the terrain of peninsular Italy was quite unsuited to the wide-ranging mobile battles fought in North Africa or Russia. Its mountainous spine and narrow coastal plains containing numerous fast-flowing rivers favoured defenders and demoralised attackers. There were 50-odd rivers on both flanks north of Salerno, and the Germans used them all to make the conflict, in Senger's words, 'resemble the static fighting of World War 1'.[27] German troops became adept at edging backwards from river to river, or crest to crest, while operating on interior lines to keep contact with industrial and administrative facilities in the north.

Then there was the weather: the men soon learned to forget the sunny tourist brochures, none of which mentioned that winter in the high mountain regions of the Abruzzi could be so severe, and the snowstorms so dangerous; the troops would sometimes

Below:
The effects of Allied bombing on an Italian railway station.
RAF Air Historical Branch

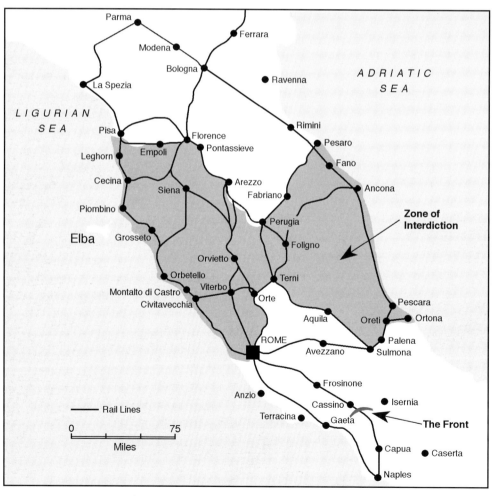

Parma

Ferrara

Modena

Bologna

La Spezia

Ravenna

*ADRIATIC
SEA*

*LIGURIAN
SEA*

Pisa

Rimini

Florence

Pontassieve

Pesaro

Leghorn

Empoli

Fano

Cecina

Arezzo

Ancona

Siena

Fabriano

Piombino

Perugia

**Zone of
Interdiction**

Elba

Grosseto

Foligno

Orvietto

Terni

Orbetello

Viterbo

Montalto di Castro

Orte

Pescara

Civitavecchia

Oreti

Ortona

Aquila

Palena

ROME

Avezzano

Sulmona

Frosinone

Anzio

Cassino

Isernia

Terracina

Gaeta

The Front

Capua

Caserta

Naples

— Rail Lines

0   75

Miles

Left:
A pair of heavy demolition bombs leave a US B-25 Mitchell over a target 'somewhere in Italy'. *IWM*

Bottom Left:
Operation 'Strangle' in Central Italy.

Below:
A trio of B-26s 'dropping their eggs' during Operation 'Strangle'. *Author's Collection*

descend towards the enemy in order to survive. Although the German soldier proved to be a tough, skilful enemy who exploited to the full his strong defensive position among steep and barren mountains and winter weather, even a German Mountain Division, fresh from the Eastern Front, had difficulty coping with the novelty of alternating rain, snow, frost and storm.[28]

During the first assault on the Gustav Line, the Fifth Army lost nearly 40,000 in battle and a further 50,000 from the weather. In deep snow or mud where nothing on wheels could move off roads, military existence was no dolce vita.

Kesselring became a master of the shrewd defence, but it was more than just holding ground. The pressure the C-in-C brought to

bear on his subordinates 'was colossal as he moved tirelessly from place to place, driving, urging and cajoling in his determination to exact every morsel of work and ingenuity from weary men and to make the best of the relatively limited resources at his disposal'.[29] Gen Lucas noted the commitment of the German élite in his Anzio diary: 'We have taken between six and seven hundred prisoners since we landed. Most of them are down in spirits but not so the Hermann Görings. These people are very young, very cocky, very full of fight, and believe they are winning the war . . .' Kesselring the Airman may have lacked aeroplanes but Kesselring the Motivator still had much to offer.

Good staff work blunted much of the efficacy of air attack. While Allied ground forces prepared for another push towards Rome, their airmen strove to disrupt German sea, rail and road communications in the roughly quadrangular area defined by Pisa, Ancona, Pescara and Rome. The central Italian terrain generated all manner of tunnels, bridges, viaducts and embankments, and it was against these engineering features that 'Strangle' was directed. Strategic Air Force being heavily engaged in attacking Germany and the Balkans, the bulk of the interdiction effort fell on the mediums and fighter-bombers. The medium bombers were

assigned to the larger bridges and viaducts, while fighter-bombers were to attack smaller structures, crater railheads, and fly armed reconnaissance in search of motor transport. Strategic B-17s and B-24s would only be called upon to bomb marshalling yards north of the Pisa–Rimini line if trains were blocked to the south, creating a log-jam of supply-laden trains.[30]

Between 15 March and 10 May, MAAF flew 21,688 'Strangle' sorties against German communications and dropped 25,375 tons of bombs in the process, though bad weather grounded the mediums for nearly half of the operation's 53 days. By the end of May, Tactical was putting 75 cuts a day in the enemy's railways, and on some days the verified cuts exceeded 100. By early April the Germans were being forced to unload their supply trains at Florence, about 125 miles north of Rome, and truck them from there. Kesselring realised that if the supply of his armies was to be assured, arrangements had to be made to bring trains further south. Four or five companies of rail engineers were brought from France, damage-reporting methods were improved and a number of mobile workshops created. By concentrating resources on the main line from Florence to Orte and two loop lines, 'it was always possible to reopen the lines for several hours or nights'. Repairs were effected expeditiously, while motor and animal transport were impressed to supplement rail transport or to carry goods around a break from one train to another. As Slessor admitted, 'I personally underrated the unsurpassed capacity of the Hun's Q staff to keep him supplied in apparently impossible conditions.'[31]

Which leads on to the last great reason why it took so long for Allied troops to move up Italy. Gen Senger gazed wistfully at Allied air supremacy which allowed 'a continuous and uninterrupted air spotting service for their artillery fire over the German lines, operating unmolested by German fighters . . . This advantage proved ineffective only because the Allied attacks moved forward too slowly, so that we always found time at night to move up the necessary reserves for counter-blows.'[32]

From the beginning in Italy, Kesselring perceived an ingrained reluctance among British generals to take risks, and a consequent tendency to play safe by 'fighting cheap' with penny-packet troop deployments on narrow fronts. Mark Clark found this exasperating: 'Yesterday I flew to see Gen Leese in an effort to co-ordinate our attacks . . . Although he professes that his attack will be all-out, it is being made by one division . . . All their actions are always dictated by their desire to save manpower and let someone else do it.'[33] While German defenders fought with a tenacious steadfastness which 'in some instances amounted to self-immolation',[34] British soldiers seemed to believe that air power should do the hard work for them.

Notes to Chapter 9

1. Churchill, Closing the Ring; p.376.
2. Molony, op.cit, p.779.
3. AHB, op.cit, p.292.
4. Twining to XII ASC, 23 February 1944.
5. No 7/9 AASC Report on the Bombing of Cassino, 23 March 1944.
6. Buckley, C.; Road to Rome; p.303.
7. Craven and Cate, op.cit, vol 3, p.367.
8. Franks, N. (ed); The War Diaries of Neville Duke; pp.147–48.
9. MAAF Report, The Bombardment of Cassino.
10. Alexander to Prime Minister, 20 March 1944: Churchill, Closing the Ring, pp.449–50.
11. AHB, op.cit, p.300.
12. Franks, op.cit, p.148.
13. AHB, op.cit, pp.302–03.
14. Gooderson, op.cit, p.181.
15. Slessor, op. cit, p.574.
16. Owen, R.; Tedder; pp.212–13.
17. Slessor, J.; The Central Blue; pp.573–74.
18. AHB, op.cit, pp.303–4.
19. Operational Research in the British Army 1939–1945; p.3.
20. Air Attacks on Rail and Road Communications, 28 December 1943.
21. Memo, MAAF A-2 Section to MAAF A-3 Section, Current Intelligence Considerations in Interdiction of Rail traffic to Italian Peninsula, 29 February 1944.
22. MAAF, Operations in Support of Diadem.
23. Arnold to Eaker, 3 March 1944.
24. Eaker to Arnold, 6 March 1944.
25. MAAF, Operations in Support of Diadem.
26. Senger, op.cit, p.218.
27. Ibid, p.188.
28. Ibid, p.189.
29. Macksey, op.cit, p.184.
30. Mark, E.; Aerial Interdiction in Three Wars; p.153.
31. Slessor, op.cit, p.570.
32. Senger, op.cit, p.218.
33. Clark Diary, 22 May 1944.
34. Maj von Brauchitsch, General Staff Report, 27 May 1944: AHB/II/117/11(A), Appendix 23, p.1.

ON TO ROME

'We were 20,000 feet over Rome. The voice of the bombardier in the nacelle sounded calm.

"Bomb doors open!"

"OK," said the captain.

"Bombs away!" came the bombardier's answer.

'That was all. I could not see the bombs drop. But I saw them tumble in clusters from the other Forts ahead . . .

'As we switched towards the sea, I could see the white ribbon of the Tiber, flowing past the Vatican, whose spirals rose in the clear sunlight far from the inferno of smoke and bomb-bursts.'
Richard McMillan

It was during April that MAAF commanders at Caserta accepted that 'Strangle' would not of itself dislodge the Germans from the Gustav Line. For all the destruction of railways and harrying of their motor transport, German ground formations continued to 'tick over' in their defensive redoubts. 'Actually,' wrote Eaker to Arnold on 7 April, 'what we need more than anything is some army support . . . What we ask the army to do is put enough pressure on the enemy to force him to discharge some ammunition and further reduce his reserves of fuel and ammunition.'

Gen Alexander was more than ready to play his part. Although the Italian campaign is now classified as a secondary sideshow, by March 1944 Alex's forces were holding down 23 German divisions including many of Hitler's finest. In planning for the resumption of his offensive, Alex was seized with the importance of assisting 'Overlord' by diverting, containing and — fate willing — destroying the maximum number of German formations.[1] But this grand scheme would flounder like its predecessors if the land element carried on in the same tedious way as before. Central Italy cried out for the decisive blow to be struck west of the Apennines, where there was both room for manoeuvre and the most important military objectives. Given that the two Allied armies had been working too separately and too ponderously to date, Alexander's most important preparation for the renewed offensive was to move the greater part of the Eighth Army into the Cassino sector alongside the Fifth. The transfer of four divisions for the Anzio landings started the realignment process, and further impetus was given to strengthening the west coast at the expense of the east by the failure of the Eighth Army to make any appreciable progress towards Pescara.[2]

Alexander decided that the Eighth Army should break through the main German front into the Liri Valley and advance to Valmontone on the German Fourteenth Army's right flank, the Fifth should advance via Esperia to the south of the Liri Valley, and VI Corps at Anzio should break out of the bridgehead to meet the

Eighth Army at Valmontone. Having finally got their act together, the armies were well placed for a new offensive; code-named 'Diadem', it was expected to be the jewel in the crown.

Although Gen Alexander was not privy to the date set for 'Overlord', he was given to understand that a mass push towards Rome in early May would suit Gen Eisenhower's D-Day operation. 'Diadem' was finally fixed for 23.00hrs on 11 May, with the breakout from Anzio scheduled for D plus four. If there were insufficient air assets to meet everyone's needs, priority in the initial phase was to go to the attack by the Eighth Army, and in the second (the thrust out from Anzio) to VI Corps.

MAAF issued the outline 'Diadem' air plan on 28 April 1944. It was drafted by the TAF commander, Maj-Gen John Cannon, and its object was 'to make it impossible for the enemy to maintain his position in the face of a combined Allied offensive'. The plan began with a chastened version of 'Strangle' designed to 'render the enemy unable to offer sustained resistance to the assault'. Known as the Preparatory Phase running up to 11 May, attacks were to be intensified on Axis rail and road bridges, motor transport and harbours. Allied aircraft were also to concentrate on supply dumps and depots identified by Ultra; those holding fuel (the Germans' greatest logistical weakness) were to be hit first, followed by those with ammunition and then other supplies. Also planned for the final days of the Preparatory Phase were enhanced counter-air operations to keep the Luftwaffe 'in its contemporary state of ineffectiveness'.[3]

Starting with Luftwaffe effectiveness, on 18 March 373 Fifteenth Air Force heavies dropped 43,000 20lb fragmentation bombs on German airfields around the head of the Adriatic, claiming 56 aircraft destroyed on the ground and 23 in the air, plus 17 shot down by escorting fighters. Strategic lost seven bombers and three escorts, including three 97th Bomb Group B-17s which went down to attacks made by 34 rocket-firing Bf109s over Udine. But once the Germans imposed stalemates on the Allies at Anzio and Cassino, the Luftwaffe curtailed the air support on offer and withdrew surplus elements for operations elsewhere.[4] The 60 Ju88s deployed in northern Italy in response to the Anzio landings returned to northwest Germany, and some 40 single-engined fighters (from I/JG53 and II/JG51) were transferred from central Italy to the Balkans, which was coming under serious threat from the heavies at Foggia.[5] The FW190s of I/JG2, which came south from the French Channel coast in response to Anzio, returned there in early April.

To show which way the wind was blowing, Fliegerkorps II — hitherto responsible for tactical air operations in Italy — was withdrawn to northern France even before the Anzio beachhead was decided. The anti-shipping units in southern France, operational control of which was temporarily given to von Richthofen and Luftflotte 2 to go against the Anzio bridgehead, went back to Luftflotte 3. The upshot was that from March 1944 onwards, there was no Fliegerkorps organisation in the Mediterranean. The German aerial centre of gravity had unmistakably shifted to the Western Front, leaving Italy to make do with what can be termed a 'fire brigade approach', the shuttling of individual Gruppen around to meet each new crisis.

Once Alexander's forces moved into gear, von Richthofen could have drawn on aircraft outside the Italian theatre, as had happened in the past. The largest concentration of Luftwaffe offensive aircraft within reach of the battlefield and Allied convoys was based in southern France. These 210 aircraft, of which 153 were long-range bombers, could not be ignored, and on 27 May 246 B-24s mauled Montpelier/Ferjorgues and Salon airfields with 515 tons of bombs. But the survivors never detached south. Even after the US Fifth Army joined up with troops moving forward from Anzio on 25 May, the OKW feared to deplete its anti-invasion forces in the west or to decrease the fighter defences of the Reich without Hitler's personal endorsement. And when it came to deploying what few air assets he had, Kesselring felt he dare not ignore the risk of further Allied outflanking movements on either the Adriatic or Tyrrhenian coasts, or an invasion of the Balkans.

So Alexander's task was made that much easier by the weakness of the German Air Force. During the 'Diadem' preparatory phase up to 25 April, MAAF Tactical aircraft were tasked to reduce German air strength by attacking their forward bases south of the Pisa–Rimini Line, while Fifteenth Air Force heavy bombers and fighter escorts attacked airfields in northern Italy and southern France. By the beginning of 'Diadem', only about 325 aircraft were available to von Richthofen to affect the battle tactically in central and northern Italy, compared with 3,960 Allied aircraft around the Mediterranean. The relative air situation on 12 May 1944 is shown on the table opposite.

On 20 February, Mediterranean Allied Tactical Air Force took over the 42nd (B-26 Marauder) and 57th (B-25 Mitchell) US Medium Bombardment Wings. As a result, TBF ceased to exist on 1 March. TBF had amassed a distinguished 28,372 sorties since its inception on 20 March 1943, and its boss throughout had been Air Cdre Laurence Sinclair. Since 10 December, the TBF had consisted of US air units only, and the fact that an RAF officer could control the operations of an entirely US air force through an all-American staff in a 'wholly workable' fashion said much about Anglo-American air co-operation.

To recap, at this stage MAAF controlled the Mediterranean Allied Coastal Air Force, Mediterranean Allied Strategic Air Forces — made up of the Fifteenth Air Force and 205 Group, RAF — Mediterranean Allied Tactical Air Forces — US Twelfth Air Force and the RAF's Desert Air Force — and an Anglo-American reconnaissance organisation. On 18 February, Ira Eaker issued a new bombing directive to his Mediterranean Allied Strategic and Tactical Air Forces. Strategic's first priority was the Combined Bomber Offensive against Germany, its second was disruption of

Above:
Sir Henry 'Jumbo' Wilson investing Maj-Gen John K. Cannon, Commanding General Mediterranean Tactical Air Force, with the Order of the Knight Commander of the British Empire. Joe Cannon's citation recognised that his 'exceptional qualities of leadership, initiative and determination have inspired all ranks of his Command with an unsurpassed spirit of Allied inter-service co-operation and aggressive action in the Air'. *IWM*

rail communications in northern Italy and third was to give such support to land forces as Mediterranean Allied Tactical Air Force might request. That gave an interesting insight into inter-service and inter-Allied co-operation. First, the 'army' in US Army Air Force was fading rapidly. Second, any request for strategic air support for the battlefield originated with 'khaki' commanders such as Wilson, Alexander or Clark, but if any of them hoped to make an impression on Ira Eaker, they had to get Joe Cannon's ear first.

The final component of the 'Diadem' air plan was to carry out normal close-support operations. When it came to dividing air support responsibility for ground forces, it was decided that a part of DAF would operate in the west with XII Tactical Air Command (XII TAC), the renamed XII ASC. The newly formed XII TAC was

AIR SITUATION, 12 MAY 1944

NORTH ITALY

Axis

Ju88	LRB	95
FW190	GA	40
Bf109	SEF	80
Ju88	L/R Recce	5
Total		**220**

SOUTH FRANCE

Axis

Do217	LRB	25
Ju88	LRB	75
Bf177	LRB	10
Ju88	TEF	10
Bf109	SEF}	40
FW190	SEF}	
Ju88/188	L/R Recce	20
FW190	L/R Recce	10
Ar196	L/R Recce	15
Total		**205**

SARDINIA

USAAF

B-26		232
P-39		52
Beau		12
	Total	**296**

RAF

Beau	23
Mosq	15
Mar	6
War	8
Total	**52**

Grand Total 348

CENTRAL ITALY

Axis

Ju87	GA	15
Bf109	SEF	30
Ju88	L/R Recce}	15
Bf410	L/R Recce}	
Bf109	L/R Recce	20
Total		**80**

CORSICA

USAAF

B-25	261
P-39	25
P-47	95
P-51	50
OA-10	6
Beau	13
Total	**450**

RAF

Spit	65
Hurr IV	8
Beau	14
Well	17
Walrus	2
Total	**106**

Grand Total 556

FOGGIA AREA

USAAF

B-17	303
B-24	421
P-38	268
P-47	88
P-51	83
F-5	9
Total	**1,172**

RAF

Lib	7
Hal	15
Well	64
Mar	15
Balt	61
Kitty	80
Must	15
Spit	152
Beau	12
Mosq	8
War	3
Wal	2
Total	**434**

Grand Total 1,606

NAPLES AREA

USAAF

A-20	71
A-36	64
P-39	96
P-40	194
P-47	113
P-51	32
F-4	2
F-5	20
F-6	21
Beau	21
Total	**634**

RAF

Bos	16
Beau	10
Spit	187
Hud	13
War	3
Wal	1
Total	**230**

Grand Total 864

BARI

USAAF

B-24	478
P-38	9
F-4	3
F-5	14
Total	**504**

RAF

Spit	23
Hurr IV	9
Well	15
Lys	2
Hal	30
Lib	3
Total	**82**

Grand Total 586

ALBANIA & YUGOSLAVIA

Axis

Do17	LRB	10
Ju87	GA	55
He46	GA}	
CR42	GA}	20
Bf109	SEF	35
Ju88	TEF	5
N.Bf110	TEF	5
Bf109	L/R Recce	25
Ns126	L/R Recce	15
Do17	L/R Recce	5
Total		**175**

TABLE 3: TACTICAL AIR FORCE SQUADRONS, 9 MAY 1944

XII Tactical Air Command, Naples Area
Four A–20 squadrons
Three A–36 squadrons
Seven P–40 squadrons
Three P–47 squadrons
One P–51 squadron
Two Beaufighter squadrons
Two Boston squadrons
Eight Spitfire squadrons
Four Spitfire Tactical Recce squadrons
1/2 Spitfire Strategic Recce squadron

TOTAL — 34 1/2 squadrons (Nationalities — 19 USAAF, 12 1/2 RAF, one RCAF, one SAAF, one FAF)

87th Fighter Wing, Corsica
Four P–47 squadrons
Seven Spitfire squadrons

TOTAL — 11 squadrons (Nationalities — six RAF, three USAAF, one RAAF, one FAF)

Desert Air Force, Adriatic side of Italy
Four Baltimore squadrons
Five Kittyhawk squadrons

One Marauder squadron
One Mustang squadron
Four Spitfire squadrons
1/2 Spitfire PR squadron
1/2 Spitfire Strategic Recce squadron
One Spitfire Tac Recce squadron
One Italian Co-belligerent Mc.205 squadron

TOTAL — 18 squadrons (Nationalities — nine RAF, seven SAAF, one Polish, one Italian)

57th Bombardment Wing, Corsica/Ghisonaccia
12 B–25 squadrons (all USAAF)

42nd Bombardment Wing, Sardinia/Elmas
12 B–26 squadrons (all USAAF)

51st Troop Carrier Wing, Sicily and Brindisi
Seven C-47 and C-53 squadrons (all USAAF)

GRAND TOTAL — 94 1/2 squadrons (Nationalities — 53 USAAF, 27 1/2 RAF, one RAAF, one RCAF, two FAF, eight SAAF, one Polish, one Italian)

Left:
A Marauder crew from Gen Robert Webster's Sardinia-based 42nd Wing go over details of the Operation 'Strangle' mission they are about to fly. The Marauder crews' hunting song, as they went repeatedly against Axis communications, was *We've been working on the railroads. IWM*

Top Right:
Beaufighters attack Axis shipping off the south of France in March 1944. *RAF Air Historical Branch*

made responsible for co-ordination with the Fifth and Eighth Armies until the course of the land battle allowed the re-establishment of the old Fifth Army/XII TAC and Eighth Army/DAF combinations.

During 'Diadem', congestion already caused in the Po Valley marshalling yards was to be exploited by the heavies. Mediums were to hit railway nodes and important installations further south, while fighter-bombers were to join the mediums against bridge targets and to hinder repair work. Roads were to be bombed around the clock and as the Germans resorted to using more coastal shipping, Strategic Air Forces were to mount heavy attacks on harbours such as Leghorn, La Spezia and Genoa plus 'any new ports expediency thus rendered interesting'. Tactical and coastal units were to hamper movement of vessels, and to bomb unloading facilities. Light bombers would do the same after dark, while enemy fuel and ammunition dumps behind the lines would come in for constant attention.

'Diadem's interdiction campaign was son of 'Strangle' with two significant differences. First, the zone of interdiction was deepened to include all rail lines crossing the northern Apennines. The aim was to put 140 miles (rather than 'Strangle's 100) between German railheads and the front, in order to impose even greater pressure on their motor transport. The second was to put more emphasis on the night interdiction light bombers of Tactical Air Force to give Axis suppliers less respite.

For interdiction missions, XII TAC was allotted the general battle area south of Rome, the central strip north of Rome to Lake Trasimene, and the Tyrrhenian coast as far north as Lake Bolsena. The Corsica-based 87th US Fighter Wing took over the west coast area running north from Lake Bolsena and demarcated in the east by a line running through Lake Trasimene, Arezzo and Florence. DAF was given the eastern area, beginning an a line east of Rome to the Adriatic, and running north to the east of Lake Trasimene and Arezzo. Tactical recce commitments were covered by three squadrons allotted to the Eighth Army, and two with the Fifth, though they could be switched if necessary.

Once the assault phase started, much would hinge on how events unfolded and so it was only possible to give general guidance to each air force. TAF was to support the offensive while Strategic was to revert to its normal role, with the proviso that it stood ready to exploit any especially good targets of opportunity which might result from a rapid enemy retreat. Coastal was to sustain its anti-shipping brief. All were to retain their anti-communications remit throughout.

*   *   *   *

'Diadem' began with a barrage of 2,000 guns shortly before midnight on 11 May. The attack caught the Germans by surprise — both Tenth Army commander von Vietinghoff, and XIV Panzer Corps commander, von Senger und Etterlin, were at home on leave. While artillery was shelling German positions, 53 Wellingtons bombed the ports of Piombino, Ferraio and San Stefano. It was small beer, as was the impact of the few Bostons

Above:
Operation 'Diadem'.

Top Centre:
RAF Baltimores and Kittybombers plaster Rieti airfield, north of Rome, on 20 April 1944. *RAF Air Historical Branch*

Top Right:
DAF Marauder after bombing the railway bridge crossing the River Asino at Chiaravelle near the Adriatic coast in May 1944. *RAF Air Historical Branch*

and Baltimores which strafed roads. Nothing was done before 23.00hrs to pre-warn of the massive air effort which was to open on 12 May and was to continue long after the fall of Rome.

On 12 May, as Gen Alexander issued an order of the day calling for the destruction of German forces in Italy, the Poles attacked Cassino while XIII Corps had 50 tanks across the Rapido by noon. On the Fifth Army front, the most spectacular progress was made by the French corps which cleared the west bank of the Garigliano. On the western flank, the US corps edged slowly forward.

The Germans counted 1,300 operational flights over the forward area, not to mention strong attacks on the central Italian railway system where the sections Brenner–Verona and Milan–Rimini were cut. In truth, nearly 3,000 sorties were flown by all Allied types that day; the average over the first three days of the offensive was 2,700, notwithstanding patches of bad weather. After taking part in a massed bomber flypast along the front to cheer the Allied

troops and dismay the opposition, 134 B-17s struck Kesselring's HQ at Monte Sorrate and that of von Vietinghoff's Tenth Army at Massa d'Alba.[6] Just under 1,000 tons of bombs were dropped on all main west coast harbours and on important rail centres. To keep Luftwaffe heads down, the B-17s and B-24s of the 99th, 463rd, 456th and 459th Bomb Groups, escorted by P-51s of the 31st Fighter Group, dropped 368 tons on the FW190 base at Piacenza and 135 tons on Reggio Emilia.

German command posts were visited by 144 French and US medium, and 48 light American, bombers. Some miles behind Cassino lay the Adolf Hitler (or Führer) Line, and as German troops congregated around it at Pico, 300 American mediums were sent to do their worst. Roads and bridges around the Pico assembly area were attacked by 168 P-40s, which also bombed troops opposing the Poles at Cassino. A dozen B-26s joined 100 US and French P-47s from Corsica in an attack on rail tracks and bridges to the north of Rome. Eighteen times during April, P-47s of the 79th Fighter Group escorted medium bombers against interdiction targets near Orvieto, Pergulia and Viterbo. Three times they were challenged by the Luftwaffe but they did not lose one of their charges.

The Germans had coped until then by sitting tight on a static front, carefully husbanding stores, obtaining food at the expense of local Italians and moving up supplies under cover of darkness by whatever means. At a time when the Allies imported stores into Italy at a daily rate of about 32,180 tons in order to sustain their

campaign, German forces facing the Fifth and Eighth Armies existed on less than 4,000 tons per day, which was 1,000–1,500 tons short of what was needed once the Allies launched their ground offensive. 'Strangle'/'Diadem' interdiction ensured that once the skies cleared, the Germans would find it logistically impossible to stop an all-out Allied ground offensive.

Throughout the first week fighters and fighter-bombers attacked lines of communication, artillery and mortar positions, command posts, vehicles and airfields, while maintaining a constant fighter-reconnaissance service. Light and fighter-bombers worked closely with ground troops in an effort to silence the Germans' two main gun areas, in the Liri Valley and around Atinia to the north of Cassino. TAC/recce units kept the guns under constant observation, and the effectiveness of the fighter-bomber response owed much to the 'Rover David' (or 'Rover Joe' in US parlance) spotters. One such atop Monte Trocchio controlled nine fighter-bomber missions on 12 May alone.[7]

The firm resistance offered initially to the Fifth Army weakened on 13 May. While some Germans stood and fought, the Allies bridged the Rapido and made useful gains. The way was now clear for 78th Division to cut Highway 6 and isolate Cassino in concert with the Poles. Under steady but firm pressure, the German right flank was finally crushed as a coherent line. What remained of the German 71st and 94th Divisions pulled back, and through the gap poured those most fearsome of doughty mountain warriors, the French Moroccan Goums.[8]

About 20 Ju88s raided Naples early on 14 May, but Coastal Beaufighters got two of them.[9] The Luftwaffe achieved much more success in a raid on the Corsican airfields at Alesani and Poretta on 12/13 May where Allied aircraft were arriving daily to participate in 'Diadem'. While a handful of bombers staged a diversionary raid on Bastia harbour, 15 Ju88s and He177s attacked Alesani, destroying eight Mitchells and damaging 12 more on the ground. The Poretta raid by around 35 bombers paid even higher dividends: 14 Spitfires and one Liberator were destroyed, and 50 Spitfires damaged. Further damage was caused to runways, buildings, motor transport and fuel and ammunition dumps on both airfields; 24 personnel were killed and 50 wounded. Someone had become complacent.

Around 20 German aircraft operated over Cassino on 14 May, but some were forced to jettison their bombs. A few Ju88s night-bombed Allied bridges over the Rapido and other positions, but although this was the first instance of Germans using Ju88s in direct support of ground troops, the experiment met with no success. It was not surprising, given that the Jabos were faring no better. During the Anzio landings, the FW190s of I/ and II/SG4 went into combat with Bf109 fighter escorts. FW190 attack formations got away without loss so long as their escorts were present, but then 40 fighters were sent back home. Thereafter, even the powerful SG4 Jabos were unable to undertake attack missions, despite accelerating out of 65° dives to air speeds of around 500mph as they bottomed out. To curb losses, SG4 tried operating

Above:
A Ju88 ready to go. *Author's Collection*

Right:
German ingenuity in the face of adversity. The racecourse adjoining Ciampino airfield southeast of Rome was used as a Luftwaffe dispersal before Allied bombing rendered it unusable. The 'horseshoes' within the racecourse were aircraft dispersal pens. *RAF Air Historical Branch*

as hit-and-run Jabos, but it made no difference. Unable to operate in the ground-attack role, the FW190s finally went back to the role for which they were initially designed, flying against Allied intruders. The change was a clear admission that the Luftwaffe in Italy was incapable of destroying advancing Allied ground forces.

On 21 May, of 24 SG4 aircraft airborne from northern Italy, seven pilots were lost in combat with Spitfires. Four more casualties followed on the 25th, and the next day the Geschwaderkommodore, Lt-Col (Oberstleutnant) Georg Dorffel, died in action against heavy bombers near Rome. Such were loss rates from Allied aircraft and ground fire that by May 1944, fully 50% of all pilots graduating from the Schlachtfliegerschule (ground attack flight school) in Germany were going to SG4.

The daily German fighter and fighter-bomber rate over the battle area would seldom better 50–75. It was not until 14 May that Luftwaffe air defenders appeared in any force, but they were then given a very hard time. The record of III/JG53 was typical. With an average of 20 serviceable 109s, it flew 693 sorties spread over 47 missions in 28 flying days. Thirteen pilots had to bale out, and over 60% of their aircraft were written off. German fighter efforts had such a limited impact that, after the first few days of 'Diadem', Strategic's heavies were released to return to their primary objectives — 'Pointblank' targets around Vienna, oil and communications in the Balkans, and support of the Yugoslav partisans.

As soon as ground troops began rolling after 14 May, Tactical's mediums returned to the interdiction task.[10] Except for a few DAF B-26s, all Marauders flew from Sardinia and all Mitchells from

Corsica, giving the Allies a potent force operating off the German right flank.[11] The B-25s went for rail lines between La Spezia and Rimini, as did the B-26s, before shifting temporarily to road junctions and then back to railways. Corsica was proving its worth as a secure aircraft carrier, and from there 87th Fighter Wing P-47s, aided by Spitfire sweeps and escort, concentrated on road and rail targets. A further 200-plus fighter-bombers attacked enemy camps and landing grounds just north of Rome on 15/16 May as German ground defences began to crack, while DAF Marauders, Spitbombers and a few Kittys flew 200 'bridge-busting' sorties on the other side of Italy. Closer to the battle, over 300 TAC fighter-bombers went for rear road bottlenecks and softened-up strongpoints. By 20 May, cuts were claimed at 92 points. Four days later, Tactical set a new record of 1,791 sorties, and now MAAF's three 'specialist' groups of bridge-busting mediums (310th, 321st and 340th) were putting one direct hit on bridges every 20 sorties.

Between 11 May and 7 June, MAAF devoted around 22,500 sorties and slightly more than 31,000 tons of bombs to interdiction. And except for periodic adjustments to keep the stipulated 140 miles between German troops and their railheads, the interdiction plan drawn up by Tactical Air Force remained unmodified. Of all the Allied fighter types pressed into service as fighter-bombers, the P-47 Thunderbolt was the most suited.

'Weighing almost seven tons (three tons more than a fully laden FW190) it could roll with amazing agility; was faster at all altitudes than either the 190 or 109, and it had no peer when plunged into a dive. It was easy to fly in formation and easy to land. It provided a stable gun platform and unlike most of its contemporaries, the front office was roomy and comfortable . . . It was truly the Cadillac of fighters.' [12]

The Jug's rugged construction and air-cooled radial engine enabled it to soak up punishment from ground fire, and it could pay back in kind through the formidable combination of eight wing-mounted 0.50 calibre machine guns plus the ability to carry up to three 500lb, or two 1,000lb bombs, or up to 10 underwing rockets. In November 1943 the 325th became the first in the Mediterranean to exchange its P-40s for P-47s, and there would eventually be nine P-47 squadrons with the DAF and XII TAC in Italy by May 1945.

US P-47s used their range to hit targets as far north as Perugia, while TAF Spitfires patrolled the battle area in strength by day. Light Bostons and Baltimores continued to intrude around Rome, bombing vehicles and creating roadblocks to restrict German mobility. On 17 May, P-47s and Spitfires hit the runway at Viterbo, Satellite No 2 — not long previously covered with fragmentation

bombs from B-25s. It was from here that the Luftwaffe launched small-scale night harassing raids with Fiat CR.42s and Ju87s brought in to replace the long-range bomber force. Manned by German crews, the CR.42 biplanes were fitted with flame dampers and armed with a pair of 12.7mm machine-guns and racks for four 50kg bombs. Success was claimed against high-value targets within the Anzio beachhead, for although the biplanes lacked the kit to operate in anything other than moonlight, they were not sitting ducks as Beaufighter pilot Peter Montgomery recalled.

'These slow-flying machines gave us quite a headache initially, for even with the wheels and flaps down the Beau tended to fall out of the sky before speeds could be synchronised and it was not possible to hold a visual contact for more than a few seconds. In addition, as it was in a period of moonlight, the enemy's practice of turning rapidly towards the Beaus as the range closed was most frustrating to our pilots when they saw the bandits passing overhead in the opposite direction, for even the tightest turn failed to regain radar contact. For a night or two this evasive action proved effective, but as the moon waxed brighter our pilots found that they were able to get their gunsights on the target during the head-on approach, and one burst was usually enough. The CR.42, when hit, just disintegrated into matchwood and after this, these machines did not reappear on our front at night.' [13]

Greater Axis hopes were placed on the inelegant night versions of the Ju87 Stuka, brought into theatre at the end of February. The British detected their presence from signal intercepts and on the night of 2/3 April, between five and 10 Stukas operated over Anzio. Allied anti-aircraft batteries claimed three, and an RAF Intelligence summary commented that 'these aircraft are reserved for harassing operations by moonlight'. In May, the same source noted that '20 or 30 Ju87s, and most probably CR.42s, operated over the battle area at points of Allied penetration, without causing significant damage'. After the 17 May raid on Viterbo, these newcomers sank into total inactivity.

Allied raids on Viterbo and Piacenza airfields wrecked any remaining Luftwaffe hopes of intervening in the battle. It was a measure of much reduced capability that nine small German bomber raids were all that were reported over the Anzio–Cassino area during the whole of May. Only on 11 days in May did German fighters intercept Allied bombers, and then only in small numbers. Overall, 'the Luftwaffe made no serious attempt to increase its scale of effort and hardly intervened in the fighting up to the fall of Rome'.[14]

By 19 May all of Cassino was in Allied hands and the Gustav Line was thoroughly breached. Three days later, the British and French broke through the Hitler Line. French elements of the Fifth Army continued their spectacular advance, while the Americans took Fondi and drove on westwards. From 19 to 25 May, 15,024 Allied aircraft were dispatched to drop 9,664 tons of bombs on missions directly related to 'Diadem'.[15] The prime tasks of cutting Kesselring's lines of communication, and keeping them cut, absorbed around two-thirds of this, and the next major commitment — bombing troop concentrations and front-line military targets — accounted for 2,368 tons.

Fifteenth Air Force planned massive support for the Anzio breakout by bombing rear areas and key points leading to the battlefield, but bad weather curtailed Tactical and Strategic efforts alike. On 23 May for example, of 504 B-24s dispatched, only 276 reached their targets; of 147 B-17s sent, only 40 were successful, and 110 B-26s had to abandon their missions. The old faithfuls — 59 Bostons, 56 Invaders, 87 Kittyhawks, 104 Thunderbolts, 123 Warhawks and a few Spitfires — all threw their weight into the fray between the bridgehead and the main army front.

The German retreat created ideal conditions for a breakout from Anzio. The bridgehead existed as such for 125 days, during which time 478,407 tons of ammunition, equipment and stores were put ashore at what was reputedly the seventh busiest port in the world under protective air cover. On 23 May, VI Corps launched an attack in a northeasterly direction, against German forces stripped of reserves, to support the southern front. Aided by more than 700 air sorties, they cut Highway 7 before noon. By nightfall on 25 May, Cisterna had fallen and infantry and tanks were facing the entrance to the Velletri Gap which led to Valmontone.

After the war was over, German commanders at Anzio were asked for their views on the effect of all this Allied air effort. The lack of Luftwaffe fighter protection was felt very keenly, as it left Allied reconnaissance aircraft free to circle at leisure over German lines. The tiny Piper L-4 and Stinson L-5 (the main aircraft used over Italy for artillery spotting) were among the most dreaded of weapons for they 'not only forced the Germans into elaborate and time-consuming measures — a brisk trade developed in constructing dummy positions to mislead the spotters — but also they engendered a contagious and dangerous feeling of impotence, of being perpetually watched'.[16] It was the Monte Cassino Monastery syndrome in reverse.

Much to the chagrin of the big-bomber men, German Anzio commanders were not worried by the effect on morale of the laboriously staged 'heavy' jamborees. It was the incessant fighter-bomber activity which most severely dislocated German leadership at all levels. The threat of yet another wave of Jabos hindered the movement of forces by day, the initiation of surprise countermeasures, the carrying out of successful flank thrusts, concentration of reserves or even the conveyance of messages: in short, commanders were deprived of the very ability to lead with drive and energy.[17]

The thrust from Anzio threatened to encircle the Germans. Kesselring had hoped to check the Allied advance at a hastily formed defensive line extending from Velletri to Valmontone but, at long last, the full impact of scientifically exploited air superiority came good. 'Never had a well-organised army been so effectively attacked from the air as was the German Tenth Army.'[18] Everything, apart from steady weather and a decent night-attack capability, were in place to enable Allied Air Forces to operate across the air power spectrum. Heavy bomber attacks between Lyons and Leghorn hindered movement from southern France, and in spite of excellent repair work by the Germans, there were 124 rail cuts north of Rome. Air power gave Kesselring's reinforcements, moving down from the north, a severe mauling. For a time, only one route was open between the Po Valley and central Italy to serve as both a supply and escape line. As Sir John Slessor was to point out, the Germans' inability to establish a 'mass of reserves, or to co-ordinate divisional counter-attacks, both of which are so vital to the halting of an offensive', owed everything to destructive Allied air attacks.

The mediums' interdiction effort made a German stand south of Rome impossible. Stocks of their two most important commodities — fuel and ammunition — fell below the danger line, and the state of their transport made adequate distribution from depots impossible. Some have argued that the Germans experienced 'no critical supply shortages . . . even during "Diadem",'[19] but the Tenth Army's War Diary begged to differ. In May 1944 it was replete with references to 'ceaseless air attacks', 'heavy fighter-bomber support for enemy ground forces', 'enemy air dominates the battlefield' and 'unremitting Allied fighter-bomber activity makes movement or troop deployment almost impossible'.

An Ultra decrypt found Kesselring reporting that on 27 May the Allies had for the first time carried out systematic road patrols using parachute flares, which greatly delayed the movement of reserves and supplies. In a review of Allied battle tactics decrypted at the end of May, Kesselring noted the delays that Allied air power had imposed upon him; on one important bridge, no less than 100 separate attacks had been made in the space of 24 hours.

The impact of Allied air power is illustrated more personally by the records of the Hermann Göring Parachute-Panzer Division.

Having been in the thick of battle for months, they were withdrawn to Pisa in mid-March to recuperate, while staying prepared to go back immediately on the attack.

'Since early May, Gen (Generalmajor) Schmalz had been stressing to Commander-in-Chief Southwest that the division's available fuel was only adequate for a range of about 200km and that, in consequence, it could not cover the 300km to its designated area of operations . . . This matter was pursued by the division with great concern, resulting in a series of requests for the release of fuel, all of which were turned down . . . At about 10.30hrs on 23 May, the chief of staff, Gen (Generalleutnant) Westphal, called the commander and gave him the order for the division to move out at once. Gen Schmalz was given to understand that the division was to see action in the area south of Rome. Wilhelm Schmalz informed Westphal that heavy losses to enemy air attacks were to be expected in the case of movement by day. Nevertheless, the request for a night departure was refused. Schmalz also pointed out that the available fuel would only allow the division to travel as far as Viterbo . . . Gen Westphal assured him that sufficient fuel would be delivered on a timely basis in the Viterbo area . . . The unit's move was spotted by the enemy within several hours of departure, and they were bombed day and night almost without pause. Initially, only 11 of the unit's 60 tanks got through. Approximately 30% of the fighting unit's motorised transport and about 20% of the heavy weapons were lost en route,

as were 18 of the armoured artillery regiment's guns . . . On arriving at Viterbo, it was discovered that the promised fuel was not in place . . .'[20]

Under the 'Diadem' air onslaught, German troop movements could only be carried out at the expense of supply, or vice versa. With his established defence lines lost, his reserves fully but vainly committed too far forward, his transportation inadequate and his forces under constant air attack, Kesselring was faced with the well-nigh impossible task of co-ordinating an orderly withdrawal on a fluid front. To rub it in, Allied ground troops enjoyed almost complete immunity from air attack and could move freely behind their own lines. Smiling Albert's battle henceforward was no longer for Rome or any other geographical feature; it was to save his armies from destruction.

Up to then, camouflage had been the Germans' salvation. A captured document made it perfectly clear to the reconnaissance pilots of 285 Wing that the Germans had been told that Allied air superiority was there to stay.

'It was part of the permanent state of affairs that had to be faced by the troops, and face up to it they did with grim determination:

Below:
'Jointery' in action — a morning conference of senior Army and Air Force officers at a field HQ, 31 May 1944. *RAF Air Historical Branch*

their concealment was magnificent, and we had to work exceptionally hard during tactical reconnaissance missions to ferret out their positions . . . Over the front line, the contrast was astonishing. In German occupied territory not a thing moved. Over our own territory, masses of tents and convoys were to be seen. That was the effect that air supremacy, or the complete lack of it, had on land forces and their everyday existence.' [21]

Lt John T. Hayden, a liaison pilot with the 339th Field Artillery Battalion, 88th Infantry Division, noted the same during his time aloft on Air OP duties:

'The Germans were masters of camouflage. During the winter, when the front was static, we could fly all over German territory and not see a thing. After a snow storm we would be looking for tracks in the snow, but seldom saw any. On the American side there were tanks, trucks and men all over the place, but on the German side — nothing.' [22]

On 26 May, Mark Clark signalled that he was 'greatly pleased with splendid air effort yesterday. We have put the enemy on the road. Good hunting to all.' Once German troops and guns were forced out 'on the road', they became very vulnerable to air attack. In the first week of 'Diadem', light bombers and fighter-bombers worked mostly against battlefield targets such as command posts, guns and troop concentrations. By the time the southern and Anzio fronts joined, there were fewer and fewer supply dumps, command posts or strongpoints to hit. Artillery reconnaissance aircraft engaged vehicles, tanks and mortars, and spotted concentrations on roads, bridges and at fords without fear of enemy air interception. Armed reconnaissance became the bread and butter fighter-bomber work for the next few weeks in the quest for transport and troop concentration targets of opportunity.

The battle was now moving too fast for 'Rover David' and 'Rover Joe', so cab-ranking aircraft increasingly had to find their own targets. 'They had acquired the art of hedge-hopping and made life hell for us,' wrote Lt Hermann, commander of an anti-tank unit belonging to the Hermann Göring Division. 'Open roads always resulted in a race with life and death. Speed and manoeuvrability were our only weapons.' [23] The record of the Kittyhawks and Mustangs of 239 Wing on 30 May was typical. Catching a group of about 200 vehicles at Subiaco, stationary and nose-to-tail, they first blocked both ends of the line with bombs and then strafed the column, accounting for 102 vehicles. Total motor transport claims by Tactical crews over the last six days of May were 1,148 vehicles destroyed and 766 damaged.

'The effectiveness of fighter-bombers,' lamented Heinrich von Vietinghoff, 'lay in that their presence alone over the battlefield paralysed every movement.' The war diaries of both German armies incessantly bemoaned the need to move at night, the damage to roads and bridges, and the resultant traffic jams. Gen von Senger was particularly distraught:

'We were accustomed to making all the necessary movements by night, but in the May breakthrough this was not good enough. In

a battle of movement a commander who can only make the tactically essential moves by night resembles a chess player who for three of his opponent's moves has the right to only one.' [24]

After Kesselring appealed directly to Hitler, the Führer ordered that one night-fighter group be sent from the Reich to protect road traffic at night.

John Slessor described the AAF's 42nd Bomb Wing with its Martin B-26 Marauders as 'probably the best day-bomber unit in the world'. [25] The 42nd got operations down to a fine art, and could bomb effectively to within 1,200ft of Allied lines without disturbing people at the 'ring side' in spite of intense heavy flak raking the formation. But not everyone was so adroit. The Gulf conflict of 1991 proved that poor air/ground co-ordination results in aircraft attacking friendly troops, and analysis back in 1944 found that such tragic incidents peaked during the transition from semi-static to mobile warfare. The theoretical answer was to establish a new demarcation line immediately in front of friendly forces, known as the close co-operation line, but as the location of this line could change as often as ten times daily, the scope for someone not getting the news in time was large. Troops in Italy were supplied with canisters of yellow smoke with which to identify themselves to friendly aircraft, but that did not stop some strafing P-40s from inflicting over 100 friendly casualties in just one incident during the advance on Rome.

In Rome itself, Allied bombs added insult to German injury. 'Strangle' raids on marshalling yards in March appeared to go clumsily astray — one woman was beheaded by the blast, the body of another was thrown on to a telegraph wire — and when a Wellington crew sent six bombs too close to the Vatican, the British Air Ministry felt obliged to issue a statement that the bomber captain, Plt Off McAneny, 'is of Roman Catholic faith'. Bombers were fitted with cameras which operated automatically as the bombs started to fall, so crews knew that any indiscipline would be noticed. Not that human error was always regarded up the chain as a hanging offence: as ACM Tedder once said to Alexander, 'Sorry to say some of the early Popes went airborne this morning.'

Alexander's intention was to close the noose on the German Tenth Army at Valmontone. It should all have been so clinical, given crumbling German leadership. Army Group Chief of Staff Westphal became ill through overwork and could not be replaced. The 57-year-old Vietinghoff fell ill too, while Mackensen was relieved of command of the Fourteenth Army on 2 June for failing to fill a vital gap in his positions: he was replaced by Panzer Gen Joachim Lemelsen. Fifth Army was ideally placed to deliver the coup de grâce while Kesselring, in the absence of any effective Luftwaffe support, was 'reduced . . . to the state of a blind man groping for guidance'.[26] But instead of building on success, and cutting off Axis escape routes to bring the campaign to a swift end,

Left:
A photograph taken at the behest of Field Marshal von Richthofen to illustrate the collateral damage inflicted on a graveyard by an Allied air raid on Rome.
Author's Collection

Below:
A couple of half-tracks fitted with 3.7cm flak guns beside Castel S. Angelo on 4 June 1944, a few hours before the first Allied troops arrived.
Author's Collection

Gen Mark Clark diverted from the overall game plan for the glory of freeing Rome.

From the beginning, the Germans had never contemplated defending Rome itself. Kesselring sought permission on 2 June to evacuate the capital, and he was directed to continue fighting to the south for as long as possible to assist evacuation of the city and withdrawal of the Fourteenth Army across the Tiber. Allied tanks entered Rome on 4 June, reaching the city centre at around 14.15hrs. President Roosevelt went on the air the next evening to celebrate the fall of the first of the 'Axis capitals'.

While Clark had his photo-calls and GI Joe had some fun for the first time in ages, Allied bombers hit the retreating Germans. Hemmed in by mountains and ravines, German motor transport made great targets. For a change, airmen tended to down-play their ground 'kills': pilots claimed the destruction of 117 motor and armoured vehicles on a short stretch of road near Forli, whereas ground observers counted 122 blown up or burned out. Over 4–6 June, as the Germans took wholly to the roads in a desperate attempt to escape north, almost 1,100 vehicles were destroyed and more than 1,100 damaged. By the end of 'Diadem' on 22 June, airmen claimed to have destroyed more than 5,000 vehicles and damaged another 5,000 in the previous six weeks.

In the end, Allied aircraft ran out of motor transport to aim at, but that did not stop a resourceful opponent. Dunkirk in 1940 showed that only an army can stop another army from getting away, and when Clark turned the Fifth Army towards Rome and away from Valmontone, the cork was out of the bottle. The German Tenth Army had been defeated at Cassino, and the Fourteenth likewise at Anzio, yet despite the havoc wrought by fighter-bombers on both as they fled north along the banks of the Tiber, the Germans lived to fight another day.

After the fall of Rome, the Germans produced a report on what had gone wrong since 1 May when a 'quite favourable situation had existed in the Army Group zone with regard to personnel and matériel.' Seventeen days after Alexander launched his 'Diadem' offensive, German losses were estimated as at least 25,000 men, 2,000 machine guns, 500 heavy machine guns, 429 anti-tank guns,

148 tanks and 295 guns. The motor vehicle situation was especially strained. The report concluded unequivocally that 'a large part of the losses suffered could be attributed to the mounting effect of the enemy air supremacy'. This was not surprising; from the beginning of 'Strangle' to 22 June, MAAF aircraft flew some 137,000 sorties and dropped around 84,000 tons of bombs, over two-thirds against Italian lines of communication and ports. The Fifteenth Air Force, although only half the size of the Eighth Air Force in numbers, almost equalled the latter in the number of sorties and bombs dropped since 1 May. Efforts by a few Ju88s to operate against Allied targets in the battle area on four nights during the last week of May paled in comparison.

Because the Luftwaffe all but disappeared from the battle area by day, there were slim air combat pickings to be had. For all the squadrons on air defence duties, the best Allied combat result recorded was the destruction of three Bf109s and two FW190s over Foligno airfield by a few Spitfires on 27 May. From 12 May to 22 June, MAAF claimed 176 German aircraft destroyed, 44 probables and 93 damaged. Against these small returns MAAF lost 438 aircraft, practically all from flak, as the Germans concentrated their anti-aircraft guns at key points along their lines of communication.

The lessons from all this were quite straightforward. First, for all the awesome air power expended on 'Strangle', the ultimate objective — to make it impossible for Kesselring to sustain his armies south of Rome — was not achieved until Allied armies forced their opposite numbers into battle. In the succinct words of USAF chief historian, Richard Hallion, '"Diadem" succeeded in draining German resources more effectively than "Strangle" alone had, because air interdiction was combined and synchronised with ground manoeuvre warfare, forcing the Nazis to expose themselves to air/land attack.'[27] As Sir John Slessor put it in an appreciation on 'The Effect of Air Power in a Land Offensive', drawn up on 18 June 1944 and delivered to Generals Marshall and Arnold when they visited Italy, air power 'cannot by itself enforce a withdrawal by drying up the flow of essential supplies' when the enemy 'is not being forced to expend ammunition, fuel, vehicles, engineer stores etc at a high rate'. Nor could air power 'by itself defeat a highly organised and disciplined army, even when that army is virtually without air support of its own'. What it could do, 'and has done in the present battle . . . is to make it impossible for the most highly organised and disciplined army to offer prolonged resistance to a determined offensive on the ground — even in country almost ideally suited for defence; it can turn an orderly retreat into a rout; and virtually eliminate an entire army as an effective fighting force'.[28]

Two further points are worth mentioning. When ground forces are rolling and encountering no effective aerial opposition, tactical air should go for an enemy's supply lines rather than give close support to ground operations — which often inflicts unnecessary casualties on friendly troops in a rapidly changing ground situation. 'Diadem' also reinforced the perennial point that 'tactical air operations are most effective when ground and air are coequal partners, neither dominated by the other but both working toward a common objective'.[29]

Notes to Chapter 10

1. COSMED, 19 April 1944.
2. Montgomery's original concept had been to wheel through Pescara to Rome.
3. MAAF, Operations in Support of Diadem.
4. For all Kesselring's status as C-in-C, 'the Luftwaffe was under the direct orders of Göring'. Kesselring, The Memoirs; p.199.
5. Strategic Air Force's contribution to 'Overlord' was to go for objectives in southern France, pin down German fighters in southern Germany and southeast Europe, sever rail links from Italy, Hungary and the Balkans to northern France, and generally to undermine German war-fighting effectiveness towards the Eastern Front.
6. Kesselring's exact command post in the Sorrate caves had been pinpointed by American spy Peter Tompkins based in Rome. Tompkins recruited a network of anti-Fascists to watch all 12 major highways in and out of Rome, and his recommendations for bombing of troop concentrations in the north were promptly carried out.
7. Mediterranean Allied Photographic Reconnaissance Wing further aided ground forces by flying around 160 direct co-operation sorties in the first week of 'Diadem'. This level of co-operation was maintained throughout the coming weeks.
8. 'These are the only troops,' wrote one German report, 'that do not shrink from mass hand-to-hand fighting in the Russian style.'
9. A few Beaufighters intruded over southern France and destroyed an He111.
10. Occasionally, Strategic did aid Tactical by hitting north Italian marshalling yards and trans-Alpine supply routes.
11. Both were given fighter escort by 87th Fighter Wing from Corsica.
12. Wörpel, op.cit, p.146.
13. Montgomery, P.; 'Italianesque'; Aircraft Illustrated, July 1970, pp.290–91.
14. AHB, op.cit, p.333.
15. TAF led with 9,081 sorties, Strategic with 4,351, Coastal with 1,447, and the Photo-Recce units with 145.
16. AHB, op.cit, pp.338–39.
17. CSDIO/OMF/M.297, 13 September 1945.
18. Ibid.
19. Sallager, RAND Corporation Report, p.19.
20. Kurowski, op.cit, pp.244–45.
21. Millington, G.; The Unseen Eye; p.127.
22. Wakefield, K.; The Flying Grasshoppers; p.77.
23. Trevelyan, op.cit, p.57.
24. Senger, op.cit, p.224.
25. Terraine, op.cit, p.587.
26. Macksey, op.cit, p.206.
27. Hallion, Strike from the Sky.
28. AHB, The Italian Campaign Vol II, Appendix 5, p.1.
29. Craven and Cate, op.cit, p.396.

AVANTI!

'The very magnitude of possible aerial offensives cries for an answer to the question, "How can we defend ourselves against them?" To this I have always answered, "By attacking".'
Guilio Douhet

Even as the last defences were crumbling before Rome, Hitler called for an all-out effort to construct the next great holding position — the Gothic Line. On 1 June, this 200-mile stretch of the northern Apennines was little more than a line on a map, so an order was issued to Kesselring, plus the General Commanding Engineers and Fortifications, telling them to make haste. Instructions were given in detail for security measures against armoured attacks, the speeding up of fortress-like construction work (blasting of caves in rock, making of embrasures and such-like), extensive mining in adequate depth, evacuation of the civil population in the forward areas, and installation of a 10km-deep barrage zone in front of the main defence line. A rock-drilling company was summoned from Norway, while construction battalions were established to supervise the Italian civilian labour force conscripted from local males on the orders of the German plenipotentiary in Italy. The only thing that the Führer's orders could not supply was time: Kesselring, past master of the spoiling fight, had to make that for himself.

Hitler had foreseen the danger of a rapid Allied follow-up as the Tenth and Fourteenth Armies withdrew in disarray, and two Luftwaffe Field Divisions had already been ordered south from Denmark and Holland. The first to arrive, together with 162 Turcoman Grenadier Division, were thrown in near Civitavecchia. Other divisions were moved from Russia and the Balkans to replace the three infantry divisions annihilated in the breakthrough into the Liri Valley and at Cisterna. The reinforcements, which totalled eight divisions, were supplemented by 12 battalions of Czechs and two Italian divisions for guard and coastal defence duties in northern Italy. The dispatch of all these troops at the very time of the Normandy invasion showed Hitler's determination to protect the southern frontiers of the Reich by 'fighting for every square mile of ground and every week of time'.[1]

The Normandy landings on 6 June — two days after the fall of Rome — stole most of Mark Clark's Roman thunder, and the projected invasion of southern France in August (Operation 'Dragoon') spoiled Alexander's enjoyment as well. As his troops pursued the Germans northwards, Alexander estimated that he could reach the Po Valley in August provided that his forces were not plundered to mount what he and Churchill both believed was an ill-timed foray into southern France. Eaker and Slessor were

strongly opposed to splitting the air effort, but their arguments fell on deaf ears. Eisenhower, who had no major port available to him in Normandy, was keen to have Marseilles and nearby ports through which his supplies and the numerous divisions still waiting in the USA could be landed.

The US Joint Chiefs, who regarded the Italian campaign as secondary in spite of all the blood and treasure they had poured into it, supported Eisenhower as did Roosevelt, who suspected a hidden British agenda in the Balkans. The removal of a complete corps then actively pursuing Germans up the west coast, including the hardened French and Moroccan fighting men, was to leave the Fifth Army seriously depleted. Great efforts were made by Mark Clark to forge new formations, especially from anti-aircraft units whose primary role had lost its significance with the Luftwaffe's virtual disappearance from Italian skies.

Below:
The Northern Italian campaign from the fall of Rome.

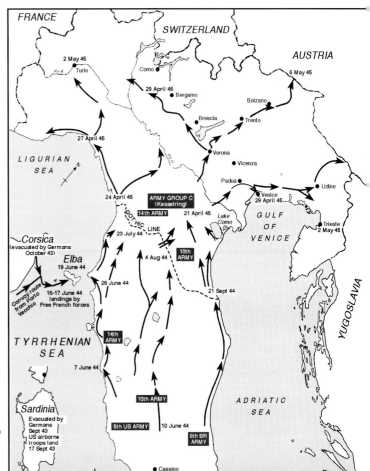

Above:
The Ju88T, fastest of the Ju88 variants, served in Italy with two Luftwaffe units. Having completed its long-range reconnaissance mission, the film container from this Ju 88T1 is about to be taken by dispatch rider to the lab for processing. *Author's Collection*

During the 12 days following the fall of Rome, the Allied Fifth Army moved forward 140km north-northwest along the axis Rome–Viterbo airfields–Siena–Arno River. Eighth Army advanced northeast along the line Rome–Terni–Foligno–Perugia, with a final curve back towards the city of Florence, while its V Corps continued up the east coast with the aim of ultimately rejoining the main Eighth. Operational control of tactical air assets for Fifth Army was by XII TAC, while DAF controlled those for the Eighth and V Corps, with operational boundaries between the two air forces and the two armies being identical.

Hand-in-hand, Allied air and ground moved north to harry the retreat. It was a ground-breaking experience in more ways than one, as the Germans did everything they could to render evacuated airfields useless to the Allies. The net effect of mine-laying, ploughing and cratering often exceeded that accomplished by Allied bombing, and the only answer to the demand for more northerly fighter and fighter-bomber airfields was to build new ones. On average, Allied engineers built a field in five days, with 6,000ft strips being required for XII TAC and 3,600ft minimum for DAF. On one occasion an engineer survey party actually got ahead of the infantry: they were captured by Fifth Army troops and held prisoner, it being difficult to convince the infantry that anything had got ahead of them.

XII TAC continued to take a heavy German toll up to 14 June, but thereafter only scattered targets of opportunity were to be found as the old cunning returned. Italian civilian carts were pressed into service, night movements intensified and surviving motor vehicles were stationed inside houses after whole walls were torn down to provide access. P-47s, B-26s and P-40s faced a growing casualty rate as remaining high-value targets were liberally protected by mobile flak batteries. DAF became so concerned about high casualties from German flak that it ordered 'no strafing missions' on 9 June.

As Kesselring received reinforcements in equal numbers to the Allied divisions being drained off for 'Dragoon', he soon recovered his grip of the situation. Gen von Senger with HQ XIV Corps was dispatched to take charge of the newly arrived divisions in the centre of the Fourteenth Army front, and from then on, the Allied rate of advance slowed down to 30km between 16 and 23 June and to just another 30km during the next three weeks. As they reached Kesselring's first main delaying position on a line running east and west through Lake Trasimene on 20 June, Allied troops found themselves up against their old enemies — the Hermann Göring, 1st Parachute and 15th Panzer Grenadier Divisions, plus sudden spells of wet weather which thwarted Tactical air's operations from 17 to 28 June.

Kesselring eventually assembled 19 divisions in the line and although most of them were seriously understrength, he also had six divisions in reserve, three of which were working hard to complete the Gothic Line. The C-in-C was quite clear in his own mind why he was still in the game. Although MAAF dropped 5,000 tons of bombs on the general battle area between 2 and 8 June, and a further 3,350 tons on communications north of the Pisa–Rimini line such that there were 78 effective rail blocks on 15 June, Kesselring believed that,

> 'the Allies utterly failed to seize their chances. Their air force was not sent in to smash the helpless targets presented them on the battlefield, especially in the back areas, nor were the Partisan uprisings supported by an airborne landing behind the battlefront. In fact, no attempt was made at a tactical landing in our rear at all.' [2]

This view was endorsed by the Hermann Göring Armoured Reconnaissance Battalion: 'From Rieti the retreat continued to Lake Trasimene. In spite of his vast superiority in armoured forces and total air superiority, the enemy pursued only slowly.' [3]

There were excuses: Strategic Air Force, which made history on 2 June by shuttle bombing targets from bases in Russia, concerned itself very little with Italy over the fortnight following the fall of Rome. And just as the Fifth Army was passing Grosseto and the Eighth took Foligno, the Allies swung wide on 17 June to seize the island of Elba. It did not take long and the Luftwaffe failed to put in an appearance, but it was a totally unnecessary operation because the advance of the Fifth Army beyond Grosseto made the German presence on Elba untenable. However, the operation boosted French morale, and showed that military logic sometimes has to go by the board to keep allies on side.

*   *   *   *

During the 36 days from 11 May to 15 June, the Allies found 290 Axis aircraft abandoned on 14 captured enemy airfields. On 5 June, Kesselring told Berlin that, 'in giving a responsible estimate of the general situation, I must report that a real easing . . . can only be expected if immediate and strong fighter and ground-attack aircraft support is provided — even if for a short time'. Fat chance. On 29 May, after 19 of their number had been destroyed by an Allied air attack on Piacenza, all FW190s were withdrawn from operations and sent to northern Italy to rest and refit. Two days later, the loss to Spitfires of Lt Günther Entress in his FW190 marked the end of the operational line for SG4 in Italy. Accepting that they were now operating 'with total lack of success as Jabos', SG4 left Italy in June for the more conducive skies of north Russia. Gen Hubertus Hitschold, Fliegerführer of Luftflotte 2 back in late 1943 and the Luftwaffe's last General der Schlachtflieger (Inspector of Ground-Attack Aircraft), considered that it was no longer possible to use his units in the West. After the war, when reflecting on the Italian experience, he noted that 'the prerequisite for successful and lasting operations of ground-attack units is air superiority'. [4]

If anything emblazoned Luftflotte 2's impotence in lights, it was that useful work was still being done in Italian skies by ancient Baltimores, almost obsolescent Bostons and outmoded Kittyhawks. Allied aircrews had the skies pretty much to themselves after all single-engined German fighters in the central Italian battle area moved north on 1 June. Kesselring followed suit after being driven out of Monte Soratte in some haste. The Commanding General of the Luftwaffe in central Italy, Gen (General der Flieger) Ritter von Pohl, left Viterbo for Siena on 7 June before moving to Florence, finally ending up at Casalecchio near Bologna. 25th Flak Division HQ settled down with the Luftflotte's Signals HQ and the main administrative authority at Treviso. Only Luftflotte 2 — now rapidly shrinking in functions — under von Richthofen stayed at Malcesine on Lake Garda, with advanced battle HQs at Monte Riceo, near Monselice, and Tabiano near Parma.

Senior members of the Luftwaffe High Command testified after the war that the primary role of their air force in Italy was now strategic, and that support for the army on the battlefield became of secondary importance. Air defence protection for the Reich being so crucial, Viterbo Fighter Control Centre withdrew its staff to Siena, radar stations were redeployed to strengthen the northern defences, and plans were made to establish new airfields in the Perugia–Siena–Pistoia area. 25th Flak Division hauled back its heavy and light guns, the former to reinforce Florence and Bologna and the latter to defend airfields. Such was German adaptability that even as these guns lumbered northwards, they were used in the anti-armour as well as anti-air role to hinder the Allied advance. Although flak contributed much to the eventually orderly German withdrawal, some 200 guns were lost between Rome and the Apennines, 90 to enemy action and the rest demolished by their crews for lack of transport to move them.

In a directive dated 23 June, Luftflotte 2 defined the tasks of its air forces, taking account of the abiding fear of further Allied landings. Its long-range reconnaissance Gruppe was ordered to photo-reconnaissance the eastern and western sea areas and Bizerta in Tunisia. In tactical support of German land forces, night ground-attack aircraft, operating from the Forli–Ravenna area with advanced landing grounds near Florence, were to attack front-line targets during the full moon period. When normal tasks permitted, aircrews were to counter Allied bombing raids and fighter operations.

Given the strategic importance of keeping an eye out for more Allied outflanking amphibious operations, Luftflotte 2's strategic reconnaissance arm, FAGr122, withdrew from Perugia to Bergamo at the end of May. The role of its Ju88s and Me410s was to cover Bizerta and the Tyrrhenian harbours that might be jumping-off points for landings, together with the seas around Italy to spot any approaching amphibious forces. The first Ju188 — a 'stretched' Ju88 — arrived at Bergamo at the end of May to help search for shipping off the Italian coasts. Beaufighter pilot Peter Montgomery recalled:

> 'One night when we were near Ancona I was on readiness when we heard through the "Y" Service [5] that a Ju188 was to make a reconnaissance sortie from the Po Valley down the Adriatic, and even the name and rank of the pilot was passed to us. The weather was foul with lots of low cloud and turbulence, so when

I was eventually scrambled I felt that I only took over from fate at about 1,000ft. After our GCI station vectored us onto the "bandit" my radar operator quickly got an echo on his set, but I felt sure that the Hun had a radio altimeter which I lacked, for after twisting and turning for nearly 20 minutes at 300mph and 250 feet over the water in pitch blackness I had to confess defeat, although the 188 did at least depart in a northerly direction.'[6]

Survivability of crucial German strategic reconnaissance assets became paramount. Radio-monitoring service operators were installed at Frosinone, alongside FAGr122's air traffic controllers, to listen in on Allied R/T frequencies for signs of an impending attack on one of their aircraft. Another precaution was never to take-off and land at the same field in case a MAAF intruder was lurking in the darkness.

FAGr122's shorter-legged brethren, the two remaining Staffeln of the tactical recce group NAGr11, concentrated their Bf109s at Florence and Forli respectively, from where they could cover coastal waters down to Civitavecchia and Pescara, as well as photographing the front. For a time, a Staffel of NAGr11 was detached to Scutari in Albania to give its 109s a clear run-in over the sea to photograph Bari, Taranto and Brindisi.

Apart from the construction of new airfields and alternate landing grounds in the far north, all bomber airfields in northern Italy were now to be prepared for fighter occupation as well; those in the areas of Milan–Piacenza–Forli–Ravenna–Vicenza had first priority. The night-flying groups' airfields moved first to Castiglione del Lago, and then to Ravenna and Forli. Outside the Arno Valley, all other Luftwaffe installations south of the Apennines and around Rimini were to be demolished.

Orders for air defence of the Gothic Line were issued to GOC Luftwaffe Central Italy. The GOC, Maximilian Pohl, was to cover and assist ground forces with close-support aircraft and flak, protect supply routes, railways and airfields in the southern area of northern Italy, and add the weight of his flak artillery to the coastal defence forces. But apart from the 15 tactical recce Bf109s of NAGr11, the only other aircraft Pohl directly controlled were the 50 Ju87s of NSGr9.[7]

To the north of Pohl's area, 25th Flak Division and Jafu (Fighter Leader) Oberitalien were responsible for all other air force commitments in Italy. 25th Flak Division's directive was to protect airfields, supply routes, railways and industrial installations in northern Italy, and its anti-aircraft artillery was to assist in the defence of the Adriatic coast to the north of the River Po. Jafu Oberitalien, Col (Oberst) von Maltzahn, had an even more daunting remit. Based at Bologna, his priority was air defence against Foggia-based Allied bomber formations entering or leaving the Reich, but he was also expected to co-ordinate air defence over the entire area of northern Italy and, whenever possible, counter Allied air attacks on the German army.[8]

The handful of Bf110 night-fighters having moved back to southern Germany on 11 June (their 20 missions had met with no success given the lack of an adequate ground control system), von Maltzahn was left with elements of three different Geschwader —

I/JG4, III/JG53 and Stab, 1 and II/JG77 — for his mammoth task. By the middle of June, an average of 45 Bf109G6s were being launched against bomber formations crossing Italy. They were too few. On 26 June, 'it was again demonstrated to Jafu and the Flotte that for the effective engagement of heavy bomber formations, it is urgently necessary for us to employ our own top cover Gruppen in Italian airspace . . .' Jafu's Bf109s could not be everywhere in sufficient numbers.

That same day, a P-47 formation was jumped by six 109s over Imola, claiming one probable but losing one definite of their own. Four days later, 12 P-47s of the 79th Fighter Group were bounced by a similar number of 109s over Bazzano. While two Thunderbolts continued on to bomb their designated stretch of railway track, the remaining 10 jettisoned their payloads and belly tanks, and turned on the Germans — two 109s were shot down and the rest 'scooted back up north'. It is arguable that the defenders achieved their goal by deterring 10 fighter-bombers from dropping on target, but such were the number of inexperienced pilots arriving to replace those shot down that, in July, von Maltzahn had to order II/JG77 to fly 'the most cautious freelance patrols possible'.

Von Maltzahn's problems did not end there. At the end of May, Luftwaffe High Command ordered that 'all Gruppen outside the Reich must immediately hand over a complete Staffel to Reich defence'. III/JG53 followed a month later, and then it was decided that personnel from both JG77 Gruppen and I/JG4 should withdraw from Italy, leaving their Bf109s behind. On 7 July, von Maltzahn officially reported that his fighters were too few to tackle heavy bomber formations passing to and fro, and on 23 July orders were given that only I/JG4 and I/JG77 would be transferred to Germany. This made Stab/JG77 superfluous to requirements — a single German Gruppe could be commanded directly by the Jafu — which left von Maltzahn with just II/JG77. To do his job, he was only going to get by with a little help from his Italian friends.

*   *   *   *

The Regia Aeronautica (the Italian Air Force) had been the pride of Fascism. The majestic freedom of flying, unhindered by stuffy established tradition, appealed to Mussolini who created a separate Air Ministry in 1924. The globe-trotting Marshal Balboa became an international celebrity and by 1937 the Regia Aeronautica had over 1,500 front-line aircraft and experience of two recent wars. It was downhill from then on, due to financial and political troubles coupled with vacillating policy. By the time Italy entered the war in 1940, she was already a lap behind in aircraft production and performance.

Yet the Italian Air Force had its moments. On 19 October 1940, four of its bombers took-off from Rhodes to fly for 15½ hours over nearly 3,000 miles to bomb British oil installations in Bahrain before landing in Italian Somaliland. The damage inflicted was pretty minimal, but the attack was every bit as audacious (and unexpected) as that mounted by the US against Libya in 1986. Although the Regia Aeronautica's bomber arm was never to be very troublesome, an Italian torpedo-bomber force operated over

Above:
The leader of the Italian Co-Belligerent Air Force mission tasked with dropping warning leaflets on Rome, reporting to Gp Capt Darwin at Foggia.
RAF Air Historical Branch

the Mediterranean with vigour and considerable success. It was clear during the Falklands conflict of 1982 that Argentinian Air Force verve and panache owed much to the Italian heritage of many of its pilots.

At the time of the Italian armistice in September 1943, the Regia Aeronautica had some 750 'efficient' aircraft at its disposal, of which 270 went over to the Allies. A fighter group was formed and sent to the Cassino front in support of the Fifth Army, and by March 1944 some 423 fighters, bombers, seaplanes and transports were operating within a national structure under an Italian Air Ministry, subject to the command of Mediterranean Allied Air Forces. At the end of March 1944, Ira Eaker felt moved to write that

'. . . in my judgement, the Italian Air Force has, during the past six months, made a wholehearted effort to contribute to its share of operations against the enemy, and I felt that this fact should be plainly recorded so that it can be placed to the credit of the Italians when the time for settlement comes . . .'[9]

The Italian Air Force was rewarded for its loyalty by a slow but steady succession of Allied aircraft, beginning with ground-attack Airacobras and progressing to Spitfire Vs and Baltimores. But to forestall any chance of Italian fighting Italian, all pro-Allied Co-Belligerent Air Force units were incorporated into the Balkan Air Force (BAF). Officially inaugurated with its HQ at Bari on 1 June 1944, BAF came under operational MAAF control but was essentially a British project with a brief to co-ordinate all air

operations in the Balkans. Once the Ancona area was secure, Strategic Air Force fighter units moved there from the heel of Italy, leaving the latter vacant for use by BAF and Co-Belligerent Air Force units.

On the German side, the main harvest after the armistice was some 200 tri-motor SM.82s which were formed into a transport Geschwader. Another 100 Macchi aircraft (some still in the factory) and about 60 SM.79 torpedo-bombers were considered usable; all other aircraft were broken up for salvage. In Mussolini's eyes, a separate army and air force were both a means of showing loyalty to the war effort and preventing the Germans from exercising undisputed rule over the territory of the Italian Social Republic (RSI). Lt-Col Ernesto Botto, an experienced fighter pilot, was made Air Force Under Secretary of State in October 1943, and he proved to be remarkably successful in appealing for pilots, engineers, armourers and other ground specialists to turn up for duty in the new Aeronautica Nazionale Repubblicana (ANR).

Botto's campaign coincided with some revival of support for Fascism. The Allies lost credibility by getting bogged down at the Gustav Line, while astute propaganda highlighted the damage being done to Italian towns by American air raids. Civilian casualties, including women and children, were too many for the

good of the Allied cause. Fascists put up large notices on bombed-out buildings: 'This is the work of your so-called liberators.' At a time when the legal government of the king was sitting impotent in the small port of Brindisi in the extreme southeast, many ordinary Italians volunteered to take up the only offer on the table to help defend their homeland. Around 1,400 pilots, 3,500 specialist trades and 2,000 officers and SNCOs answered the call. A further 30,000 soldiers joined the ANR anti-aircraft artillery, and 45,000 more enlisted directly into Luftwaffe flak; and these were on top of the 40,000 men demanded by von Richthofen to labour on his airfields.

Discussions in Berlin led to the Göring–Botto agreement whereby ANR tasks were defined as defence of RSI territory by fighter units, offensive action by torpedo-bombers and support action by transport units to facilitate common war efforts. There was to be no over-land offensive capability so that no Italian would have to bomb Italy. On his return from Germany, Botto gave orders to start recovering assets to the relative safety of northern Italy, wherein lay the bulk of the Italian aircraft and aero-engine industry.

It was hoped to replace the once formidable but now outclassed SM.79 torpedo-bombers with Ju88s, but production of the latter was discontinued in favour of the Ju188 and every one coming off the production line was needed by the Luftwaffe. A Staffel of elderly SM.79s was operating against the Anzio landings and convoy sailings by February 1944, but in the absence of adequate instruments the SM.79s could operate only on moonlit nights in good weather. They were hammered. The strength of Allied anti-aircraft defences at Anzio, the loss of their commander and 11 aircraft at the hands of four P-47s of the 57th Fighter Group, plus damage caused by an Allied air attack on their base at Gorizia, all forced the SM.79 out of battlefield activity. SM.79 torpedo-bombers continued to operate in the anti-shipping role, and two transport groups supported the Eastern Front, but the main raison d'être of the ANR became defence of the shrinking Fascist homeland.

For all Mussolini's aspirations, HQ Luftflotte 2 was firmly responsible for the birth, development and operations of the ANR. Like their Luftwaffe patrons, ANR units were organised in Gruppi composed in turn of three Squadriglie. It was intended that the Gruppi Caccia (pursuit groups) would be equipped with the most up-to-date fighters Italian industry could produce — Macchi 205 and Fiat G.55s. 1ª Squadriglie was declared ready for action and transferred to Mirafiori at the end of December 1943. On 3 January 1944, it was launched to intercept a 99th Bomb Group formation of B-17s in the process of bombing the Villar Perosa ball-bearing factory near Turin. The Macchi 205s claimed to have dispatched three American P-38s, but there were still some wrinkles to iron out — on 30 January, a JG77 pilot misidentified the commandant of I Gruppo and shot him down. Worse was to follow. In the first five months of fighting alongside German Jagdgeschwader, I GrC lost 35 aircraft and 28 pilots.

It was not all bad. After Mussolini presented colours in April 1944 to RSI battalions then under training in Bavaria, crowds flocked to greet the Duce on his return train journey to Lake Garda. With Italy reduced to a great power battlefield, Communists approaching from the east, and air raids destroying large swathes

of Italian towns, Mussolini seemed to offer the reassurance of a familiar father-figure who might yet lead people into the light.

But the fall of Rome changed the atmosphere. I and II Gruppo Caccia were up and running as follows by June 1944:

Iº Gruppo Caccia
Commanded by Maj Adriano Visconti
1ª Sq Asso di Bastoni ('Ace of Clubs') — Lt Guiseppe Roberto
2ª Sq Vespa Arrabbiata ('Angry Wasp') — Capt Amedeo Guidi
3ª Sq Arciere ('Archer') — Capt Pio Tomaselli

2º Gruppo Caccia
Commanded by Lt-Col Aldo Alessandrini
1ª Sq Gigi Tre Osei (nickname of a former ace) — Lt Ugo Drago
2ª Sq Diavoli Rossi ('Red Devils') — Capt Mario Bellagambi
3ª Sq Gamba di Ferro ('Iron Leg') — Lt Guiseppe Gianelli

But they were running out of Italian aircraft. Allied bombing took its toll of the Macchi and Fiat production lines, and Fiat output was not helped by the decision to start removing much of the company machinery to Germany on 21 June. Allied bombs fell on the Fiat works the following day, and 40,000 workers came out on strike,

thus showing, according to a police report, 'the existence of a link between the strike and the enemy air force'.[10] The workers returned after concessions, but Mussolini's heartland had given a pointer to the future with all its political implications.

For all its prowess at high level, the Fiat G.55 was not best suited to mixing it in the weeds; and with fewer and fewer Italian aircraft to go round, the logical decision was taken to standardise on German fighter aircraft beginning with II Gruppo. As Jagdgeschwader crews returned to Germany, they left their Bf109s behind for the ANR. The USAAF officially discovered the existence of Italian-flown Bf109s on 29 June when a dozen P-47s of the 64th Fighter Squadron and 57th Fighter Group, ran into two II GrC 'Gustavs' near Bologna.[11] After a chase up and down local valleys, 'Lt Mannon saw his tracers striking the fuselage of one enemy aircraft that was blue-grey in colour with Italian markings . . .'

RSI airspace was divided into three defensive zones — West, Centre and East — held together by an overarching radar system controlled by the Luftwaffe. The two ANR Gruppi were essentially independent entities. I Gruppo maintained the time-honoured Italian air defence tradition of individual bravado and aerobatic skill, while II Gruppo modelled itself along more collective Luftwaffe lines — by July, an Occhio di Lince (Lynx Eye) section of four aircraft was providing top cover for II Gruppo's main formation. Differences apart, ANR air defenders developed into quite an effective little force, and their crews were keen and on the whole efficient, even when the struggle was lost in all but name. But their priority was air defence of the Reich and the RSI industrial and population base.

By August 1944 the Fifteenth Air Force had reached its full fighting strength of 21 heavy bombardment groups (six with B-17s and 15 with B-24s) and seven fighter groups (three with P-38 Lightnings and four with P-51 Mustangs). Even without the five 205 Group wings, this made a grand total of 1,957 aircraft and 81,000 personnel. With barely 100 Italian and German-manned fighters in theatre to take on that lot (of which no more than 70 were serviceable at any one time), the Jafu could offer little succour to the army. Kesselring, having proved pretty adept at fighting a successful defensive campaign virtually without air support, was left to make do as best he could.

*   *   *   *

'With the Germans retreating north of Rome, and a sharp falling off in Luftwaffe activity, our Spitfires were fitted with racks to carry a 500lb bomb. After practising dive bombing at 60° over the sea we began operating, securing results which were agreed to be effective on a number of targets. This bombing was not without its occupational hazards, however, and it was dangerous when the bombs hung up. The South African Du Toit was killed when a bomb would not release but fell off and exploded when he landed, blowing his aircraft to pieces. He was a fine chap and it was very bad luck. Once, when attacking a level crossing, my bomb hung up during a dive and fell off while I was dodging round some trees avoiding flak, exploding under the aircraft and throwing it about so violently that I thought the flak had connected.'[12]

Around Lake Trasimene, where Flaminius and his legions had been routed by Hannibal, tactical air kept up an average of 1,000 sorties a day against German lines of communication and supply movements. Medium bombers attacked railway and road bridges

well to the rear; fighter-bombers operated along the bombline over secondary roads leading northwards and more distant rail targets; light bombers attacked supply dumps; fighters were out in their hundreds on armed recce patrols and artillery reconnaissances, and there was much light bomber and fighter defensive counter-air activity at night.

Italian airspace served as a laboratory for many air power techniques, and one innovation which underlined the extent to which the Allies had the skies to themselves was the use of light aircraft as a forward air controller. In May, XII TAC had established a system, dubbed 'Pineapple', to seek out and destroy Axis motor transport operating between the front line and the bombline. 'Pineapple' allowed aircraft put on patrol for transport hunting to be called in by any aircraft — such as the F-6 photo-recce version of the Mustang — that spotted vehicles below the bombline.

One day, an artillery-spotting L-5 pilot low on fuel landed next to a XII TAC controller, Capt William H. Davidson. The pilot asked why no one had thought of using an L-5 to direct fighter-bombers onto a target when artillery was unavailable. The name of this L-5 pilot was never recorded, but his suggestion was passed up the line and by mid-June, VHF radios had been fitted into the L-5s supporting VI Corps. With their radios tuned to army frequencies, L-5s and their crews began operating as airborne forward air controllers. This innovation was known as 'Horsefly', and it became usual for two L-5s to be assigned to each corps. 'Horsefly' aircraft carried an infantry observer to identify friendly troops and differentiate between friendly and enemy armour and flew at 3,000–4,000ft. 'Horsefly' aircraft carried smoke bombs to mark targets, and they were of particular value when artillery was unavailable for the task. They acted as an easily located orbit point for the fighter-bombers, sometimes up to 20 miles behind German lines, and the L-5 observer was well placed to determine the results of any air strike.[13]

The battle astride Lake Trasimene lasted 10 days. Three days in, on 23 June, von Pohl ordered intensification of night ground-attacks against Allied targets near the front. NAGr9 responded with their robust Stukas, supported by anti-aircraft batteries and searchlight nuclei. 'The creation of this night harassing attack force, although an emergency measure not without a certain nuisance value when weather permitted, acted favourably on German morale at a time when all hope of audible and visible air support was nearing zero point.'[14] Bf109s made spasmodic attempts to support Pohl's directive, and as many as 30 of them were reported in the Ancona area on 29 June. But as the

small fighter force was fully committed to the interception of heavy bombers further north, there was little German air activity worth recording over the front line from the end of June to the entry into Florence.

After a typically bravura performance which imposed severe delays in the hill country on either side of Lake Trasimene, the Germans melted away. Stubborn German resistance and extensive demolition activity throughout July held successive natural defensive positions for a few days at a time, so although the French were in Siena by 3 July, Arezzo fell on 16 July, the Poles captured Ancona two days later and on 19 July the Americans entered

Below Left:
A very brave Piper Cub pilot prepares to take-off for another stirring day flying far behind enemy lines to check on the accuracy of Fifth Army artillery fire. *IWM*

Right & Below Right:
The fruits of Allied air supremacy in 1944. *(right)* Eighth Army reserves nose-to-tail, waiting to move forward during the advance on the Gothic Line. They could only act this way in daylight because the Luftwaffe was no longer a force to be reckoned with. *(bottom right)* On the other hand, this was the penalty of moving in daylight without air superiority: French troops are passing the wreck of a German column spotted by Allied airmen and destroyed by combined air/artillery attack in the Esperia defile. *Author's Collection*

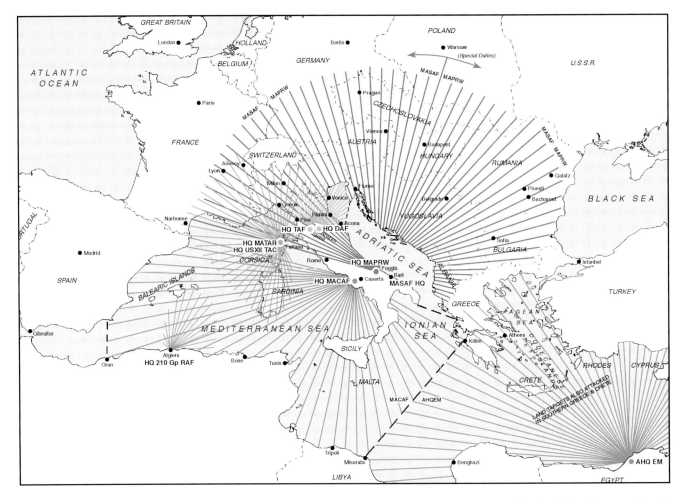

Leghorn. The Allied advance to the Arno was slow and laborious — and as the summer days ran out, US tactical units moved to Corsica on 18 July to participate in the 'Dragoon' invasion of southern France.

HQ MATAF moved to Corsica and began to function there on 19 July. Maj-Gen Cannon continued to control the two USAAF medium bomber wings of XII TAC in Corsica and DAF on the mainland. Cannon left his deputy, AVM D'Albiac, plus a small staff to form a subsidiary HQ on the mainland to be known as HQ Tactical Air Force (Italy). DAF, under AVM Dickson, worked to a general directive from Cannon which included responsibility for providing air support for both Fifth and Eighth Armies from 05.00hrs on 20 July. Dickson kept his Advanced HQ DAF alongside HQ Eighth Army, while creating 'Ops A' alongside HQ Fifth Army. Requests for air support were discussed by Fifth with Ops A, which then passed them to HQ DAF where arrangements were made to meet them, depending on the resources available and Eighth Army's requirements. Defensive fighters were controlled by No 1 Mobile Operations Room Unit (MORU) 'A' on the east coast, and No 1 MORU 'B' on the west.

Notwithstanding the impending invasion of southern France, XII TAC was to operate very effectively over western Italy from

Corsica for the next two weeks. Back in June, senior air commanders believed that there would be no quick Gothic Line breakthrough without knocking out the bridges between the Apennines and the Po. The principal river of Italy, the Po wound through a broad plain for some 420 miles, and because it was hemmed in by protective embankments running in many places high above the plain, it formed a natural obstacle across the north of Italy. All routes leading northwards to the Reich had to cross it.

The airmen came up with a plan code-named 'Mallory', which maintained that the destruction of six railway bridges over the Po, another across the River Trebbia at Piacenza and the viaduct at Recco on the west coast, would stop all rail traffic from Germany, Austria and France reaching south of the river and east of a line from Genoa to Florence. 'Mallory' was ready to go on 17 June, but bad weather intervened and then the plan was dropped because Alexander and his senior land commanders expected a quick sweep through the Gothic Line and up to the Po, in which case they preferred to occupy the bridges intact. But once it became clear that Allied ground forces would not have such an easy ride, the army lifted its veto on attacks against road bridges across the Po — which had been based on the hope that at least one bridge on each front could be seized by airborne forces, Arnhem-style. The aim

Left:
The range and flexibility of air power as demonstrated by Mediterranean Allied Air Forces during July and August 1944.

Above:
Leghorn after Allied air attacks on 20 June 1944. *RAF Air Historical Branch*

now was to bring the Germans to battle between the Apennines and the Po, driving them back against a bridgeless river. On 11 July, the air forces received a revived directive for what was renamed Operation 'Mallory Major'.

'Mallory Major' sought the destruction of all bridges over the Po from Piacenza eastwards to the sea — five rail, two rail and road, and 14 road bridges — plus rail and road crossings over the Trebbia and continued interdiction of bridges between La Spezia and Genoa. Eleven were permanent structures, some over 2,000ft long, built of steel lattice girders with masonry or concrete arches; the rest were pontoons. As the heavy bombers were pretty much occupied with targets in Germany, the Balkans (especially the Ploesti refinery) and southern France, the job of knocking out the bridges was assigned to TAF.[15]

The mediums of the 42nd and 57th Bombardment Wings began their sustained campaign on 12 July, the B-26s taking the westerly,

and the B-25s the more easterly bridges. Fighter-bombers supplemented these attacks to prevent hasty German repairs and destroy any pontoons. Flying conditions were so ideal that almost 300 missions were flown daily. After four days, 12 bridges were either totally destroyed or had gaps in them more than 500ft long. Eight more were cut, blocked or otherwise so damaged that they were closed to traffic. Only one, a reinforced concrete and steel structure at Ostiglia on the Bologna–Verona line, remained open in spite of four attacks. No north–south rail traffic was possible eastward of Piacenza.

'Mallory Major' as such ended on 15 July, but then the scope of medium bomber operations was expanded to try to interdict all north–south traffic by cutting the Po bridges west of Piacenza, and to paralyse east–west traffic by cutting other key bridges through the Po Valley. By 4 August, Genoa was isolated, communications eastward of Turin were limited, all railway lines from Milan to the south and east were cut, and all but two routes along the northern Apennines were useless.[16]

None of this was as easy as it sounded. The excellent design and construction of many Italian bridges presented a strong challenge to bomber crews who lacked the wondrous laser-designation devices of today. Some B-25s and B-26s had received the famous

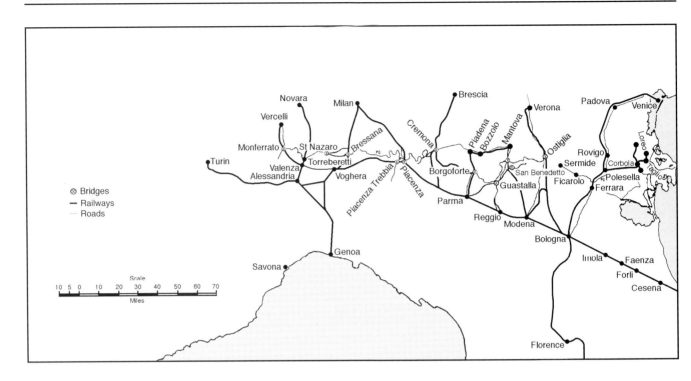

Above :
Po River Bridges attacked during operation 'Mallory Major', 12-27 July 1944.

Left:
The result of Allied air attack on a railway line near Florence in July 1944. *Author's Collection*

Norden bombsight in response to the more unfortunate bombing errors earlier in the campaign. The aircraft leading the basic bombing formation of six carried the Norden-enhanced bombardier, who sighted for range and deflection. But for all the considerable accuracies achieved from 9,000–12,000ft, the Norden was a visual bombsight: it could not see through cloud and it had certain disadvantages at night. The narrowness of some bridges and pontoons explained why one squadron of fighter-bombers often succeeded where formations of mediums failed.[17] Given that the Po included some of the heaviest structures ever bombed in the Mediterranean theatre, a solidly-built bridge, solidly defended by flak, was no pushover: it took 11 attacks with a total of 482 tons of bombs to create permanent blocks on the parallel road and rail bridge at Piacenza.

By the time Allied forces entered southern Florence on 4 August, there was much air-inflicted paralysis on the Po. At times, Kesselring was virtually isolated from the rest of Europe, yet for all the hardship and disruption, the German forces south of the river did not disintegrate. They kept going by skill, ingenuity and a massive railway repair effort which relied on Italian labour units and repair materials pre-positioned along the most important lines. The Germans assembled pontoon bridges at night, used them and dismantled them before dawn. Ferries were used at more than 50 points along the Po, supplemented by the cunning use of cable railways to carry supplies across the river without using fuel. German front-line troops were kept supplied by whatever could be moved under cover of darkness or bad weather, and great use was made of camouflage. The very complexity of the communications

network in northern Italy helped Kesselring, because Allied air forces could not simultaneously interdict all lines. Notwithstanding the great achievements of an enhanced 'Mallory Major', it did not prevent the Germans from stopping the Fifth and Eighth Armies at the Gothic Line.

'Dragoon' landed on the French Riviera on 15 August, supported by 'the greatest air effort in the Mediterranean to date'.[18] Senger noted 'a considerable relief to us in the Italian theatre when strong elements of the enemy's air force were withdrawn',[19] and John Terraine noted 'the lamentable effect that such a diversion of strength was bound to have on the forces in Italy; how it might affect the air can be judged from one single statistic — the 4,249 sorties flown by MAAF on the first day of 'Dragoon' alone'.[20] But in all honesty, Alexander had all these sorties and more available for months before 'Dragoon'. They did not prevent the squandering of that great window of opportunity immediately after the fall of Rome, when only shattered units and mostly third-rate newcomers stood between the Allies and wrapping up the Italian campaign.

It was not lack of air power which plagued Allied operations in Italy during the summer of 1944, rather it was the lack of a coherent strategy applied with sufficient resolve. 'I am rather disappointed,' wrote Chief of the Imperial General Staff Sir Alan Brooke to 'Jumbo' Wilson on 2 August, 'that Alex did not make a more definite attempt to smash Kesselring's forces up whilst they are south of the Apennines. He . . . seems to be deliberately driving the Germans back on to that position instead of breaking them up in the more favourable country. I cannot feel that this policy of small pushes all along the line and driving the Boche like partridges can be right.'[21] Such an approach enabled the Germans to take cover in good order on the Gothic Line.

Notes to Chapter 11

1. Warlimont, op.cit, p.430.
2. Ibid; p.206.
3. Kurowski, op.cit, p.272.
4. Interrogation Latimer House, England, 24 October 1945.
5. The interceptors of Luftwaffe radio and telephone traffic.
6. Montgomery, P.; 'Beaufighter Ban Yan'; Aircraft Illustrated, January 1970, p.27.
7. Night Harassment Wing.
8. Directive to GOC Luftwaffe in Central Italy from Operations Division, Luftflotte 2, 11 June 1944.
9. AHB, op.cit, Appendix 14, p.2.
10. Deakin, op.cit, p.206.
11. Until December 1944, every Bf109 in Italy was a G6 variant.
12. Duke, N.; Test Pilot; p.120.
13. The British only adopted the Air Observation Post concept in Italy in the late autumn of 1944, when Austers manned jointly by the army and RAF were first employed to direct RAF fighter-bombers on to close-support targets such as German tanks.
14. Von Pohl Interrogation reports.
15. Though on the second day of 'Mallory Major', Strategic's entire effort was directed against Italian oil storage facilities and communications. Soon after midnight on 13 July, Halifax pathfinders led 22 Wellingtons and Liberators to drop 62 tons on the Brescia yards. Later in the day, 196 Strategic heavies severely damaged four railway yards and the rail bridge at Piacenza.
16. Report on Operation 'Mallory Major', MATAF, 15 January 1945.
17. RAF Desert Air Force Study (1944), Fighter-Bombers.
18. Craven and Cate, op.cit, p.430.
19. Senger, op.cit, p.262.
20. Terraine, op.cit, p.597.
21. Bryant, op.cit, p.204.

Below:
It was wryly said by Allied footsloggers that 'Jerry's retreating all right, but he's taking the last ridge back with him.' This German, who perished at Zollara on the Gemmano Ridge, died in September 1944 helping to hinder the Allied advance so that his comrades could retreat in good order to the next great defensive position — the Gothic Line. *RAF Air Historical Branch*

AGAINST THE GOTHIC LINE

'The Army was to be given more close support if possible and more attacks were to be made on communications immediately behind the lines. This was uneconomical, but it must be remembered that the army had grown so used to air superiority and all it implied that close support in large quantities had become an almost physical necessity.'
RAF Official History

In aeronautical terms, two types of Allied wings mattered in Italy: the organisational and the structural. An RAF 'Wing' was the equivalent of a USAAF 'Group'. The number of squadrons in AAF groups and RAF wings varied according to role and circumstances, but the US heavy day-bomber group normally consisted of four squadrons of eight aircraft each, while a fighter group consisted of

75 aircraft divided between three squadrons. US groups were assembled into a wing, as were French and Brazilian air force units.[1] RAF and Dominion squadrons were of similar size but their wings were more varied in make-up: three to six squadrons made up a wing, and around five to six wings comprised a group.

The other crucial wings were those that generated enough lift to keep aircraft in the sky. Aircraft were given a major role in the original plan to break the Gothic Line, which envisaged a concentrated drive by four corps (totalling 14 divisions) from Florence to Bologna. Then, on 4 August, Alexander and his chief

Below:
Alexander's final plan for the offensive against the Gothic Line, August 1944.

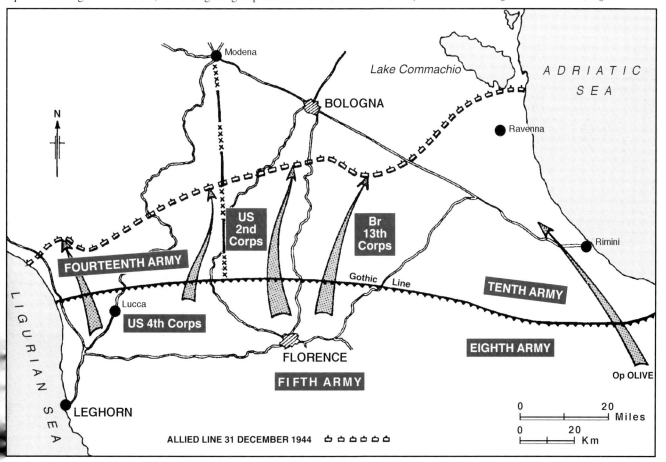

Left:
Sir Charles Portal, British Chief of Air Staff (centre), models the latest designer shorts while leaving a Spitfire Wing ops room in August 1944. Sir John Slessor, deputy Air C-in-C (left), tries to avoid stepping on something. *RAF Air Historical Branch*

of staff met Eighth Army commander Oliver Leese on Orvieto airfield. So improvised was this meeting that it took place under the wing of a parked Dakota transport to give some shade from the August sun. 'Leese managed to persuade Alexander and Harding that their well-matured concept for forcing the centre of the Gothic Line should be jettisoned at the last moment in favour of a wholly undeveloped plan in which the Eighth Army would cross the Apennines and attack on the Adriatic coast, supported by subsidiary attacks by the Fifth Army on the Florence–Bologna axis.'[2]

This new plan, known as 'Olive', suited Alexander's penchant for the 'two-handed punch'. The rationale was to attack two points equally vital to the enemy, thereby splitting the reserves available for defence. If the Eighth Army hit first up the east coast, followed within the week by five divisions striking through the central mountains towards Bologna, it would be the boxer's 'one-two'.

Yet for a time it looked as if Alexander would have to box clever without many of his vital wings. Although by the end of August Eisenhower had 103 air groups under his command as against 46 in Italy, the transfer of the entire Twelfth Air Force to France was repeatedly under discussion during the second half of 1944. The British viewed this prospect with grave concern, but Gen Eaker was equally worried that US air and ground troops would stagnate if the Italian front became static. On 21 August, Eaker advised Arnold that he should support any plan to move the Twelfth out of Italy and furthermore he recommended that the Fifth Army be moved to reinforce the effort in France.[3] When Alexander appealed directly to Sir Alan Brooke, the latter could only reply, 'It is not possible to send reinforcements to the Mediterranean and you will have to continue to live on your own resources.'[4]

Eighth Army's offensive on the Adriatic flank, which began on 26 August, was so successful initially that the Fifth's prospects of

driving to Bologna looked very rosy. Generals Wilson, Eaker and Spaatz met late in August to discuss the allocation of air forces between southern France and Italy, and as it seemed foolish to make any changes while things were going so well, the ultimate fate of the Twelfth was postponed until the outcome of 'Olive' was known.[5]

When XII TAC was withdrawn from Italy in July for the impending invasion of southern France, DAF became the sole close-support authority for the hard slog up to the Arno. By redistributing its Mediterranean assets, the British Air Ministry raised the total strength of AVM Dickson's DAF to 29½ squadrons supporting both Fifth and Eighth Armies. DAF's fighters and fighter-bombers, and its light and medium bombers, mounted over 500 sorties on 15 August — D-Day for 'Dragoon' — but they managed to cope from coast to coast only because the Luftwaffe conceded battlefield airspace. During the period of relative Italian quiet, 4–25 August, DAF was largely confined to softening the Gothic Line defences and disrupting communications in the area bounded by the Genoa–Pavia railway in the west, the Po in the north and the east coast.

Air support for 'Olive' started at D-Day minus 7. The night-bombers of 205 Group were used over four nights to attack targets such as the Ravenna and Bologna marshalling yards. Given the scale of the interdiction effort to date, the Germans were expected to be short of fuel and ammunition; the goal now was to attack their forward reserves and dumps. But the canny Germans took to nocturnal replenishing and redeploying, and although Allied tactical air reconnaissance often witnessed its start in the evening, this came too late to allow any bombers dispatched to land in daylight. The flow of night-capable operational aircraft into the Italian theatre remained too low to sustain the 24-hour capability that was essential if the German logistic chain was to be really severed.

Given that the greater part of the Eighth Army was in the central sector when 'Olive' called for them to breach the eastern Gothic Line, a mass transfer was necessary under conditions of great secrecy over tortuous mountain roads. So an elaborate system of misinformation started, aimed to convince the locals that the 11,000 vehicles moving every day to the assembly areas at Ancona were nothing more than normal road traffic. DAF had to behave likewise. To avoid giving the game away, only a limited ground support programme could be mounted: DAF devoted a mere eight to ten missions daily against long-range guns that would most threaten Allied troops when they went into action.

Squadron crests, previously carefully painted on all vehicles, were equally carefully removed. In an effort to fool the German intercept service, wireless stations on the west coast maintained normal radio traffic, even if most of it was rubbish, while no new stations on the east were allowed to start activity before time. To pass messages from coast to coast other than by teleprinter, air couriers plied twice daily between Siena and Jesi. To counterbalance increased aerial photography of the Adriatic coast, 285 Wing regularly flew dummy PR missions over the Futa pass which led directly to Bologna.

Until D minus 3, DAF was to fly from its current airfields against dumps and communications. From D minus 2 to D plus 5, ground parties were to move across to the Adriatic. Aircraft were to fly over on the morning of D-Day to start intensive operations. And after the majority of DAF units moved to airfields on the east coast, a proportion would have to be switched back to support the Fifth Army attack.

The official records found it 'hard to say how successful our deception methods were'. German long-range reconnaissance was a high priority task and the Ju88s and 188s, flying high at night with their Hohentwiel radar reconnaissance kit, struggled to make sense of what was happening below. It was indicative of reduced Luftwaffe flying training standards that no fewer than seven of FAGr122's Ju188Ds were lost to accidents in September. Day reconnaissance was left to the few up-to-date Me410s flying out of Bergamo over the Ligurian Sea, Corsican harbours and occasionally down the Adriatic Coast as far as San Benedetto. The close reconnaissance Bf109s drew the short straw; they were most directly concerned with keeping a watch on the Fifth and Eighth Armies, and they suffered heavily in the process.

Between 9 and 24 August, no German air reconnaissance was noted, but numerous Ju88s and 188s covered the air concentration areas in the Adriatic sector. At last light on 25 August, two aircraft were plotted on what must have been an NAGr11 tactical recce mission. Kesselring, in his postwar memoirs, claimed that after the middle of August, 'there was no longer any doubt that the British Eighth Army was getting ready for a decisive outflanking attack on the Adriatic'.[6] Yet for all his stout words, Kesselring was completely surprised when, on the morning of 26 August, Eighth Army launched its attack across the Metauro River.

From first light, almost the entire DAF effort directly supported the advance which occupied Fano the next day. Of the 664 sorties flown on the first day, over 180 light and medium bomber sorties flew against guns and defences still under construction, while waves of fighter-bombers attacked guns and strongpoints. Nineteen artillery reconnaissance missions were flown, 11 hostile batteries were engaged under Rover direction and 114 Marauders bombed roads and bridges in the Apennines to create road blocks.

It was indicative of the short-termism inherent in much of the Allied strategy that even as the first V1 flying bombs fell on London in June, Churchill felt the need for advice on 'the prosecution of the war after clearing the Pisa–Rimini line. Were we to head for Vienna according to Alex or were we to launch another expedition into France?'[7]

As it happened, the last great defensive line before the Brenner, with its 2,376 machine-gun posts and 479 anti-tank gun, mortar and assault gun positions, neither started in Pisa nor ended in Rimini. In the west, La Spezia was well protected by defences in depth which stretched back to Carrera on the coast. From there the Gothic Line ran across the mountains, with strongpoints prepared astride the routes leading to the wide plains of the Po Valley. Finally, the Gothic Line turned east to follow the River Foglia to Pesaro. This last sector, covered only by low foothills, was well developed with anti-tank ditches, extensive minefields and deep bunkers as well as dug-in tank turrets. The ancient town of Pesaro (one-time home of Lucrezia Borgia) was a key German position and the Eighth Army much preferred to see it neutralised from the air while the army by-passed it. But the presence of the German 1st Parachute Division around and in Pesaro — where the physical defences were known to be strong — could not be ignored. Pesaro had to be softened up, and as the Corsica-based mediums were preoccupied with 'Dragoon', the task was handed to 205 Group RAF.

After four months in Bari alongside HQ Fifteenth Air Force, HQ 205 Group moved to the Foggia area in April 1944 to be closer to its flying units. The four RAF wings — 231, 236 and 330 with Wellingtons, and 240 flying Liberators and Halifaxes — were increased to five in July with the arrival of the Liberators of 2 SAAF Wing. Twenty seven of Slessor's 119 squadrons came from the South African Air Force and to reinforce the Springbok dimension, Brig J. T. Durrant of the SAAF took over command of 205 Group on 3 August from Air Cdre Simpson. His arrival coincided with the inauguration of a new 'Gee' chain 'liberated from all offending gremlins'; while on 23 August three Liberators were fitted with the H2S navigation and bombing radar. It was hoped that these devices would reduce, if not prevent altogether, embarrassing bombing errors in future.[8]

Thus enhanced, 205 Group undertook maximum harassing attacks on German troops 'throughout the night' without touching the town of Pesaro, which was marked by a red target indicator dropped on its centre, while green indicators defined the target area perimeter. On the first night — 26/27 August — the South Africans kicked off with a three-minute 'blitz', whereupon 39 Wellingtons, 21 Liberators and six Halifaxes 'harassed' the area behind the front line for eight hours on end. The next night the harassing continued, interspersed at 23.00hrs by a three-minute 60-aircraft 'blitz' against troops, equipment and supplies to give the Germans no rest. A third attack on 28/29 August closed the series, by which time nearly 2,000 tons of bombs had been dropped behind the narrow Pesaro front.

Three days passed before Gen Lemelsen realised what he was up against, and on 30 August Allied patrols crossed the Foglia and captured the first positions in the Gothic Line. A 'Backs to the Wall' order of the day was issued and German reinforcements rushed in, but they were swept back and all commanding features cleared. Polish Corps was supported by a large air effort, including concentrated fighter-bomber attacks on pinpoint targets between 16.00hrs and 18.00hrs.

On 1 September, DAF's support effort reached 690 sorties. For the first three days of the month, Spitfires, Kittyhawks, Mustangs, Baltimores and Marauders carried out a general 'blitz' on German defences just ahead of Allied troops.

'It was urgent that enemy stores, petrol and ammunition should be bitten into, confusion sown in the distribution system and the enemy's freedom of tactical command neutralised. To this end, continuous armed reconnaissance was flown by day and Beaufighters patrolled by night. On the first two days, road movement was agitated and some 36 lorries, two locomotives and a barge were reported destroyed and more damaged.'[9]

Notes on the technique for an Air Blitz (September 1944)

(a) Bombline

The principle of the air blitz is the establishment of a bombline, in front of which aircraft can operate freely on any target that presents itself.

The bombline will be marked by blobs of white smoke made and maintained by artillery smoke shell. These will be about a mile apart, extending across the whole front, as nearly in line as the natural features of the ground will allow.

The bombline line will be 3,000yd in front of the forward troops. The bombline will move forward as a whole, on a timed programme, lifting about every 15min.

There will be a flying controller whose role will be to report on the effectiveness of the smoke bombline through 'Rover David'. The controller will also control the aircraft engaged on the blitz.

(b) The Air Attack

The air blitz will be about two hours' duration. It must be intense. The principal methods of attack will be fragmentation bombing and strafing.

After the blitz, a lull in air attacks for about two hours must be accepted.

By 2 September, 1st Canadian Division was over the River Conca and V Corps' two armoured divisions were about to be launched towards Rimini and beyond. Kesselring was down to his last mobile reserve — the 29th Panzer Grenadiers — which moved across from Bologna to join 1st Parachute and 26th Panzer Divisions. Heavy rain on the morning of 3 September put all the forward DAF airfields out of action — those in the Adriatic sector were very susceptible to rain, and PSP was in short supply — but around 250 sorties were somehow flown by other aircraft. Among them was a lucky No 241 Squadron Spitfire pilot who scored a hit

Above:
The cavalry is coming – US Mitchells on their way to support the Fifth Army.
RAF Air Historical Branch

on a petrol and ammunition train, which blew up.

The very heavy rain that blighted DAF flying efforts lasted for three days. Advancing Allied tanks, guns and vehicles got quickly bogged down and air support was seriously constrained. From 4 to 12 September, on a ridge before the town of Coriano and at Geminano five miles to the south, three German divisions managed to hold their ground against all Allied attacks in some of the bitterest fighting of the whole campaign. The few recce Bf109s that came within range, and eight Ju87s that attempted night harassment bombing, fared badly at Allied hands, but dense German flak around Rimini proved a growing menace, damaging 60 Allied aircraft on one day. Aerial photographs viewed in DAF Advance HQ revealed as scarred a landscape as anywhere in Italy bar Cassino. It was time to unleash the Fifth Army on what should have been Kesselring's weakened centre.

To conceal the main point of the Fifth's attack, the medium bombers and Corsica-based fighter-bombers, plus those of the 350th Fighter Group, concentrated on bridges and communication targets: priority was given to the River Po crossings and rail bridges below Lake Maggiore, where all five bridges across the Ticino River were destroyed. Nine B-25s of the 321st Bomb Group were going for the Polesella railway bridge across the Po when they were attacked by four 109s belonging to JG77. While one Mitchell was damaged, the Americans shot down a 109 killing

the junction point between the German Tenth and Fourteenth Armies, was captured and the opposing line broken. German reinforcements failed to stop the Fifth Army from capturing Firenzuola on 21 September but a week later the advance was halted by violent counter-attacks and communication difficulties. Mark Clark recorded that 'we switched the direction of our main attack . . . to Route 65, leading to Bologna, and pressed slowly forward against stiff resistance'.[11]

The bulk of the medium bomber close-support effort had passed to the Eighth Army front on 16 September, where DAF was making a tremendous and sustained effort to support the drive for the famous seaside resort of Rimini. From Kesselring's perspective, the Florence–Bologna sector was a worry, but much less so than his left flank. If the Germans were to be forced off the Apennines, they had to avoid being driven into a corner formed by the Allied Seventh Army in southern France and the frontier with neutral Switzerland, leaving the northeastern approaches to the Reich still open. Any withdrawal from the Gothic Line had to take the form of a wheeling back of the right flank while tenaciously holding the left. This explained why, during the first two weeks of September, when the Allied right flank was slowed down by determined resistance and early winter rains, Kesselring amassed no fewer than 10 divisions in the Rimini sector, in part by robbing the centre.

These defenders held firm as the Eighth launched an all-out assault on the night of 12/13 September, supported by sustained efforts from DAF and TAF's two medium bomber wings. DAF operational intensity peaked on 13 September when over 900 sorties dropped over 500 tons of bombs, including an attack by 22 Spitbombers on 26th Panzer Division HQ. The 800-plus sorties flown the next day concentrated on German troop movements, though 84 DAF Marauders and Baltimores flew sorties against gun areas and defended positions outside Rimini. In addition, three waves of B-25s flew 122 sorties to drop 10,895 20lb fragmentation bombs and 215 demolition bombs (totalling 163 tons), on German troop positions, covering around 60% of the target area.

The 700-plus daily DAF sorties over the following three days were devoted mainly to close army support. While erratic weather on 15 September thwarted bomber attacks, some fighter-bomber pilots operated five times that day. But although weakened by air and artillery bombardment, the tenacious Germans clung on and Allied troops suffered grievous casualties themselves.

There followed some of the bloodiest and most expensive fighting of the whole Italian campaign. The battle for San Fortunato sector — with its six good German divisions — amounted to the battle for Rimini. From first light to 07.45hrs on 17 September, 132 DAF Kittyhawks and Spitbombers ceaselessly bombed and strafed guns, mortars and strongpoints on the forward and reverse slopes of the last ridge defending Rimini, to soften up the opposition before the ground troops went in. Thereafter close-support missions, with 'Rover David' much in evidence, were maintained throughout the day; 144 light and medium bombers of TAC and 96 from DAF participated, with 244 Wing's six squadrons of Spitbombers doing 'everything humanly possible to meet the increasingly clamorous army requests for close air

Officer Cadet Volke. Another German pilot, Cpl (Gefreiter) Burgstaller, also died in combat that day. They were probably the last Jagdflieger to die in theatre, because the final Luftwaffe fighter unit was about to leave Italy.

Once the Fifth Army opened its assault on 9 September, B-26s shifted their attacks from the Po to the railway lines leading from Piacenza, Rimini, Ferrara and Verona directly into Bologna to isolate the battle area. But the bulk of medium and fighter-bomber effort was devoted to blasting a path through the Gothic Line for the Fifth Army. The 42nd and 57th Bombardment Wings began a series of attacks on supply points, barracks and reserve areas south of Bologna, 'in which Fifth Army saw the mirage of safe, spacious and comfortable winter quarters ahead of them'.[10]

From 9 to 20 September, when bad weather started to restrict operations, DAF fighters flew around 240 sorties daily against encampments, command posts, assembly areas and supply depots around Futa and Il Giogo. The strongest German defences being in the Futa pass, Mark Clark decided to make his main thrust to the east, up the Firenzuola road through the Giogo pass. As II Corps began its main attack on the morning of 13 September, the B-25s and B-26s shifted their efforts to defences north of the passes. Although weather halted their efforts two days later, on 16 September 132 B-25s spread 237 tons of phosphorus bombs around motor transport repair and supply depots, storage facilities and a fuel dump.

At first Clark's attack made little progress, but XIII Corps used the time well to cross the almost trackless mountains to establish themselves on the watershed. On 17 September, Monte Pratone, support.' The gun area west of Rimini was hit by 162 TAC bombers hit while DAF attacked three major gun areas in the afternoon.

By ensuring that the gun batteries attacked by fighter-bombers were the batteries that were troubling Allied troops, this timely and flexible use of air power gave Alexander's troops the encouraging boost they needed, with many fortified positions being hit and the area becoming studded with fire and explosions. But it was not all good news: the Germans were masters of camouflage and used all available cover, including haystacks and church towers, to conceal their guns or observation points. The only Luftwaffe retaliation was a reported attack by two aircraft — probably recce Bf109s — on 56th Division troops at 11.15hrs.

Table 4: Luftwaffe Order of Battle in Italy, 20 September 1944.[12]			
	Type	Strength	Serviceable
Close Recce			
I/NAGr11	Bf109G	11	9
II/NAGr11	Bf109G	13	12
Long-Range Recce			
2(F)/FAGr122	Me410	6	3
4(F)/FAGr122	Ju88/188	9	7
6(F)/FAGr122	Ju188	9	6
Night Ground-Attack			
Stab/NSGr9	Ju87	1	1[13]
1/NSGr9	Ju87	10	6
2/NSGr9	Ju87	12	9
3/NSGr9	Ju87	9	7
TOTAL		**80**	**60**

Tactical and Desert Air Forces put up 804 sorties between them on 18 September. This crowning day began with two concentrated early morning attacks on San Fortunato ridge, the first carried out between 06.00hrs and 07.00hrs by three entire wings of fighter-bombers. Spitbombers flying at 10-minute intervals, interspersed with Kittyhawks and Mustangs, delivered synchronised bombing and strafing of both forward and reverse slopes. The second wave from 07.00–07.45hrs saw a change in tactics: while a very heavy artillery concentration came down on the forward slope, air bombing and strafing were confined to the reverse slope with a No 145 Squadron Spitbomber pilot scoring a direct hit on a house serving as an ammunition dump.

All this effort was reinforced by prearranged light and medium bomber attacks on gun areas, and fighter-bomber cab-ranking in support of Canadian and V Corps. While the Spits of 244 Wing worked at full stretch in the Fano area, 239 Wing Mustangs and Kittybombers from Jesi made their name by attacking slit trenches and gun positions pinpointed by those most affected: one squadron reported Allied troops cheering as their Kittys went in. It all helped the Eighth establish a firm foothold on the ridge by the close of 18 September.

The weather completely deteriorated by 20 September, bringing air operations to a virtual standstill for some days. Few airmen

minded. From 13 to 18 September, which included two bad weather days, the DAF flew over 4,000 sorties. The strain of the intensive air effort from 26 August started to tell on flight commanders, while aircraft serviceability was dropping noticeably. Fortunately for the Allies, the formidable German force along the east coast was gradually being siphoned off as the Fifth Army's threat to Bologna grew in seriousness.

On 21 September, the stubborn defence of Rimini was broken and the Greek Brigade occupied the city. Gen Leese took this opportunity to express his appreciation for the part played by the air forces in the assault, particularly the bombing of the German gun positions on 17 and 18 September to which he attributed the negligible shelling received by the Eighth Army in its subsequent attack. But the Germans had managed to deny Eighth Army an entry into the Po Valley until winter rains arrived to prevent full exploitation of the breakthrough.

*   *   *   *

The successful outcome of the Italian land campaign depended on all manner of supplementary air activity; North Africa, the Middle East, the Balkans, Malta and Sicily all had to be defended against air attack. There was also the need to co-ordinate all air transport criss-crossing the skies.[14] Eight years after General Franco initiated the first mass aerial movement of troops directly to the battlefield, the transfer of 3,000 troops requested by Mark Clark from Eisenhower began at first light on 25 October. Every available Dakota was sent to France, and it took 203 round-trips over three days from two airfields in the Cherbourg Peninsula to Pontedera in Italy to complete the task, with five C-47s being lost in the process. Unfortunately, the Fifth Army assault was halted before the new troops could be fed into the line.

Apart from Operation 'Hasty' on 1 June, when 11 Dakotas of 8th Troop Carrier Squadron dropped 61 real paratroopers east of the Avezzano–Arce road plus 199 dummies to fool the opposition, the transfer of urgently needed personnel from Normandy was the first diversion from the normal Italian air transport tasks of evacuating wounded personnel, hauling stores and ferrying passengers. Throughout 1944, the two groups (comprising four squadrons each) of the 51st Troop Carrier Wing moved 163,535 passengers, 30,800 troops and over 54 million pounds of freight. The evacuation of no fewer than 121,889 Allied patients and casualties by air in 1944 must have been even more morale-raising.[15]

Then there were the constant anti-submarine patrols, which were both massively boring and massively essential. Standing watch had also to be kept and attacks carried out on the multifarious German-directed shipping, which continuously expanded as roads and railways came under attack from the air. It was a measure of German lateral thinking that they managed to bypass many of the breaks in over-land communications by feeding substantial supplies to the front line through the Tyrrhenian and Adriatic Seas. During the first four months of 1944, 8,000–12,000 tons was received by the Fourteenth Army along the west coast, and 4,000–6,000 tons delivered to the Tenth along the east coast, amounting to an impressive 12–18% of the total supplies for both armies.

The shrinking of the German front, the cumulative effect of air attacks, the virtual disappearance of Luftwaffe air defence cover and increased Allied control of the west coast following the success of 'Dragoon' all reduced the potential for German resupply by sea. Yet in spite of growing difficulties, the Germans kept La Spezia, Venice and Genoa working until their evacuation. Allied air tried to halt this activity. For example, on 4/5 September 164 B-17s dropped 490 tons of 500lb bombs on Genoa harbour. One torpedo boat capsized, a destroyer and corvette were sunk, three submarines were destroyed and many other vessels, including a German hospital ship, were damaged. But even these heavy air attacks interrupted loading and unloading for only a short time. The hubs of Genoa, Trieste and Venice were never attacked with sufficient aerial weight to cause a complete breakdown in shipping supply, and the Allies found it more effective to attack ships than harbour installations.

It was against this background that RAF 328 Wing[16] was set up at the end of August to deal with coastal traffic as part of the US 63rd Wing. A good deal of shipping was sighted, but scoring definite hits against barges and coasters proved more demanding. Large and distinctive targets such as the Rex were a rarity. The 51,000-ton Rex had been the pride of the Italian merchant marine, holding the transatlantic Blue Riband in 1933. With her sister ships which plied the warmer southern route, Rex pioneered the great lido decks and outdoor pools which are standard on cruise ships today.

After the Italian Line service to New York was suspended in 1940, the Rex lay in Trieste protected by anti-aircraft batteries. On 4 September, an Allied photo-recce pilot spotted her leaving harbour towed by two tugs with a destroyer escort. She was sighted southwest of Trieste two evenings later, and Allied intelligence deduced that the intention was to use her as a blockship either at Trieste or Venice. As the Allies hoped to capture both intact, it was decided to put Rex out of action. The task was given to No 272 Squadron, whose Beaufighters left Borgo in Corsica for Falconara near Ancona on 7 September.

Eight No 272 Squadron Beaufighters, with an eight-ship Mustang escort, got airborne at 10.25hrs the following day. As the formation approached the Rex, by then lying close inshore off Capodistria, a German E-boat opened up intensive fire, but it was speedily seen off by the Mustangs. Despite very potent flak from Trieste harbour, no one had thought to man the guns where the multi-coloured umbrellas had once stood on the liner itself. The Beaufighters pressed home their attack, scoring 59 25lb rocket projectiles hits, all but four of which were reported as being below the waterline. The Beaufighters returned to base safely, and although they left a burning and fatally wounded Rex, it needed the added efforts of eight Balkan Air Force Beaufighters to finish her off with 64 RPs.

The British did not have all the fun. Admiral Cunningham, Naval C-in-C Mediterranean, also feared that the Italian liner Taranto would be used to block La Spezia harbour on the west coast. In response to the admiral's plea that it be sunk, Gen Cannon called forward the highly efficient 340th Bomb Group. On 23 September, an 18-ship B-25 formation was sent over, six being briefed to attack the stern, six the middle and six the bow. Post-attack photography showed three separate clusters completely covering the Taranto which sank within 25 minutes. Cannon reported that this was the 62nd consecutive pinpoint attack that the 340th had mounted without a miss.

*   *   *   *

While Allied troops moved further up Italy and France, senior airmen were busy reorganising. As German air and sea threats disappeared, Mediterranean Allied Coastal Air Force lost much of its previous importance. Its strength having fallen steadily from a peak of 56 squadrons at the start of the year to 33, MAAF decided to offset the loss of XII TAC by withdrawing XII Fighter Command from Coastal and reconstituting it as a tactical air command responsible for close-support operations on the Fifth Army front. The new command was officially up and running on 20 September under Brig Benjamin W. Chidlaw, which freed DAF to revert to its former responsibility for the Eighth Army area. However, the two air commands were mutually supporting when the situation demanded. This was just as well; with initially only the six squadrons of the US 57th and 350th Fighter Groups and one night-fighter squadron in Italy, Fighter Command had to watch DAF fighter-bombers flying twice as many sorties in support of the Fifth during the third week of September. As a stopgap, Chidlaw's command was strengthened by the addition of the two XII TAC P-47 fighter groups remaining in Corsica.

The early and successful conclusion of 'Dragoon' enabled Seventh Army to advance up the Rhône beyond the range of Twelfth Air Force, liberating air units for the still desperate battle in Italy. On 16 September, the Chiefs of Staff Committee approved the split of the Twelfth Air Force between Italy and France: HQ XII TAC together with some fighter, tactical recce and support units were to remain in France, while all other elements were to return to Italy. The final detailed arrangements were thrashed out at a conference at Caserta on 27/28 September, with combat units returning from France in early October. The former DAF-administered US 79th Fighter Group was not overjoyed at the prospect. 'The ground crew moved to a staging area outside Marseilles, to await formation of a convoy to take it to the land of no spaghetti, starvation, filth, disease, and the monuments to precision bombing as typified by the shambles of what were once clean, proud buildings.'[17] On 19 October the command, now fully established in Italy with 25 squadrons, was officially designated XXII TAC.

British and American administrative HQs existed side by side in MAAF HQ, in which were also accommodated an integrated Operations, Plans and Intelligence Division and a combined Signals Division, all under unified command. HQ Tactical Air Force had an integrated AAF/RAF staff, but its various commands — the US medium bomber wings, Desert Air Force and the new US Tactical Air Command — were either entirely USAAF or entirely RAF, except that some RAF units were to be placed under operational control of XXII TAC. All US units within Tactical Air Force remained part of the US Twelfth Air Force; Commanding

By the end of September 1944, the German defensive line covering Route 65 had been pulled back to Monghidoro which stood on high ground astride the road 30km south of Bologna. The rush was on for Gen Mark Clark's troops to reach the Po Valley before the rains turned to snow but despite artillery and air support assistance, the reduction of the Monghidoro line took four days, averaging an advance of about a mile a day against stubborn delaying tactics. US Fifth Army troops finally entered the battered little Italian town of Monghidoro on 3 October 1944, having discovered once again – if the wrecked buildings were not evidence enough – that the Germans did not evacuate a defensive position without a fight. The capture of the town was just one more laboured Allied step up Italy. *RAF Air Historical Branch*

General TAF was also Commanding General Twelfth Air Force, and Gen John Cannon maintained a totally separate Twelfth Air Force HQ. HQ MATAF therefore co-ordinated operational policy, but exercised very little direction over organisational or administrative matters: these tended to conform to national policy within British or US forces comprising the Tactical Air Force.

After the fall of Rimini on 21 September, the scope for fighter-bomber attacks on strongpoints, guns and troop concentrations decreased. Consequently, the crews raised their sights to communication targets immediately behind the front line to try to hinder German movement, regroupings and transfer of supplies. Ten Stukas from Villafranca took advantage of bright moonlight to attack their former base at Rimini on 30 September, but few seemed to notice. The Eighth Army was advancing towards the Germans' next line of defence along the Savio River, so the main aerial bridge-busting effort was directed there. Fighter-bombers also cut railway lines in the Ferrara–Bologna–Ravenna triangle while light and medium bombers attacked the marshalling yards that fed Bologna. It was indicative of the prevailing co-operative spirit that, on the first four days of October, DAF's Kittyhawks, Mustangs and one Spitbomber wing flew most of their sorties over XXII TAC's area on behalf of Fifth Army's thrust towards Bologna.

On the Adriatic flank, a dozen or so river courses ran directly across the Eighth Army's line of advance. The early and heavy autumn rains ensured that this former reclaimed swampland quickly became the 'richest' mud in the whole campaign, bringing tracked and wheeled vehicles to a complete standstill anywhere off the few roads. The Fiumicino, 'normally a shallow trickle' but now swollen to a width of over 30ft, was but one river in spate which, together with high flood banks, gave the Germans both observation and ready-made defensive positions. Violent storms at the end of September thwarted any chance of a breakthrough here, though there still seemed a chance of the Fifth Army clearing the mountains up Route 65 to Bologna.

Throughout October, DAF flew over 7,000 sorties and XXII TAC about 5,000, but all MATAF operations were severely restricted by weather. Although almost the entire XXII TAC effort was given over to support of the Fifth Army's offensive during the first 11 days of October, the dogged German defence held. Eighth Army was along the line of the Savio River and steadily pushing towards Ravenna and Faenza, but the Fifth was stopped short of Bologna as Kesselring swung divisions away from the Adriatic to beef-up his centre. By so doing, the Germans put a big spoke in Allied strategy — which hinged on the Fifth Army breaking through Kesselring's centre and fanning out north of Bologna to act as the left pincer to trap the German armies in Italy.

Air operations in the centre peaked on 12 October when 177 B-25s (out of 213 dispatched) dropped 1,011 500lb bombs on four targets, including two supply concentrations, a barracks and a fuel dump, while 698 heavies (out of 826) spread 1,271 tons of 20lb fragmentation and 100lb, 250lb and 500lb bombs among 10 assigned targets. Having the skies to themselves, many bomber crews attacked assigned targets 'in a timely, accurate and cost-effective manner', and the air assault was credited with raising the morale of Allied troops. XXII TAC also flew more than 300 sorties a day between 14 and 20 October, when weather brought air operations to a virtual standstill. But by now the Fifth Army was too weakened to exploit the advantage gained; by 26 October, both sides had come to the end of their strength after fighting steadily for six weeks. Although the Allies were only nine tantalising miles short of Bologna, there was no alternative to the stalemate but to go on the defensive and make preparations for a future resumption of the offensive.

*   *   *   *

From August until the end of October, it appeared that Kesselring would have to retire across the River Po. The extent of Allied presumption was typified by the Air Force HQ Weekly Intelligence Summary for 25 September which proclaimed,

> 'There can now no longer be any question of the enemy's re-establishing himself on the line of the Apennines . . . tenacious as he is, Kesselring must now be exploring the prospects of conducting an orderly withdrawal.'

Consequently, Allied air forces pursued a double-edged strategy: to block German escape routes by knocking out bridges and other crucial road and rail points, and then to work closely with the ground-pounders to drive said Germans back against these blocks where they could be annihilated.

When he subsequently came to analyse the Allied assault on the Gothic Line, Gen von Vietinghoff identified five factors that primarily influenced events. First, the Allies had seized and retained the initiative. Second, although the Germans believed they had forecast Allied intentions correctly, they lacked sufficient air reconnaissance and in-place intelligence assets to confirm or exploit their theories. Third, difficult mountain terrain prevented rapid redeployment of forces. Fourth, commanders lacked air support and suffered from shortages in personnel and equipment. Finally, Allied air forces imposed a damaging strain on the German supply system.[18]

This was a pretty daunting list of deficiencies, yet the high morale and excellent performance of German fighting units offset the lack of German aircraft overhead and frustrated Allied plans to break into the Po Valley and stop Kesselring's army withdrawing through the Alpine passes before the onset of winter.

The balance of forces when the battle for the Gothic Line opened was 26 German divisions, plus about six Italian, against 21 Allied. Although he received some compensation for his losses to Seventh Army in southern France, Alexander had five and a half divisions

fewer than at the fall of Rome. On the other hand, Kesselring's strength in Italy grew to no less than 28 German divisions, of which 20 were committed south of the Po. The good news was that none of these left Italy for the Western Front, but although their aircraft ranged at will, the Allies lacked the ground power to exploit breaks through the Gothic Line in the face of appalling weather conditions, supply difficulties over inadequate roads, lack of reinforcements while playing second fiddle to 'Overlord', and stubborn German resistance. The onset of early winter 'where mud ruled' finally prevented the Allies from reaping the benefit of their main advantage — air supremacy.

The Gothic Line battles cost the Germans 8,000 prisoners. On 15 September, LXXVI Panzer Corps reported that, since the start of the battle on the Adriatic flank, it had suffered 14,500 casualties. From the fall of Rome to 15 August, Fifth Army lost 17,959 killed, wounded or missing, while in the three months from July to September, Eighth Army suffered 19,975 battle casualties, of which 8,000 came between 25 August and 9 September. Having also lost some 210 tanks, with even more bogged down or beyond local repair, in just over three weeks' fighting, the Eighth Army was set back seriously for many months to come.

Maintaining the Allied air interdiction programme through another winter remained as important as the weather would allow. Kesselring understood this when he wrote:

> 'In view of the importance of the bridges across the Po and the water obstacles in front of it, the Allied air force would certainly do everything possible to smash our communications. This might have a fatal effect on our supplies and the conduct of our operations in the spring of 1945.'[19]

On 22 October, Kesselring held one of his regular meetings with Reich Armaments Minister Albert Speer at Tenth Army HQ. Speer's greatest skills lay in administration and organisation, and as the supply situation became more critical, he reorganised and extended the upper Italian inland water transport system on which Transportflotte Speer barges carried essential materials and armaments. Kesselring was interested to hear Speer say that he had never experienced such artillery fire or air raids in France as he had in Italy.

Governing Kesselring's every moment, according to his biographer, '. . . was the task confronting him, from which he never sought to escape'. The C-in-C had a regular schedule according to one of his staff officers, Dietrich Beelitz. 'About 8am, the Field Marshal received the daily reports and worked in general until midnight with a short break at lunchtime. On at least three days a week, and sometimes more, the Field Marshal went to visit units at the front . . . at dawn.'[20] On 23 October, the schedule was no different:

> ' . . . after a short night's rest I started out at 5am and drove from one division to another, beginning with the right flank. I was welcomed everywhere and . . . I got the impression that the crisis had passed and that we would be able to hold the northern slopes of the Apennines. Harassed throughout the day by British

aircraft, I was driving along the main road from Bologna to Forli [the Via Emilia] in the late afternoon on my way to visit the last two divisions when my car, passing a column, collided with a long-barrelled gun coming out of a side road. I received severe concussion and a nasty gash on the left temple . . . Soon after my accident, the story got about that the field marshal was doing well but that the gun had had to be scrapped.'[21]

It was such affability combined with an unerring sense of duty which so endeared 'Smiling Albert' to his troops. By shaping the operating environment in which Kesselring had to travel, Allied air power put the German C-in-C into hospital for nearly three months, leaving von Vietinghoff in command of the Army Group. After so much hard slog, some feared that Kesselring's example and unfailing optimism had left just when they might be needed most.

Notes to Chapter 12

1. Brazil was the first South American state to declare war on Germany and Italy on 22 August 1942. A 25,000-strong Brazilian Expeditionary Force joined Mark Clark's Fifth Army as partial compensation for the loss of his 'Dragoon' divisions, supported by the 1st Brazilian Fighter Squadron. This Thunderbolt fighter-bomber unit, with its motto Senta Pua — freely translated as 'Up and at them!' — came under US operational control.
2. Jackson, The Mediterranean and Middle East, Vol VI, Pt II, p.119.
3. Letter from Eaker to Arnold, 21 August 1944.
4. Bryant, op.cit, p.287.
5. Even so, Marshall advised Eisenhower on 6 September that he should not hesitate to draw on the Mediterranean for such additional air resources as he felt were needed.
6. Kesselring, op.cit, p.212.
7. Bryant, op.cit, p.177.
8. Gee enabled a navigator to plot his position relative to a ground station and its introduction began the process of turning aerial navigation from an art into a science. But Gee's accuracy, and that of its US equivalent Shoran, was measured in miles; much more precise navigation and weapon-aiming had to await the introduction of the self-contained H2S radar, so-called because it either stood for 'Home Sweet Home' or from the first official response to the concept, 'It stinks!'
9. AHB, op.cit, p.73.
10. Ibid, p.76.
11. Clark, op.cit, p.373.
12. German Air Force Quartermaster Returns.
13. Stab and 1/NSGr9 opposed the Eighth Army, while 2/ and 3/ faced the Fifth.
14. The Naples-based HQ Mediterranean Air Transport Service, an integrated American and British organisation, co-ordinated air routes.
15. Of which 67,714 were American and 37,590 British.
16. Comprising Squadrons Nos 272 (Beaufighters), 14 (Marauders), 458 RAAF (Wellingtons), 17 SAAF (Venturas) and 284 (Marauders and Walruses).
17. Owen, op.cit, p.229.
18. The Fourteenth Army's Withdrawal to the Northern Apennines, Part B.
19. Kesselring, The Memoirs; p.214.
20. Macksey, op.cit, p.190.
21. Ibid, p.218.

Left:
Kesselring, then aged 59, and his chief of staff, Lt-Gen Siegfried Westphal.
Author's Collection

SPLENDID ISOLATION

'These, Scheisskopf, are the Germans. They're dug into these mountains very solidly in the Gothic Line and won't be pushed out till late next spring, although that isn't going to stop those clods we have in charge from trying.'
Joseph Heller, Catch-22

From the Low Countries through France, northern Italy, Hungary, the Balkans and East Prussia, the Allies were driving back the German defensive perimeter. But the least mobile sector of them all was Italy, where the Germans continued to resist in great strength with seasoned troops and armour. Bologna (the home of Mussolini's grandfather) had become one of the strongest fortresses in the world. Allied airmen tried to make the difference, mounting Operation 'Pancake' — as its name implied, to flatten the defences — during the fierce ground onslaught from 10 to 23 October.

On 12 October, 697 heavy bombers (out of 800 launched), 300 medium bombers and 277 fighter-bombers dropped 1,661 tons of bombs on 74 targets. The effects were devastating: damaged roads tied up engineers, traffic jams were everywhere and movement delayed, command posts were hit, supply chains choked, artillery damaged and gun crews dispersed, bivouac areas scattered, panic caused, strongpoints hit and defences softened. US II Corps

reported back on the tonic effects of 'Pancake' on American ground morale, but the Germans — completely without air support — hung on.

From 20 September 1944 to 12 January 1945, the Eighth Army made a slow, costly advance from the Marecchia to the Senio, river by river, in worsening weather conditions. On most days, the cloud base was 2,000-3,000ft at best, which made a nonsense of Spitbomber dives from 8,000ft and light and medium bomber attacks from 10,000ft; even Kittyhawk and Mustang dive-bombing was impracticable. And behind the Senio lay the Po, the Adige and then the Brenta guaranteeing line after defensive line. One irony — given how much high explosive was being hurled at the German supply chain — was that by 13 November there was just about enough British ammunition in theatre to sustain current Eighth Army operations and an all-out offensive of no more than 15 days.[1]

The failure of the Fifth Army to take Bologna at the end of October reinforced the appeal of air interdiction to deny supplies to a stubborn foe, but it was not just to be more of the same. Allied air had battered bridges for months, but as the mirage of a wholesale German evacuation faded, it became clear that there was no mass paralysis of the Po Valley. Germans and Fascist Italians were ingenious enough to pass supplies by night ferries, pontoon

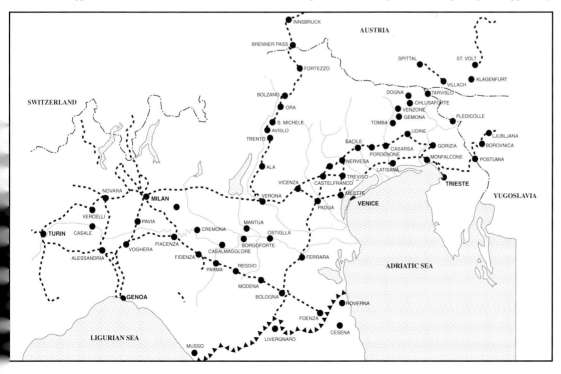

Left:
The principal rail lines of northern Italy.

bridges and pipelines, and they continued to move troops with relative impunity as and when required.

Axis forces on the French frontier and around the Gulf of Genoa were reduced from nine to five divisions, the other four being transferred to the main front with comparative ease via routes south of the Po interdiction belt, invalidating at a stroke most of the Ticino cuts and the high priority accorded to the Po. Moreover, the Germans were doing more than simply moving troops: they were sending back trainload after trainload of loot, food, industrial equipment, metals and so forth by all routes to the Reich. On some days in September, 33 trains were reported passing northwards towards the Brenner Pass. During October, a daily average of 28 trains left Italy on the Brenner and Tarvisio routes combined. By late October it had become all too apparent that Kesselring was winning the battle of logistics on the Po.

If Allied air learned anything, it was that attacks against supply lines must be continuous to have any long-term effect. At the end of October, Tactical Air Force Intelligence was arguing that,

'[as]the enemy is not being forced to withdraw from the Po valley, our bombing programme during this winter... be directed to denying all movement by rail to and from Italy ... The effect of such a programme will, it is submitted, be the gradual wearing down of the enemy's potential power to resist in northern Italy. By isolating Italy from the Reich, it may be possible to turn the scales ...'

This argument was so persuasive that isolating Italy from the Reich became bombing policy on 3 November.[2] Ground forces were no longer to be given any meaningful air support, except in isolated cases where limited air assistance might be required to gain local objectives or to counter successful enemy thrusts.

The most overused simile throughout the Italian campaign was to compare the peninsula to a human leg. The mountain ranges running down the country were likened to the bones, the coastal plains to part muscle, part sinew, part fat, and the roads and railways were the arteries and veins. The whole aim of the interdiction campaign was to starve the leg of life-sustaining blood.

In the summer of 1944, four principal rail arteries connected Italy with the Reich — the French, the Swiss, the Yugoslav and the German. By November, the French route was out. However, it was arguable that the Swiss, for all their proclaimed neutrality, were turning a blind eye to the passage of militarily significant cargo such as scrap iron and chrome,[3] not to mention coal to fire Italian industrial plants making munitions for the Germans. But although Eaker felt moved to recommend on 22 November that the Swiss be given an air ultimatum — stop the war traffic by 1 January or the St Gothard and Simplon lines would be bombed — the Swiss route was relatively unimportant.

That left three German and four Yugoslav lines. It was not individual lines that mattered so much as their interrelation, and how the weight of attack on one would react on the others. On this basis, Allied air planners grouped targets under three arbitrary headings — the Brenner, the Venetian Plain and the northeastern frontier. Of these, the most important was the one which accounted for 50% of all supplies — the Brenner.

At this stage the combined strategic bomber offensive had moved away from aircraft production lines which by now were too widely dispersed to be economical targets. With Allied armies in France drawing close to the German border, bombardment against the railway system of Germany was given a strategic priority second only to oil. On 11 November, Gen Eaker relieved Strategic Air Force of all responsibility for attacking communications targets in Italy so that it could concentrate instead on the Reich. After 16 November, no target on the Italian peninsula was to be attacked without a request from, or approval by, Gen Cannon at Tactical Air Force.

Apart from the important Innsbruck control centre end of the Brenner line which remained with Strategic Air Force, the medium bombers of 42nd and 57th Wing were given the following list of interdiction priorities: the Brenner Pass; the northeast Italian lines (Piave, Brenta, Tagliamento Rivers); the Po and Adda Rivers.

Table 5: 42nd AND 57th BOMB WINGS — ORDER OF BATTLE, 1 NOVEMBER 1944		
42nd Bombardment Wing		HQ Borgo
17th Group		
34th Sqn	B-26	HQ Poretta
37th Sqn	B-26	HQ Poretta
95th Sqn	B-26	HQ Poretta
432nd Sqn	B-26	HQ Poretta
319th Group		HQ Serragia
437th Sqn	B-26	HQ Serragia
438th Sqn	B-26	HQ Serragia
439th Sqn	B-26	HQ Serragia
440th Sqn	B-26	HQ Serragia
320th Group		HQ Alto
441st Sqn	B-26	HQ Alto
442nd Sqn	B-26	HQ Alto
443rd Sqn	B-26	HQ Alto
444th Sqn	B-26	HQ Alto
57th Bombardment Wing		HQ Prunelli
340th Group		HQ Alesan
486th Sqn	B-25	HQ Alesan
487th Sqn	B-25	HQ Alesan
488th Sqn	B-25	HQ Alesan
489th Sqn	B-25	HQ Alesan
321st Group		HQ Solenzara
445th Sqn	B-25	HQ Solenzara
446th Sqn	B-25	HQ Solenzara
447th Sqn	B-25	HQ Solenzara
448th Sqn	B-25	HQ Solenzara
310th Group		HQ Ghisonaccia
379th Sqn	B-25	HQ Ghisonaccia
380th Sqn	B-25	HQ Ghisonaccia
381st Sqn	B-25	HQ Ghisonaccia
428th Sqn	B-25	HQ Ghisonaccia

The Brenner Pass railway line was a 168-mile stretch of standard gauge electrified track running from Verona to Innsbruck. There were 33 targets on the Lower Brenner, which ran from Verona north to Trento along the Adige River, but the only bridge over 135ft long was the heavily defended one at Verona. The 10 other bridges were sturdy masonry structures spanning small streams.

On the Middle Brenner north of Trento, the valley floor widened slightly on the way up to Bolzano. One of the most vital points along it was the 3,000ft-long, 35-span masonry viaduct at Lavis. It was attacked five times, and on four of the attacks spans were destroyed. Three miles further north of Trento, at San Michele All'Adige, the track crossed to the west bank of the Adige, proceeded 15 miles northward, then recrossed to the east bank at Ora. Two of the best targets were the 350ft steel bridges over the Adige at Ora and San Michele, so the Germans set 5,000 men to work to complete the diversion Ora–San Michele by 5 December. Thereafter, 48 attacks had to be made against the diversion.

The Upper Brenner from Bolzano to Innsbruck presented the most acute problems for aircrews. A way had to be picked through peaks often reaching 13,000ft, and although the best targets were in the upper Brenner — aircrews loved to create a good landslide — the combination of rugged mountains, V-shaped valleys, outcroppings, haze and smoke, made identification and attack difficult. Some targets could be approached only along one axis, were often visible only three or four miles from bomb release point, and were too small and shadow-screened to permit last-minute run-in corrections.

In mountainous country with long, steep gradients, electric power is much more efficient than steam locomotion. Large transformer stations, spaced some 20 miles apart, fed the wires between Verona and the Pass; as the line got steeper, there were sub-stations every 10 miles. The system was so designed that even if two consecutive stations broke down, a limited service was still possible. To stop everything, Allied air had to eliminate three adjacent power stations.

German Army Group C's daily minimum supply requirement was estimated at 5,500–6,000 tons, of which some 3,600–4,000 tons normally passed over the Brenner and Tarvisio routes. The chief mechanical engineer on Italian State Railways advised that if the Germans were forced to change from electricity to steam, Brenner line capacity would be reduced to no more than 10 trains (6,000 tons) daily. Winter having brought operations to a virtual halt, the German basic requirement could be met by one-third of that. But the long-term hope was that when the fighting season came round again, the Germans would have as little spare capacity to resist an Allied onslaught as they had back in May after 'Strangle' and 'Diadem'.

On 4 and 5 November, the weather was good enough to allow TAF mediums to make 25–30 cuts in the Lower Brenner. Hundreds of rolling stock units were trapped and all traffic on the southern section of line was completely disorganised. It was a good time to launch 'Bingo' — the operation authorised by HQ MAAF on 27 October to 'destroy' the Brenner line electrical system[4] and Allied air went in mob-handed on the morning of 6 November.

The four transformers between Verona and Trento were divided between DAF and XXII TAC fighter-bombers, and 57th Wing B-25s. The stretch between Verona and Trento was given to the 42nd Wing B-26s. Strategic Air Force made a guest appearance to attack the three stations north of Trento, as well as to try to pothole the line up to Innsbruck and create blockages. The whole 'Bingo' operation was co-ordinated by TAF, with XXII TAC providing general fighter cover.

Early assessments of bombing results showed that the heavies fared badly; bombing from altitude, most missed their mark, enabling the Germans to continue using electrical power at the northern end of the line. Nearer home, two Kittyhawk squadrons from 239 Wing and the rocket-firing P-47s of the 86th and 87th Squadrons, 79th Fighter Group — each 4.5in underwing rocket[5] had the power of a 105mm howitzer — claimed 18 direct hits on the main buildings and 23 on the transformer of a station southwest of Verona. Vivid blue flashes streaked a dense pall of black smoke to give the pilots a vision of the inferno.

More prosaically, von Vietinghoff reported to the OKW that Allied bombers were operating 'as if at a sporting event'. Ground agents reported that only steam traction could be used on 12 November, and five days later the Germans were having to use motor transport to move supplies from Ora to Verona. Sub-station

A soldier's-eye view of an American P-47 passing over German lines. The Thunderbolt carried twice the bomb load of the Spitbomber, as well as six Rocket Projectiles. *Author's Collection*

Above:
Hail Mary, and pass the ammunition! *Author's Collection*

repair work between Verona and Trento was halted on 23 November, and by 25 November damage to the four stations was such that only steam locomotives could operate. PR aircraft flew an average of three sorties daily over the Brenner, weather permitting, and their pictures confirmed the agents' reports. Only steam trains were observed and, on occasions, long motor convoys were seen to parallel apparently unserviceable sections of rail track.

From 1 to 19 November, some 44 medium bomber missions were flown against the Brenner. 57th Wing carried the main weight of the Brenner campaign, including striking hard at the loop line running southeast from Trento to Vicenza to block it for six weeks. Interdiction of the rail routes across the Venetian plain was also maintained through most of November, and by the end of the month, the Nervasa bridge was the only one open between Udine and Padua.

But the Germans and Italians living off the rich granary of the Po Valley survived. The Axis repair organisation was made highly mobile, with material dumps skilfully dispersed and camouflaged near vital points susceptible to air attack, rather than stockpiled where any bombardier could see them. As the weather became

more hostile, Axis repair gangs used the respite from air attack to show their guile and demonic energy: the Ala bridge on the lower Brenner was kept working despite being destroyed seven times in 24 air attacks. Traffic increased on the northeast routes in the last week of November, partly because a substantial part of the medium bomber effort was diverted between 21 and 24 November to support the Eighth Army advance on Faenza. Lousy flying weather in December limited the mediums to five missions against northeast routes, allowing the Germans to open at least one bridge or bypass over the Brenta, Piave, Livenza and Tagliamento rivers.

Another factor which weakened the interdiction campaign after 19 November was the removal of 42nd Wing HQ and two of its B-26 groups to France. The good news was that surviving 319th converted to B-25s and joined the 57th Wing; the bad news was that TAF's strength was further reduced the following month when Washington withdrew the 319th and its new B-25s for deployment against the Japanese. Given the static nature of the front, Ira Eaker felt that this group could be spared, but he urged that no further withdrawals be made from his tactical air force given the importance of maintaining the assault on the extensive road and rail nets supporting the German armies in Italy.

Diminishing medium bomber numbers raised the importance of fighter-bombers to the interdiction campaign. From 26 November to 2 December, 148 sorties were flown against the line, with operations being extended north of Trento. On one of the early flights, a strafing attack near Sant' Ambrogio blew up a train and lifted 280yd of track skywards. On 28 November, 46 P-47s blew 10 gaps in tracks over a 40-mile stretch of the lower Brenner, isolating small 'islands' of rolling stock. All through December, an average of 20 P-47s flew up and down the Brenner as far north on occasions as San Michele, attacking yards and claiming 149 cuts in all.

In the meantime, DAF began to supplement medium bomber attacks over northeast Italy. Particularly good results were achieved against rolling stock along the northern route to Udine and against bridges across the Piave and Livenza. With the loss of 42nd Wing, and the hindering effects of deteriorating weather on the remaining mediums and night intruder A-20s, low-level fighter-bomber efforts became indispensable to the maintenance of the blockade of Italy.

Although frequent bad weather broke the continuity of attack operations during December, by 15 January the Germans had abandoned hope of restoring electric current south of Trento, concentrating their efforts elsewhere.[6] Operation "Bingo" did not, and was never expected to, terminate all traffic through the Brenner Pass, but it did considerably reduce the volume of traffic to a point where, with periodic interruptions by bombing, it could more easily be kept below the essential minimum.' From now on, not even Mussolini could make the trains run on time.

*   *   *   *

As the Allies could not stop all supplies from getting through, on 3 November TAF gave a definite priority to attacks on the enemy's accumulations in storage dumps. The anticipated resumption of Fifth Army offensive operations argued for a concentration on

Above:
A Polish fighter pilot awaits the chance to get airborne and add to his 'kills'.
RAF Air Historical Branch

ammunition dumps, and given that it was both a communications hub and storage centre, 'the little university town of Bologna was doomed to a pounding from the air which its medieval school of law had done nothing to deserve'.[7]

Gen Alexander was justifiably proud of the fact that '26 nations contributed contingents to my command in Italy', and that took no account of the different nationalities serving in the US forces. One such was Witold Rodzinski, born in Warsaw and son of Artur Rodzinski who was conducting the New York Philharmonic in Carnegie Hall when the Japanese bombed Pearl Harbor. The young Witold became a bomber pilot and found himself posted to the B-25 base in Corsica immortalised by Joseph Heller in Catch-22. Rodzinski (later to become Polish ambassador to London) always insisted that the book was a faithful documentary, devoid of fantasy or exaggeration. And if Heller, a Mitchell bombardier, lived out a recurring nightmare through his alter ego in Catch-22, it was the prospect of returning to Bologna.

'The B-25s they flew in were stable, dependable, dull-green ships with twin rudders and engines and wide wings. Their single fault, from where Yossarian sat as a bombardier, was the tight crawlway separating the bombardier's compartment in the plexiglas nose from the nearest escape hatch . . . Yossarian longed to sit on the floor in a huddled ball right on top of the escape hatch inside a sheltering igloo of extra flak suits instead of hung out there in front like some goddam cantilevered goldfish in some goddam cantilevered goldfish bowl . . .

'There was no escaping the mission to Bologna once Colonel Cathcart had volunteered his group for the ammunition dumps there that the heavy bombers on the Italian mainland had been unable to destroy from their higher altitudes. And to prove to Yossarian that they bore him no animosity, they even assigned him to fly lead bombardier with McWatt in the first formation when they went back to Bologna the next day. He came in on the target, confidently taking no evasive action at all, and suddenly they were shooting the living shit out of him!

'Heavy flak was everywhere! He had been lulled, lured and trapped, and there was nothing he could do but sit there like an idiot and watch the ugly black puffs smashing up to kill him. There was nothing he could do until his bombs dropped but look back into the bombsight, where the fine cross-hairs in the lens were glued magnetically over the target exactly where he had placed them, intersecting perfectly deep inside the yard of his block of camouflaged warehouses before the base of the first building. He was trembling steadily as the plane crept ahead. He could hear the hollow boom–boom–boom–boom of the flak pounding all around him in overlapping measures of four, the sharp, piercing crack! of a single shell exploding suddenly very close by . . . The engines droned on monotonously like a fat, lazy fly. At last the indices on the bombsight crossed, tripping away the eight 500-pounders one after the other. The plane lurched upward buoyantly with the lightened load. Yossarian bent away from the bombsight crookedly to watch the indicator on his left. When the pointer touched zero, he closed the bomb doors and over the intercom, at the very top of his voice, shrieked:

"Turn right hard!"

'McWatt responded instantly. With a grinding howl of engines, he flipped the plane over on one wing and wrung it around remorselessly in a screaming turn away from the twin spires of flak Yossarian had spied stabbing toward them . . . He levelled McWatt out with another harsh cry just as the bombs he had dropped began to strike. The first one fell in the yard, exactly where he had aimed, and then the rest of the bombs from his own plane and from the other planes in his flight burst open on the ground in a charge of rapid orange flashes across the tops of buildings, which collapsed instantly in a vast, churning wave of pink and gray and coal-black smoke that went rolling out turbulently in all directions . . .

'Behind him, men were dying. Strung out for miles in a stricken, tortuous, squirming line, the other flights of planes were making the same hazardous journey over the target, threading their swift way through the swollen masses of new and old bursts of flak . . .'[8]

The flak in question belonged to the Commanding General of the Luftwaffe in Italy (Kommandierender General der Deutschen

Luftwaffe in Italien). In September, the last Luftwaffe fighter unit was withdrawn from Italy as Mussolini came to the end of a full year as leader of the Salo Republic. Despite his vigorous protests, the Germans were dismantling and removing much valuable industrial machinery, not least the Innocenti works in Milan; and what was left was getting bombed too often. The Duce lost faith in the founder of the Aeronautica Nazionale Repubblicana, Lt-Col Botto, after a heavy daylight raid on the factories of Turin, and wrote angrily to him:

'You put up no defence against the attack, not a gun-shot nor an aeroplane. Nine fighter planes on the Turin aerodrome did not take off. Our pilots were out of action in the hotels. This inaction must stop, or we shall never be able to overcome the passive demoralisation of the Italian people.' [8]

Shortly afterwards Mussolini sacked Ernesto Botto, replacing him with Gen Arrigo Tessari. When Tessari too was dismissed, von Richthofen intervened 'as the Duce had replaced ANR's chief of staff too many times without asking anyone's permission'. Seizing on the fact that there was next to no link between the bureaucratic Air Ministry and front-line units, Richthofen decided to disband the ANR. Early on the morning of 25 August, Lt-Col (Oberstleutnant) Dietrich, liaison officer to Italian Fighter Command, called on the Under Secretary of State for Air, Col Manlio Molfese, and told him that the Luftwaffe was taking possession of all ANR airfields, stores and barracks. The ANR was to be disbanded, and its personnel — there were 2,300 in front-line units — given the option of enrolling in an Italian Air Legion which would be an integral part of the German Armed Forces, or posted to anti-aircraft units.

Mussolini, having no prior knowledge of this dismemberment of his air force, immediately contacted Hitler, who, with uncharacteristic resolve, moved von Richthofen. Disagreements apart, what aerial assets remained in Italy were too few to justify the full panoply of a field marshal and an air fleet, so it made sense anyway to withdraw von Richthofen and his staff to Vienna.[9]

In their stead, the staffs of Mittelitalien Command and Luftgau XXVIII were merged under the Commanding General of the Luftwaffe in Italy, Gen von Pohl, who had a reputation for dealing far more diplomatically with his Italian allies. On 15 September Maxi Pohl and his staff of 600 moved into the former Luftflotte HQ at Malcesine on Lake Garda, from where they were directly responsible to Luftwaffe High Command for all German flying units, flak and ground organisation, and for servicing the reconstituted ANR. Preference was given to the II GrC because its pilots were more familiar with the Bf109 and had a less troublesome history than I GrC, which had become noted for several morale crises and disciplinary problems. A few weeks later, Luftwaffe High Command agreed to provide I GrC with 109s and the Gruppo's pilots were sent to Germany to covert because the Italian theatre was no longer considered safe. The upshot of this change and disruption

Left:
The newly appointed Under Secretary of State for Mussolini's Air Force, Gen Tessari, with Lt-Col Dietrich. *IWMT*

Above:
An Italian anti-aircraft unit guns near Verona. Such flak batteries were in direct communication with the Jafu's radar controllers who could warn of incoming bandits. *Author's Collection*

Right:
Gen von Pohl with the smallest member of a flak battery in the Abruzzo Mountains. *IWM*

was twofold: it stimulated suspicion and distrust between German and Italian airmen, and ensured that for several months, defence of Italian airspace fell squarely on the flak batteries.

In September, Col (Oberst) Eduard Neumann took over as Jafu Oberitalien. He inherited an operational HQ on Castle Hill near Verona together with sub-HQs at Udine and Milan, a radar early warning system and a plan, cunningly code-named 'Threatening Danger South', to deploy four fighter Gruppen south in the event of another amphibious landing.

In November 1944, Jafu controlled three main sectors — the Central, Western and Eastern — defended by some 2,500 flak guns. The Central sector up to the northern frontier, including the Brenner, was covered by 25th Flak Division; 3rd Flak Brigade looked after the Western; while 22nd Flak Brigade covered the Eastern sector over the Venetian plain. Despite heavy losses in anti-aircraft guns during the hectic summer retreat past Rome, flak intensity around priority sites actually increased through shrinkage in the total area to be defended.

And these guns did not just blast away. Axis informers often watched Allied formations take-off and communicated the fact up north by radio. By the time potential attackers had climbed to height, they were getting within range of the best German long-range early warning radar in theatre, Wassermann, which could see high flying aircraft out to about 190 miles and provide a height-finding capability. Information from Wassermann, and the 14 Freya surveillance radars in Italy which had a range of 100 miles, was put together in the filter and plotting room at Verona air defence HQ. This overall air picture was used to alert the civilian population, and bring the relevant area Flakführer up to readiness by radio and telephone. He pre-alerted his heavy batteries, and the mobile radar operators and gun crews stood by.

There could be anything between four and 12 guns in an Italian flak battery. The usual manning ratio was 60–70% German and 30–40% Italian: the one exception was Verona, which was all-Italian manned. Normally, when a battery picked up a target, radar tracking was used for range and optical tracking for direction. Defended areas were divided into sectors, one for each battery, whose commander fired on any hostile aircraft approaching the target in his sector. Only the Flakführer could order any given sector to fire into another. Around important targets in the Brenner were Grossbatterien, complexes of two or more heavy batteries. They had centrally located fire control systems, consisting of two complete sets of kit which allowed the simultaneous tracking of two separate aircraft formations. The Rhonrad switching device permitted rapid transfer of gunfire from one formation to another.

Smoke, camouflage, searchlights — there was nothing like being coned in by a searchlight to put a bombardier off his aim — chaff and fancy routeing were just some of the subterfuges and devices employed in the flak battle of wits over northern Italy during the winter of 1944-45. US P-47s were now regularly demonstrating their superior firepower, range and resilience over the Spitfires and Kittyhawks. P-47 crews developed an antidote to flak by skilfully executing low-level machine gun and rocket attacks against batteries which were concentrating on a simultaneous medium bomber raid. Prisoners of war confirmed that the new rocket projectiles and napalm bombs were even more successful than had been hoped in temporarily demoralising flak crews. And reducing the normal size of a P-47 flight formation, from 12 to eight or often four aircraft, permitted greater manoeuvrability and hence accuracy of aim while drawing less flak fire.

*   *   *   *

German fighter opposition was so slight in September 1944 that TAF adopted the unprecedented policy of sending out its mediums without fighter escort. But on 19 October, the ANR's II Gruppo came back into action. Fourteen Bf109s of the 2nd and 3rd Squadrons took-off from Villafranca, and eight from 1st Squadron at Ghedi, to intercept a group of 30 Marauders out to bomb a Mantua railway bridge. The first pass against the 320th formation proved fruitless but the second, against the less numerous 319th, cut a flight of B-26s in half. As three B-26s went down, the astonished cry of 'Italian fighters' over the radio reflected that this

was the first enemy attack the unit had experienced in eight months. Medium bomber waist and nose guns were immediately reinstalled, while the Gruppo's achievements on its 'first' mission were rewarded with personal congratulations from Kesselring.

By 2 November, II GrC boasted 42 109s, its highest number since June. Three days later, three more B-26s were lost and six damaged as 23 ANR 109s scrambled to jump a 320th Bomb Group formation about to bomb the railway at Rovereto. In response, A-20s of the 47th Bomb Group were detailed to fly intruder missions against one or more enemy airfields almost every night for a fortnight, and on 14 November MATAF rescinded its policy of not requiring fighter escorts for medium bombers.

The whole of II GrC moved to Aviano on 12 November, in part to get away from the attentions of Allied fighter-bombers. From there, they were brought to battle using the 'Giant Wurzburg' Ground Control Intercept radars located at Mantua, Padua, Genoa and Treviso. One Wurzburg directed the defenders while another plotted the raiders,[10] which from now on included the heavies.

Strategic Air Force was now fully based in the Foggia–Bari area, fed by the aviation fuel pipeline from the port of Manfredonia. Fifteenth Air Force and 205 Group were well placed to strike at those targets UK-based heavies could not reach, and the lack of comparable facilities and the means of supporting large numbers of additional units in France dictated that Strategic's bombers would remain in Italy. They seemed to have the high-level skies to themselves as they concentrated on the synthetic fuel plants, crude oil refineries and fuel stores in what remained of the Greater Reich.

Then, on 16 November, heavy bombers returning from a raid on Germany met their first serious opposition over Italy for ages. At noon, Capt Drago led eight 1st Squadron, ANR Bf109s from Aviano into a 10-minute engagement with scattered groups of B-17s and P-51 escorts in the Udine area between 24,000ft and the deck. As this battle was winding down, 2nd Squadron, ANR sent up another eight fighters led by Capt Bellagambi which ran into a group of escorted B-17s near the mouth of the River Livenza at 13.10hrs. Four heavy bombers were reported missing from the operation, while Italian records show the loss of two Bf109s.

At a briefing conference at Supreme Headquarters on 6 November after the first 'Bingo' onslaught, Gen Jodl stated that Allied air forces were using Italy as a bombing training area. Vietinghoff had begged to be allotted, at least temporarily, 'a couple of hundred fighters' but Hitler refused. Presumably with reference to the concentration of forces for the forthcoming Ardennes offensive, Jodl advised that 'we have nothing more to give Italy'.[11] This was not strictly true, for on 5 October it was decided to transfer 18 FW190s to upper Italy. Four were to operate alongside NAGr11 out of Udine in an over-water/coastal recce role, while the other 14 were ground-attack aircraft. The latter belonged to Sonderverband Einhorn (Special Force Unicorn), which had a brief to train to attack targets within a radius of 150km at twilight with 'the heaviest load' using the Egon blind-bombing system.[12] When these newcomers were added to the ANR fighters, Allied Intelligence believed that it was seeing around 100 air defenders with renewed aggression on the hardstandings at Aviano, Vicenza, Villafranca and Udine.

Above:
Wreckage of a US B-24 Liberator brought down behind German lines.
RAF Air Historical Branch

Strictly speaking, these airfields were within TAF's area of responsibility, but Gen Twining decided to devote a day of his heavy metal to helping sort the problem. During the night of 17/18 November, 205 Group deposited 212 tons of bombs on Campoformido and Vicenza, though this was insufficient to prevent a pair of tactical reconnaissance aircraft from getting off at 08.15hrs the next day to cover the Adriatic down to Pola. On the morning of 18 November, Fifteenth Air Force joined in, hitting the same two fields, plus Villafranca and Aviano, with 952 tons of bombs: the Germans estimated that B-24s dropped 7-8,000 fragmentation bombs on Villafranca. Eleven people died, along with a horse and seven cattle. An FW190 and three Ju87s were burnt out, and more damaged. In mid-afternoon, three P-47s shot up the dispersal, destroying another Stuka. It was reckoned that the landing ground would be unusable for 24 hours.

The same destructive story was repeated elsewhere. Of 15 aircraft at Ghedi, only two were left undamaged, while about 100 Italian civilians (probably Organisation Todt workers) were killed. At Aviano, Sgt Mjr (Sergente Maggiore) Bonopera, an armourer with II GrC, noted that 'when, just before 10 o'clock, the bombardment ceased, the field looked like it had been ploughed and almost all our aircraft had been hit and damaged'.[13] No

opposition was encountered, although 186 P-51s patrolled the target areas just in case. From post-attack photographs, MAAF estimated that they had accounted for 50–60 aircraft.

According to the papers of Gen Karl Koller, the last German Chief of Air Staff, throughout 1944 the Luftwaffe in Italy flew a total of 28,664 sorties and lost 966 aircraft — one for every 30 sorties. The Allies worked on higher figures (see Table 6).

Table 6: Allied Estimates of Axis Air Losses in Italy 1 January–22 December 1944			
	Destroyed	Probables	Damaged
In Air Combat	3,753	899	1,262
On the Ground			
Transports	84	—	38
Bombers	212	—	85
Fighters	322	—	134
Type unknown	1,220	—	886
Total Losses	5,591	899	2,405

When they totted up the Axis losses for 1944, Allied observers noted smugly that they had 'put paid to any effective activity by the Fascist flyers for the rest of the year and further limited the small German Air force effort'. Pohl's problems were compounded when Berlin ordered that half his available fuel be returned to Germany.[14]

But little was ever clear-cut in Italy. Notwithstanding the 18 November raids on Axis airfields, II GrC was back at Villafranca two days later taking delivery of new 109s. Once others were repaired at Aviano, the Gruppo was back to combat readiness and awaiting I GrC to help bear the airborne defence burden. And the ANR was not alone. When the battle of the Brenner opened on 4 November, there were some 366 guns clustered around the four key points of Verona, Trento, Bolzano and Innsbruck. On their own initiative, von Vietinghoff and von Pohl decided that 'nerve centres' such as Verona, Bolzano and Innsbruck must be protected by heavy flak concentrations, even at the expense of the front and other vulnerable points in the Po Valley. Eventually, about one-third of all the heavy flak guns in Italy came to be concentrated along the Brenner. After the war, von Pohl maintained that credit for keeping an emergency flow of traffic through the Brenner was due first to the 'unceasing and heroic' work of the railway engineers, and next to the flak crews, whose efforts were likened to the defence of the Messina Straits in the summer of 1943.

Which helps explain why the Mediterranean Allied Tactical Air Force lost no fewer than 713 aircraft in 1944 totally destroyed by flak. Furthermore, life was not going to get any easier. By 29 March 1945, German flak strength in Italy had grown to 1,012 heavy and 2,194 medium/light AA guns, all of which forced bombers to fly higher, which reduced their chances of hitting precise targets. Kesselring the airman may have lacked aeroplanes, but Kesselring the former gunner troubled Allied air operations to the very end.

Notes to Chapter 13

1. From the Allied point of view, the Italian campaign was an 'ammunition' rather than a 'fuel' war. By the end of 1943, British forces alone were expending shells at the rate of 22,000 tons a month, compared with 10,000 tons a month in North Africa from Alamein onwards.
2. No 21 Operational Directive.
3. 4,773 metric tonnes of the former and 988 tonnes of the latter passed southbound during September — memo from General Eaker to SACMED, 16 November 1944.
4. HQ MAAF Operation Instruction No 14.
5. There was a cluster of three under each wing. Beside the first recorded use of Rocket Projectile attacks on land targets on 7 October, another aerial 'first' was recorded on 3 October when the Napalm fuel tank incendiary bomb was introduced operationally in Italy.
6. Survey of Transformer Sub-stations on the Lower Brenner Line. Report by Engineer Righi, Italian State Railways, May 1945.
7. Owen, op.cit, p.179.
8. Copyright Joseph Heller 1955, and quoted with the permission of A.M. Heath & Co Ltd on behalf of Random House UK Ltd.
9. Lamb, R.; War in Italy,1943-1945; p.273.
10. Richthofen was invalided out of the service in November 1944 after developing a brain tumour.
11. The single Benito Pylon long-range direction finding radio system north of Udine was used to plot the interception of escort fighters.
12. Warlimont, op.cit, p.474.
13. Egon relied on two Freyas interrogating the aircraft's FuG 25 IFF transponder and triangulating on its position, the ground controller using these plots to guide the pilot.
14. Beale, N., D'Amico, F. and Valentini, G.; Air War Italy; p.126.
15. The British Air Ministry estimated that a large Luftflotte used 2–300 tons or 274–411cu m of aviation fuel daily. Of 3,600cu m held at the beginning of October, Pohl had to dispatch 2,066 to Germany. Of the remainder, recce aircraft used 300cu m while Italian Bf109s got just 35cu m, barely enough to fill their internal tanks.

WINTERDICTION

'Direct or indirect, the major air tasks were all in support of the Army Group . . . But this was not always appreciated by those who preferred to see their aircraft rather than read about them.' RAF Official History

On 27 November 1944, Sir Harold Alexander was promoted to field marshal, backdated to 4 June when his troops entered Rome. This charming, affable man, who had a reputation for defeating enemies without ever making any, was the Americans' favourite general, and there was no dissension when he replaced Sir Henry Maitland Wilson as Supreme Allied Commander Mediterranean on 12 December. Command of Allied armies in Italy was assumed by Gen Mark Clark. Lt-Gen Lucian Truscott returned to Italy to command the Fifth Army, in parallel with Lt-Gen Sir Richard McCreery who had taken over the Eighth Army in October.

For all his considerable attributes (including personal bravery), Alexander was no original thinker. His plan for December was a 'two-handed punch' aimed at Bologna and Ravenna, to split the German defences. The Eighth Army would breach the line of the River Santerno, and then launch a concerted drive on Bologna with the Fifth Army. As it transpired, the Eighth Army bore the brunt of fighting in December. By dawn on 5 December Ravenna had been taken, but then the troops faced a row of defended waterways at a time when the weather was never quite good enough for precise fighter-bombing. It took the Canadians from 13 to 22 December to cross the fiercely defended Naviglio Canal, even though DAF had put an unusual deception plan into operation.

The aim was to get as much armour as possible across the Old Canal, so at 15.00hrs on 12 December — while divisional artillery put down a dense barrage of mixed smoke and high explosive to

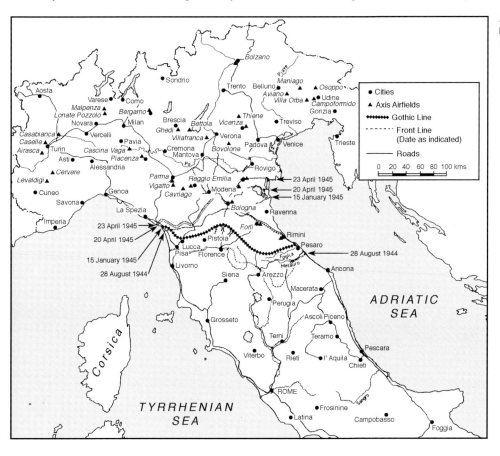

Left:
Italian airfields and operations, 28 August 1944–23 April 1945.

hide the tank crossing — fighter-bombers flew low-altitude attacks to drown the noise of tank tracks moving up the metalled road. This ploy was first used by the Royal Flying Corps in the first week of the Battle of the Somme in 1916, and 21st Tank Brigade reported it as being 'entirely successful'.

However, air support for the fighting around Pergola and Faenza 'was by no means all that had been hoped for. The fierce weather was a major handicap.' The same was true when it came to try crossing the Senio — by 18 and 19 December, bad weather inhibited all flying. Profiting from a lift in the cloud on 22 December, Spitfires and Kittyhawks attacked guns and strongpoints along the river banks. Thunderbolts and Mustangs performed impressively against a headquarters and occupied buildings, the former dropping bombs and the latter napalm on the ruins to make doubly sure.

But the fireworks changed nothing. Despite 40 close-support missions flown on Christmas Day, and many more the day after when the light bombers managed to get airborne, the Senio defences were every bit as strong as feared. By 27 December, DAF managed to take advantage of a cold, clear sunlit day to come to the aid of two desperately engaged divisions. Spitfires subsequently put a big German motor repair depot near Castel Guilfo out of action, adding to Axis supply problems, but it was too late. The nullifying effects of rain, snow and low cloud cancelled out Eighth Army's advantages in armour and air power such that it failed to reach the Santerno River. Worse than that, Bologna was still too strong, as von Vietinghoff held four divisions in reserve. Hitler was not prepared to weaken his Apennine positions. When two infantry divisions were sent to meet a crisis in Hungary, they were immediately replaced: one replacement division travelled nonstop from Norway to Italy.

The German C-in-C in Italy differed from his Allied opposite number in that his command was neither unified nor all-powerful. Von Vietinghoff could request assistance from the navy and air force, and in practice often obtain it — but he could not, as Field Marshal Alexander could — command it. Yet von Vietinghoff was a more enterprising man than Kesselring was later to concede. In the face of the Allied push beyond Ravenna, it took a special sort of leadership to harden and engender desperate aggressiveness among the German forces.

Eighth Army troops pushing towards Ravenna on 4 December had been supported by 93 DAF missions flying 613 sorties. It was a DAF record to date, and it dwarfed the Axis air effort for the entire month. But it was a measure of von Vietinghoff's spirit that the relatively few Luftwaffe air-to-ground-attackers made their presence felt. Stukas, flown by experienced low-level men such as Sgt (Feldwebel) Kaspar Stuber with 311 operations to his credit, were never a pushover. They operated in groups of up to nine along the front, and a No 600 Squadron Beaufighter which ran into four Ju87s in line-astern with a fifth to port on 1 December was set upon with great aggression and forced to take violent evasive action. The following day, a Staffel of six Ju87s machine-gunned Forli airfield ineffectively, and then bombed Eighth Army's Cesena HQ not so harmlessly. Communications with the three Corps — V, Canadian and Polish — were restored within an hour, but 'in view of an imminent Canadian attack, this was highly inconvenient'. The size of the Stuka mission was laughable compared to the numbers DAF and XXII TAC were putting into

Left:
Air crewmen load a belt of machine gun ammunition into a Twelfth Air Force Thunderbolt wing on 3 January 1945. The P-47 is being prepared for a dive-bombing and strafing mission against Axis installations in the Po Valley.
RAF Air Historical Branch

the sky, but the episode showed that even a small aerial force had the potential to achieve disturbing results, and that Axis resolve was never to be dismissed lightly.

Another factor which forced the issue was the Duce himself. The old showman was still captivating the Milanese masses as late as December 1944, and in seeking a 'spectacular' success for his divisions newly arrived from training in Germany, he persuaded von Vietinghoff to launch an attack against the left flank of the Fifth Army early on 26 December. The joint Italian–German assault by some five battalions on the wild and romantic Serchio Valley succeeded beyond all expectations, and by noon there was a big gap in the Allied lines. Given von Rundstedt's recent Ardennes offensive, there was fear that Axis forces could threaten the supply base and port of Leghorn. 92nd Division being no longer capable of offering organised resistance, XXII TAC dispatched several small Thunderbolt missions. They bombed road and rail bridges in the reported sector, and missed them all.

After a quiet night, Allied intelligence started to get a handle of what was going on. While the 19th Indian Brigade came to occupy a new defensive position astride the valley, a dozen small Thunderbolt missions did what they could. P-47s of the 86th and 350th Fighter Groups set a dump on fire while three missions by 8th SAAF Wing Spitbombers scored a number of hits on occupied areas. The Luftwaffe did not put in an appearance; although 8th Indian Division reported a few bombs falling on their positions, Allied aircrew were the most likely culprits. By the time 'Rover Joe' arrived, and the Allied air effort rose to 145 sorties,[1]

Below
Two 310th Bomb Group B-25s cross the Po as other members of their formation flatten a bridge. *Author's Collection*

the Indians had restored the situation. The last three days of 1944 saw a steady withdrawal by Germans and Italians harassed along both sides of the river by Indian artillery and XXII TAC Thunderbolts. But as Truscott had moved three of Fifth Army's divisions from the main battle area just in case, and heavy snow was now falling on the mountains, Fifth Army's attack on Bologna was called off and Alexander issued orders that both armies should pass to the defensive.

*   *   *   *

Air forces comprising some 280 squadrons now became the most potent weapon in the Mediterranean. Consequently, their instructions were revamped. First, the northeast zone of interdiction was deepened to cover the frontier routes through the Alps above the Venetian Plain. Second, those DAF Baltimore and Marauder squadrons then operating almost exclusively south of the Po were committed to the blockade. Third, there was to be an all-out fighter-bomber effort against crucial stretches joining Italy to the Reich as soon as they could decently disconnect from the armies. 'The aim was dual: to starve the forces which the enemy might choose to leave in Italy, and to prohibit the escape of those which he might wish to withdraw.'[2]

At the height of the Ardennes offensive, an urgent appeal went out from Tooey Spaatz to Generals Cannon and Twining urging them to immobilise the Brenner and Tarvisio routes as fully as possible. This was the most important contribution Mediterranean air forces could make to the battle in the west, and its implications were formalised in Operational Directive No 23, dated 9 January 1945. As little ground activity was foreseen in Italy for the next

Left:
Col Arthur Agar, CO 15th Fighter Group, with Generals Twining, Spaatz and Eaker on 3 January 1945. *IWM*

Right:
Bird's-eye view. *Author's Collection*

three months, the Directive eliminated ground support as a major responsibility and redefined Tactical Air Force's primary task as maintenance of the isolation of northern Italy while destroying all enemy means of transport, including fuel, whenever possible. The 57th (B-25) Wing's priorities were first the Brenner; then in succession the Venetian railway bridges over the Brenta, Piave, Livenza and Tagliamento Rivers, and the group of three northeastern lines — the Tarvisio, Piedicolle and Postumia. The bulk of XXII TAC and DAF effort was directed at crucial stretches joining Italy to the Reich. From now on, international routes replaced the army-focused Po Valley network as the primary communications goal.

In the Fifth Army sector, there had been only restricted operations for some months and troops had grown used to limited direct tactical support. Not so Eighth Army, which objected strongly to the new air directive; while admitting the case for less close support, it pointed to DAF's role in preventing the build-up of counter-attack forces and the engagement of hostile batteries. V Corps was particularly upset, having been haunted by river defences over the previous year. It argued passionately for a regular three or four-day close-support 'fix' every month to flatten all buildings that the enemy could be occupying within 1,000 yards of the Senio. In response, the air staff at Army Group HQ pointed to the high priority accorded to the anti-communications programme in the north, the seriously falling aircraft serviceability rate, the obsolescence of some types and the stuttering aircraft replacement flow. If DAF was to build up adequately for a spring offensive, it must conserve.

The argument continued with no little heat, and feathers were not smoothed by an order on 23 January confirming that the only close air support targets to be engaged were heavy guns out of

range of Allied artillery. The refusal of Air HQ to alter its decision led to a period of estrangement, leaving airmen with the impression that the army had become too addicted to air support. However, few aviators would appreciate that even in this three-month 'static' phase of the ground campaign, 582 Eighth Army officers and men would lose their lives, 3,027 would be wounded and 331 would be reported missing. These were a tenth of the total casualties for the whole period from 9 August 1944 to 31 March 1945, and probably none of them ever understood the finer points of the air war against unseen communications.

Across the whole of northern Italy, precise German records showed 1,020 cuts in all, of which 754 were made by aircraft attacks, 154 by partisans and 112 by accidents. Analysing these into degrees of permanence, 831 cuts were on open stretches and stations, and only 189 at bridges. But 31 December 1944 was typical in that some German traffic was always moving. From now on, airmen were asked to destroy bridges, not just pothole tracks.

After two days of bad weather, the B-25s struck Lavis viaduct and other bridges. On 4 January, the heavies attacked Trento marshalling yard and blocked it. For the rest of the month, in and around bad weather, the mediums reduced the flow of rail traffic to fits and starts between cuts. These air attacks drove an increasing volume of traffic onto Italian roads. One agent's report stated that road traffic in the first week along the east bank of Lake Garda had increased to 750 motor vehicles southbound and 940 northbound. This state of affairs was confirmed by photo-reconnaissance over the lake and all along the Adige Valley on 17/18 January. Given the Axis shortage of vehicles and petrol, plus the relative inefficiency of substitute motor fuels, this was a rewarding sight.

Kesselring was back in post by mid-January, and although he could offset the interdiction campaign by juggling his reserves, no

such salvation was forthcoming further afield. On 12 January, the Russians opened their winter offensive which would get them to within 35 miles of Berlin by 3 February. The Russian High Command was just as anxious as Eisenhower that German reinforcements should not be allowed to switch from Italy to their fronts. This was where interdiction helped ground forces far beyond their range of vision. Within a week, 356th Division was removed from the Italian front and the first elements sent off in a northeasterly direction through Verona. Three weeks later, the last elements had still not cleared Italy.

The 16th SS Panzer Grenadier Division had a similar experience as air attacks rendered movement schedules chaotic. They began to move at the beginning of February, but ground agents saw them soon afterwards moving on foot and then held up in the Adige valley when their lorries ran out of fuel. One unit was said to have been reduced to buying fuel on the black market. Troops leaving the Reich for Italy fared no better. Under normal conditions, the journey from the Austrian border to Bologna (a distance of 330 miles) took 12 hours. Now it took three to four weeks of changing, marching, hitch-hiking, waiting for long hours on roadsides or in tunnels, and often living off the land. The ethos of making do was no way to fight a credible war on several fronts.

February marked the turning point in the interdiction battle. Over 1,000 mediums made 73 attacks on 20 out of 28 days, and while many were against all the familiar targets on the Lower and Middle Brenner, after 14 February their reach was extended to reach Bressanone, only six miles south of the Austrian border. The closure of the Bressanone bridge for nine days was a triumph of the B-25s' range and their crews' flying skill because it was 'one of the most difficult of all possible air journeys'. South of Bolzano, Lavis viaduct was hammered: by the close of the month, 450ft of viaduct

was missing in a series of four gaps. The Axis never succeeded in bringing it back into use although 700 men were employed in making a long, winding diversion on the flat.

Four serious blocks had been created on the Brenner line by 8 February; at the end of the month, there were 10. Up until February, the Germans had been able to maintain forward railheads in the Ora and Trento area; thereafter, the increase in weight and range of concerted air attacks pushed the blockages northward of Bolzano. As the depth of interdiction increased, so did the requirement for motor transport to provide transhipment, adding to the difficulties of radio-directed railway repair crews who were forced to travel further to do their work. More and more German supplies had to be held along the upper Adige and Isarco valleys until transport could be released to move them south. As if the Germans did not have enough problems, Strategic Air Force intervened over four February days and nights to stomp on the marshalling yards that had long been abandoned by TAF.

On 8 February, the Tactical Air Force achieved a record by being the first force to have flown 500,000 sorties. The Germans, on the defensive, resorted to every ingenious device to overcome the handicap of air inferiority. Bridges were built under a few inches of water so that airmen could not see them. Another ingenious ruse was the 'night-operational' bridge. A damaged structure would be repaired to a point just short of completion, leaving one span missing so that aerial reconnaissance would class it as impassable. At night, however, a specially prepared span would be dropped into place so that traffic could pass over.

Another stratagem was the close timing of Allied air attacks. Captured records of air raid alerts in Verona showed a decrease in attack around twilight, when the day boys had finished and the night-bombers were not yet airborne. That interlude was marked

Table 7: Mediterranean Allied Tactical Air Force Sorties [3]						
Mission	Nov	Dec	Jan	Feb	Mar	Apr
Blockage	1,844	3,185	4,725	6,364	8,162	4,162
All Other Communication Targets	6,624	5,788	5,220	3,148	5,220	8,746
Other Combat Sorties	10,937	12,513	9,380	8,995	14,089	25,881
Total	19,405	21,486	19,325	18,507	27,471	38,789

by feverish repair activity which, unbeknown to the Allies, explained why the railway network around Verona continued to function. Throwing manpower at the problem was another solution. Under Col Schnez, Chef des Transportswesen Italien, was a repair organisation employing over 55,000 men, reinforced by an unknown, fluctuating but certainly large amount of impressed Italian labour, plus troops on leave commandeered for three days' service when trains were held up by bomb damage.

On no less than 16 days in March, TAF flew over 1,000 sorties. One result was that in that month the Brenner route was completely impassable between Bolzano and Trento, and open for only two days between Trento and Verona. The northeastern routes were impassable for the whole month and in the Inner Belts, only one line was open for only one day. Schnez's repair organisation, though never immobilised, was gradually outfought, exhausted and hounded by partisans at the end.

    *   *   *   *

By the end of February, 57 pilots of I GrC had returned from training in Bavaria with 54 Bf109s. Their planned bases were Lonate and then Gallarate, to supplement the efforts of the more active II GrC which now had 82 pilots divided between Aviano and Osoppo. For the loss of five aeroplanes and two pilots, II Gruppo claimed the destruction of five B-25s and three P-47s engaged on interdiction missions in February.

Allied records noted 'rather more German fighter reaction' during the month, but this often only reflected reconnaissance activity. On 23 February, a 2(F)/122 Me410 was out of Bergamo heading for the front when it ran into some P-47s of Orchid Section, 347th Fighter Squadron, 350th Fighter Group, 20 miles south of Parma. The P-47s were returning from dive-bombing the Ora rail diversion, and 2nd Lt Jim Young recalls:

'[I] turned and gave chase. When the German saw us he hit the deck . . . I remember using water injection to get enough speed

to keep up with the 410. The enemy plane tried to use evasive action by pulling straight up to 900–1,100ft, then pushing the nose back to the deck. I kept firing small bursts . . . and could see some hits on the 410. I remember we flew 10–15 minutes (it seemed that long) at top speeds. Finally he was treetop level with his port engine trailing smoke, and my ammo finally hit his starboard engine. The plane dipped its right wing and hit the ground in a big ball of flame.'

P-47s could get away with this because the combination of wing and belly tanks gave them the legs to reach targets many miles beyond normal bombing range. The downside for outfits like the 79th Fighter Group was that, when sporting the full interdiction loads of 1,000-pounder and belly tanks — or wing tanks, rockets and belly tanks — the concrete runways at Fano were 1,500ft shorter than that required for a 'safe' take-off. And that was not the only flight safety hazard. There were six British and three US squadrons at Fano, and another six British squadrons based at Forli. Serious airfield congestion was eased only by allowing aircraft to take-off and land in either direction to minimise taxi distances and bring aircraft as close to their dispersals as possible.

Allied records state that over 1,000 mediums made 73 attacks on 20 out of 28 February days for the loss of 15 aircraft to flak. Luftwaffe and Italian gun crews were more upbeat, claiming 104 Allied aircraft shot down with the army adding two and the navy 21. Another 14 came down in German-held territory for reasons other than combat damage. Yet those losses must be set against the 18,507 missions flown that month (see Table 7).

By March, the run-up to the forthcoming ground battle was absorbing the greatest proportion of the tactical air effort. But long before that, it was clear from the statistics that an appreciable medium, light and fighter-bomber effort was being devoted to targets other than Italian communications as a whole.

One important subsidiary commitment was the air supply to resistance movements in northern Italy. The mood of life in what remained of Mussolini's domain was exemplified in the executive order authorising construction of defensive positions in the foothills of the Alps:

'The fortifications . . . will be constructed by means of a levy on the population in accordance with the principles of total war. This can be accomplished only through intervention of the political authorities.'[4]

Such an authoritarian approach drove more and more Italians to rebel against their former ally. Many turned to partisan resistance, whereupon the Germans and their Blackshirt colleagues carried out reprisals which more often than not only injured the innocent, alienating yet more Italians who wanted nothing more than to survive. Shrewd observers like Gen von Senger realised that 'the war had moved from a purely military setting into a politico-military one — a sure sign of its impending termination'.[5]

So it came about that the 885th Heavy Bomb Squadron (Special) became the only four-engined heavy outfit in the Mediterranean theatre never to drop a bomb. The 885th pioneered what are now known as 'counter-insurgency operations' and by the time the conflict was over, its B-17s and B-24s had flown 2,875 sorties to drop 501 agents, 9,571,581 tons of supplies and 355,370lb of leaflets, for the loss of 17 aircraft and 16 crews.

The growth in partisan activity was such that between 22 November 1944 and 8 May 1945, close on 5,000,000lb of supplies, freight, personnel and propaganda leaflets were dropped by 51st Troop Carrier Wing. All this effort was not wholly selfless. Whereas front-line troops when captured usually spent the rest of the war in captivity, many Allied aircrews who baled out after being shot down by flak had a chance of escaping capture. Supplies dropped to the partisans helped the creation of safe havens and strengthened the escape and evasion organisation.[6]

As the Italian locals had little enough food to spare for escaping aircrew, HQ Twelfth Air Force accepted responsibility for supplying fugitive air personnel with food, clothing, supplies and money. On 10 October, one fully armed B-25 and crew from 57th Bombardment Wing was assigned to the resupply task and, on occasion, lifting them from clandestine air strips. This Combat Search and Rescue B-25 became known as the 'Lazzarone Air Force' — the beggar's air force. Operating at low attitude during daylight, the drops were most carefully co-ordinated and pinpointed. From its first flight in October until the end of the campaign, the 'Lazzarone Air Force' undertook 64 resupply missions and completed 35 escapes.

But the largest items on the air programme from November to March, besides the interdiction of Axis land and sea communications, were to reduce the flow of supplies from existing dumps to Axis forces on the Italian front and 'destroy the enemy's means of transportation'.

Life is about priorities, and technology helped to meet air priorities in Italy. Two technical innovations introduced in February were the use of delayed action anti-personnel butterfly bombs to hamper German repair work, and the successful use by the Americans of their 'Shoran' blind bombing aid. On 15 February, 18 B-25s used this device to bomb the German

ammunition depot at Spilimbergo, generating large columns of smoke and concussions from exploding bunkers which were felt by the attackers flying at 13,000ft. But the bombers with the most sophisticated navigation and bombing kit tended to be based in England. The Italian theatre was forever a poor relation in this respect; it did not enjoy the advantages conferred by radar-directed bombing until the final stages of the campaign, and only a few aircraft were converted from the by then obsolescent Norden bombsight to something better. Notwithstanding the strict priorities laid down in the November and January air directives, the winter weather of 1944-45 often forced aircraft to bomb where they could, rather than where HQ might have wished.

If the weather stopped operations on the isolation of Italy programme, medium bombers were to concentrate on the permanent railway bridges over the Po and Oglio Rivers, the latter aimed at interfering with the evacuation loot from the industrial heartland around Milan and Turin.[7] The myth had taken root in some quarters that Operation 'Mallory Major' had completely destroyed all the permanent Po bridges for all time. This was untrue, as post-attack aerial photographs began to reveal. The PR Spitfire Flight was kept exceedingly busy, determining whether a bombing mission had to be repeated and, if so, how quickly.

To give some idea of the intensity of Allied photo-reconnaissance achievement in Italy, the grand total of prints produced during 1944 was no less than 3,350,000 for all purposes. And they were not given to some computer for interpretation: every shot of potential interest had to be physically viewed by a photo-interpreter. From this analysis, air attackers now concentrated on the night operational pontoon bridge and night ferry system, a task made easier when DAF transferred two Baltimore squadrons to nocturnal operations and the P-61 Black Widow and A-26 entered the theatre as night-bombers and intruders.

Night intruder missions doubled to 2,903 in March, which together with the growing number of day sorties managing to bomb through overcast or mist, gave Axis personnel little rest or hope for continued protection from weather or darkness. Nowadays, TV footage illustrates the technologically precise nature of modern air attack, but life was much more rudimentary back then. Lt Charles V. Wilson, a bombardier-navigator flying Invaders with the 86th Squadron of the 47th Bomb Group, recalls:

'. . . most of our missions were dispatched to strike targets of opportunity. These usually were enemy airfields, bridges, marshalling yards and motor transport. On clear nights convoys could be sighted rolling along the highways . . . We usually travelled to the target by dead reckoning and then used the visual bombsight. When there was cloud cover, we used our ground radar stations to put us over the target and we bombed on their direction . . . About the only way we had to learn of enemy fighters was by monitoring the frequencies of the local RAF night-fighter network. However, even when we knew that there were German fighters in the area, there was little that we could do about them. One of our greatest dangers was a mid-air collision with one of our own aircraft that was "freelancing" in

the same area . . . If we lost our radio or navigation aids, we were abetted in finding our course home by flare pots that would be lit at night in the mountains of northern Italy. These would serve as guides to get us back home to our base in Pisa. There were occasions when the Germans would pass us false radio homings to lure us out over the sea to become lost and finally be forced to ditch.'[8]

It is worth following DAF from sunset on 5 March to sunset the following day to appreciate the breadth of its air power capability. As darkness fell south of the Po, six Bostons of 232 Wing and eight 253 Wing Baltimores bombed a factory and stores dump under radar control, interspersed by a propaganda leaflet drop. Thereafter, road and rail reconnaissance occupied them until the gooseneck flares dimmed in the early morning light. North of the Po, a No 256 Squadron Mosquito intruded over the airfield at Udine, but haze prevented any sightings. Bostons and Baltimores were over the road and rail systems of northeast Italy and barge routes between the Po and Caorle, dropping bombs on Monselice and Rovigo marshalling yards. Small clusters of lights indicated enemy transport moving between the Piave and Tagliamento rivers. One Boston did not come back.

Life got worse for the Germans come the dawn. Two 7 Wing Spitfires on an early morning recce north of the Po reported about

Top Left & Left:
Damage assessment prints taken during and after the Operation 'Bowler' raid on Venice harbour, 21 March 1945. A warehouse full of landmines erupted *(top)* as a No 680 Squadron Spitfire passed overhead. The damage after the smoke had cleared *(left)*.
RAF Air Historical Branch

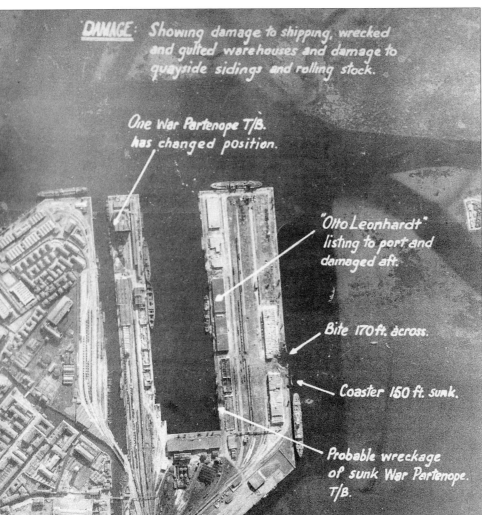

DAMAGE: Showing damage to shipping, wrecked and gutted warehouses and damage to quayside sidings and rolling stock.

One War Partenope T/B. has changed position.

"Otto Leonhardt" listing to port and damaged aft.

Bite 170 ft. across.

Coaster 150 ft. sunk.

Probable wreckage of sunk War Partenope. T/B.

800 wagons on a length of railway track near Conegliano. The chokepoint was attacked by 39 Marauders from 3 SAAF Wing whilst 244 Wing and 7 SAAF Spitbombers, 79th Fighter Group P-47s and 239 Wing Mustangs and Kittyhawks claimed 58 wagons destroyed and 79 damaged. Attacks further up the line destroyed or damaged a locomotive and 50 wagons, while line-cutting missions left 15 cuts at different points in their wake. 239 Wing Kittyhawks destroyed the southern span of the bridge at Longhere, and scored direct hits on the western approaches of the bridge at Gorizia. 79th Fighter Group P-47s knocked the centre and western span out of Montereale and destroyed the northeastern span at Citadella diversion.

Barges on the waterways were attacked by Spitbombers, Thunderbolts and Kittyhawks. All three Spitfire wings flew escorts for the mediums and TAC recce aircraft of 285 Wing. Anti-flak missions were flown by 7 SAAF Wing and 79th Fighter Group. South of the Po, Spitbombers attacked two gun positions. 285 Wing meanwhile undertook tactical and artillery reconnaissances, and provided oblique photographs of the Senio River on behalf of the Eighth Army. Across Italy, XXII TAC was performing similar feats.

*   *   *   *

Particular emphasis was laid on the Po between 16 and 20 March, when XXII TAC intruders bombed 17 of the crossings. One quarter more motor vehicles were destroyed in March than in February, though less motor traffic was now in evidence. The interdiction campaign was working so well that no operations worth recording were mounted over northwest Italy. It did not matter that the

Germans could move freely there, so long as they were being dammed up at more critical points — one of which being enemy coastal shipping.

A feature of the 9 January directive was the introduction of shipping as an important weather alternative. For some time, the army and navy had been opposed to the bombing of German-held ports because they foresaw the need to rely on these facilities themselves before too long. So priority was given to the bombing of shipping in and around harbours rather than harbours themselves — a rather demanding differentiation given the bombing accuracy of the time.

Between June and August 1943, DAF mediums were bombing point targets with a probable radial error of 330yd. Twelve months later, the crews of TAF mediums had honed their skills to within an error of 170yd. Bomb density achieved by mediums was generally two and a half times greater that that of heavy bombers, but bomb density did not mean that a target was likely to be hit. From operational data compiled in the Mediterranean theatre, it was calculated that to ensure a 95% chance of hitting a bridge occupying 6,000sq ft, TAF mediums needed to drop 600 bombs.[9] That risked a lot of bombs landing far away from a target as small as a coastal vessel tied up alongside a quay.

By February, Strategic was running out of meaningful targets to hit outside Italy, so it was sent against Adriatic ports. The cumulative bombing of Trieste, Pola and Fiume had two notable results. The first, which should have come as no surprise, was that these missions inflicted 'appreciable destruction and damage' on port facilities as well as naval and merchant shipping. The second was a general exodus of shipping from these ports to concentrate in and around Venice. Final delivery of supplies from there to the front line was by barges which were routed through the southern entrance of the Venetian Lagoons into the canal system of the great Po delta.

For too long, precision bombing of Italy had meant the area bombing of precise targets. But the chance now came to give a display of precision bombing. After watching Venice harbour on a daily basis, weather permitting, the cerulean-blue PR Spitfires noticed quickening activity by 18 March. The SS Otto Leonhardt, a 340ft-long vessel of 3,200 tons which had been there since 29 January, was taking on stores, while nearby was an equally busy group of two torpedo boats, a coaster and a number of barges. TAF looked on Venice as an obvious base for supplies by sea (particularly of fuel) to the Tenth Army front, so when a 200ft-long coastal tanker moved up ahead of the Otto Leonhardt, sailing time seemed near. Yet having done so much harm to the unique monuments of Italy already, it would have been inexcusable to batter any part of historic Venice with the war almost won. An order went out that the only area that could be hit was the shipping basin and surrounding docks, measuring 650 by 950yd. AVM Foster, commander DAF, made it plain to his pilots that he would be 'bowler-hatted' — compulsorily retired — if any bombs fell wide of their mark. From then on, the attack became known as Operation 'Bowler'.

Venice was bathed in sunlight on 21 March. The initial requirement then, as it would be against Iraq in 1991, was to silence the air defences, so 16 No 260 Squadron Mustangs and 20 79th Fighter Group Thunderbolts went in first at 15.30hrs to attack the 45 flak positions defending the port with bombs, rockets and machine gun fire. Then came the Kittyhawks of No 250 Squadron led by Wing Cdr George Westlake, which scored direct hits on the Otto Leonhardt, two warehouses on the quay and a near miss on a torpedo boat. The second wave found the target area partially obscured by smoke, but they scored direct hits on the coastal tanker and three adjacent warehouses. By the time the last wave went in, Otto Leonhardt was ablaze and the air thick with smoke and dust. In all, 24 Kittyhawks and 40 Mustangs (16 of which were anti-flak) dropped 69 1,000lb bombs and 31 260lb bombs on the dock area in the space of 20 minutes. There followed a major explosion, which was felt by the PR Spitfire sitting overhead at 20,000ft. Everyone returned home bar one pilot, who was rescued after baling out.

Post-raid damage assessment revealed a clearly accomplished task. The Otto Leonhardt was so severely damaged that it sunk two days later. One torpedo boat and the tanker were sunk, several warehouses were gutted, tracks were cut and wagons damaged. Only one bomb out of the hundred dropped fell outside the target area, destroying what appeared to be a small private dwelling. The bowler hat stayed on the peg.

As DAF tended to have shorter-range aircraft, they were given the calls to support both Fifth and Eighth Armies. This freed American P-47s to attack further afield, and as they increasingly moved northwards up the Brenner, they in turn enabled TAF mediums to attack targets still further north. This creeping development culminated in the first successful Italian-based medium bomber raid on Greater German soil on 11 March 1945. It put a bridge east of Lienz, on the line connecting the Brenner and

Tarvisio routes, out of action for 10 days. But the onset of spring weather heralded the fact that it was the land campaign that would decide matters; and like all modern armies, the German depended for its fighting power on the fuel that fed its engines of war.

The heavy bomber offensive from the UK and Italy in the first half of 1944, coupled with Russian advances later in the year that occupied Ploesti, had dealt a crippling blow to German oil production. Fortunately for Axis forces in Italy, natural gas and oil wells close to the front were put to good use. By themselves, these would not have sufficed were it not for the fact that the Germans thinned out their petrol with alcohol obtained from sugar beet molasses and grape pressings. MAAF decided that the most effective counter was to go for the sugar beet refineries, which forced the Germans to hoard their diluted petrol for battle only.

It is worth asking why the massive and continuous expenditure of Allied air effort failed to cripple the Axis road transport system completely. The answer lay in the steps Germans and Republican Italians took from August 1944 onwards to convert their vehicles to wood, charcoal and methane gas. It was a laborious process but the Germans carried it through with their usual single-mindedness, to the extent that in Army Group C's area at the end of the campaign, 2,800 vehicles had been converted to run off wood gas generators. Wood gas, like methane, did nothing for vehicle performance, but constant air attacks slowed the tempo of transport operations anyway. Wood and gas alternatives, plus the use of light motorcycles, horse and ox-drawn vehicles, bicycles and extensive use of towing, sufficed so long as the battle front was relatively static.

*　　　*　　　*　　　*

Given that ground forces, short on manpower and ammunition, were unable to generate an offensive until April 1945, and in Field Marshal Alexander's words the navy's functions were 'largely auxiliary to the other two forces', air power was a vital factor in bringing about final defeat.[10] In fact, during the closing months of the war 'it was by far the most potent Allied weapon in the Mediterranean'.[11]

Back in 1943, Professor Solly Zuckerman's view that it was more profitable to attack large railway centres containing important repair facilities and concentrations of rolling stock rather than road and rail bridges, formed the basis for the Allied air onslaught on French rail centres in the run-up to the Normandy invasion. But whereas the principal marshalling yards in northwest Europe were fairly concentrated and relatively near to the battle front, rail communications in Italy were extended, presenting a number of small and widely dispersed targets. In other words, during Strategic Air Force raids in mid-1944 on such rail centres as Turin, Pisa, Piacenza and Florence, 'too few bombs were dropped on too many places, too few times'.[12]

The subsequent controversy over the respective merits of attacking marshalling yards or bridges was, as Sir John Slessor observed realistically, 'somewhat unreal'. The fact that a certain doctrine worked on one occasion did not necessarily mean it would ever be thus again.

'It depended on a number of things — the time factor, how quickly one wanted results, and on the forces available. The thing to do was adapt one's thinking to the conditions of the time and to the developing capacity of aircraft and weapons, making full use of the flexibility of air power to attack the enemy's transportation system in the way that seemed most likely to be profitable in the conditions with which we were faced, and with the resources we had at our disposal.' [13]

Previous operations such as 'Strangle' and 'Diadem' had absorbed all the air effort available, but now with slightly less strength, Allied air crews flew more sorties, achieved greater accuracy, dropped more tons of bombs on communication lines, destroyed or damaged more locomotives, rolling stock and motor vehicles, wrecked more bridges and cut many more tracks. The difference between the interdiction effort in early 1945 and what went before lay largely in the depth and distribution of effort. With the Axis confined to the top of Italy, at long last the scale of the task coincided with Allied capability to deny freedom of movement and access to sources of supply.

The return of fine flying weather came at the right time to put the seal on an Allied air campaign which, by the end of March 1945, had virtually paralysed Axis lines of communication and faced Kesselring with an acute shortage of every kind of propellant fuel just as his army group was about to meet the expected Allied spring offensive. Yet when media pundits today give the impression that a few cruise missiles plus economic sanctions are all it takes to bring an errant regime to heel, the Italian interdiction campaign throughout the winter of 1944–45 gives food for thought.

Despite the deposition of 10,267 tons of bombs by 6,839 sorties on the Brenner line in six months, the long intervening periods, worsening weather, longer nights and highly efficient German repair system went a long way towards neutralising the early diffuse efforts. After February, Kesselring was deprived of his best southward lines from Verona and there was a decline in the repair rate. 'But the line was never completely and finally cut up to the very end. That supplies were cut off was much more due to the conditions obtaining in Germany than to the state of the railway on the Italian side.' [14]

Mark Clark was equally objective. 'Our Air Force blasted the mountain tunnels in northern Italy, bombed railways through narrow passes, and performed other modern miracles of destruction. It hurt the enemy without question, but it never kept him from reinforcing or supplying his Italian armies up to the very end of the war.' [15]

Although February turned out to be an above average flying month, the Allies still lost 323 aircraft across the theatre. [16] Italy proved that even with air superiority, it takes thousands and thousands of missions — flown continuously and around the clock for months — to break a resilient foe's supply chain and keep it broken. To expect to do it any more easily and with minimal cost today is to rely on a wing and prayer.

Notes to Chapter 14

1. 60 by the 350th Fighter Group, 75 by 86th Fighter Group and 10 by 1st Brazilian Squadron.
2. Craven and Cate, op.cit, p.478.
3. AHB, op.cit, p.177.
4. OKW, WF St/Op/772641/44, 29 July.
5. Senger, op.cit, p.270.
6. By the end of the war, 241 Fifteenth and 495 Twelfth Air Forces' aircrew were rescued from Italian soil.
7. Milan housed over 100 firms making the turbines, engines, vehicles, cables and precision instruments that are essential in modern war, and its central station was the most important junction in peacetime Italy. Six railway lines also converged on Turin, a centre of mechanical engineering whose products included tanks, aircraft engines, locomotives, cables and chemicals.
8. Hess, W. N.; A-20 Bostons at War; pp.113–14.
9. Godderson, op.cit, p.130.
10. Report on the Italian Campaign, 12 Dec 44-2nd May 45, draft p.6.
11. Craven and Cate, op.cit, p.442.
12. Richards and Saunders. vol ii, p.364.
13. Slessor, op.cit, p.568.
14. Report on the Battle of the Brenner; Oberst Schnez, formerly General des Transportswesen Italien.
15. Clark, op.cit, pp.273–74.
16. One per 123.6 sorties: Jackson. Vol VI, Pt III, p.183.

THE FINAL ROUND

'One great "if" of history may be: "If Hitler had been a corporal in the Luftwaffe . . ."'
Roderic Owen

At the end of 1944, the Luftwaffe Commanding General in Italy made it clear to Berlin that his defences against vastly superior Allied air power were quite inadequate. On an average day in good weather, von Pohl estimated that the Allies sent against him around 1,000 ground-attack aircraft, 250 mediums, 70 fighters (excluding escorts), 80 tactical recce aircraft, 20 night-fighters and 20 intruders, not to mention 700 strategic bombers passing through his airspace and which might occasionally hit Italian targets.[1]

It was bad enough that Maxi Pohl had neither the equipment nor the aircraft to fight or reconnoitre, but also his airmen were being withdrawn to be used as soldiers and he was too dependent for supplies on the caprice of Air Fleet Reich. But there was a way out:

Pohl had read reports on the performance of new jet-propelled fighters, and he saw great merit in his being given a Me262 fighter Gruppen. If integrated with an Italian fighter wing, the combined force would compel the Allies to use an increased number of bomber escorts. Although Pohl admitted that a jet-enhanced force could not hope for any sensational success against powerful and heavily escorted bomber formations, the appearance of up-to-date German jet fighters would provide a fillip to the morale of heavily pressed ground troops. Interestingly, this was also an argument that Allied armies were constantly pointing out to their air forces.

Gen Eaker had also read reports of forthcoming German jets, and on 4 October 1944 he had written that 'I believe our best antidote, aside from all-out attacks on the factories building these

Below:
An Arado Ar234 being towed at Osoppo. *Author's Collection*

planes, is to have available on forward aerodromes by April 1st several groups of our own jet-propelled fighters.'

Two Lockheed P-80 Shooting Stars were subsequently assigned to Italy for operational evaluation and training purposes, but it fell to the Luftwaffe to deploy the first operational jets to Italy. By February 1945, total Axis aircraft in various states of serviceability in northern Italy fluctuated around 130. There were 66 Bf109s and FW190s at Udine, Aviano, Lonate and Osoppo, 20 TAC recce 109s and 190s at Udine, 18 long-range recce Ju88s, 188s and Me410s at Bergamo and Ghedi, and 33 night-attack Ju87s and FW190s at Villafranca and Ghedi. These major airfield complexes were masterpieces of German construction — it is no coincidence that they underpin NATO operations over the former Yugoslavia today — and into Osoppo in late February flew the first of three Arado Ar234s.

At the time, Gen Lemelsen's Fourteenth Army was positioned on the western part of the front, from south of Bologna to the Tyrrhenian Sea, while the Tenth Army held the eastern flank from the Adriatic to Monte Grande. Although the Tenth and Fourteenth still contained some of Germany's best divisions (now up to strength and thoroughly rested), neither Kesselring nor his commanders believed they could hold their main front against a major Allied offensive enjoying complete air superiority in fine spring weather. 'Diadem' had shown what would happen as soon as Allied tanks, guns and aircraft were free to move again, refreshed, replenished and retrained after the winter break.

To complicate matters, Kesselring perceived a definite threat of an Allied amphibious landing on his Adriatic flank.[2] If that happened, and given Allied air supremacy, the German C-in-C believed he stood considerably less chance of getting his troops back intact across the Po than at the start of winter. Consequently, once Allied offensive operations were seen to be imminent, he proposed to initiate Herbstnebel — a controlled retreat to, and withdrawal across, the Po. His divisions in the western Alps would fall back to the Ticino slowly, so that the industrial centres of northwest Italy could be protected for as long as possible. In Kesselring's view, his army group was well poised for such a withdrawal, and although he did not say so, it had two years' experience in the art. But success would depend on two factors — predicting Allied intentions, and securing OKW approval for Herbstnebel.

Without aerial reconnaissance, Kesselring's chances of discovering Allied intentions were slender, which explained why a trio of Ar234B twin-turbojets and pilots were in place under the command of Flg Off (Oberleutnant) Erich Sommer by mid-March. Operating at altitudes between 29-39,000ft, these jets were unstoppable as they made regular photo runs over the front. Erich Sommer was pleased to receive a radio intercept of a P-51 pilot trying to intercept him and frustratedly reporting, 'He's too bloody fast!' The Ar234s were well supported by their more conventional colleagues. Recce Bf109s achieved up to eight sorties a day down the east and west coasts in the first half of March, supplemented by 38 nocturnal missions and FW190s flying armed recce. No 600 Squadron, RAF, which by early 1945 was flying Mosquito XIX night-fighters, noted on 2 March after the third

unsuccessful pursuit of low-level Ju188 or Me410 contact that week:

'These reconnaissance aircraft have had a long spell of success. Their chief advantage appears to be that they are equipped with every aid . . . their ability to fly right down low is due to their being equipped with a really efficient radio altimeter. They have a fast aircraft . . . plotted at 385mph on the deck, and backward-looking AI of a range from two to four miles. Plus, there is no doubt that their crews are well trained and really know their business.'

In sum, Kesselring described his air arm as 'a mere skeleton. All the same, a few modern reconnaissance aircraft — the Arado 234, superior to anything the enemy possessed — brought back useful information and very slightly lifted the curtain over the enemy's back areas and the sea area near the front.'[3] But even more difficult than deriving intelligence was acting upon it. Once he was finally convinced that Allied armies were advancing, Kesselring gambled on quickly being able to persuade Hitler that a stand south of the Po was beyond the resources of his armies. Yet when that crucial moment did arise, Kesselring had been long gone to replace von Rundstedt as C-in-C West. From mid-March 1945, von Vietinghoff was back in command of Army Group C, bound by orders he dare not defy until it was too late.

*   *   *   *

The harsh realities of Luftwaffe life were spelt out in a letter dated 9 March 1945:

'TOP SECRET
To:
Commanding General, Luftwaffe in Italy
Headquarters Luftflotte 4
Headquarters Luftflotte Reich

For information to:
Adjutant to Reichsmarschall Göring
OKW/Armed Forces Operations Staff (Air)

Luftwaffe forces in the Reich and on the Eastern Front are so heavily engaged that the transfer of units to other fronts is no longer possible. Moreover, transfers of any appreciable scale could not be carried out owing to the difficult fuel situation.

The plan to dispatch reinforcements to the Commanding General, Luftwaffe in Italy in the event of an enemy landing must therefore be cancelled. Defensive operations will be carried out with the forces at present available to the Commanding General, Luftwaffe in Italy.

Christian
OKL Operations Staff'

For all their remaining pockets of expertise, Axis airmen in Italy were up against a combined Allied Strategic and Tactical front-line strength of 4,393 aircraft. Strategic Air Force had 117 squadrons — 109 US day squadrons and eight 205 Group night units, supported by seven Lightning and Mustang escort fighters groups — based on fields from Foggia to Rimini.[4]

Tactical Air Force consisted of 42 USAAF, 44 RAF and Dominion, one Brazilian and two Polish squadrons: among the most important of these was the US 57th Bomb Wing which controlled 12 squadrons of B-25s about to move from Corsica to the Fano area. Then there was Coastal Air Force with its 17 squadrons. Extras such as the 12 Dakota squadrons of the US 51st Troop Carrier Wing brought the total up to 258 squadrons under MAAF operational command.[5] Even though two Twelfth Air Force fighter-bomber groups — the 27th and 86th, totalling 150 aircraft — had been withdrawn from the Italian theatre in January, in March 1945 130 Axis aircraft faced odds of 30:1.

On 21 February, Berlin decreed that the German Air Force in Italy be restricted to nine tons of fuel per day, as against 407 tons on the Eastern Front and 403 for the Reich/Western Front. Nine tons of fuel per day did not go far, but Allied intelligence admitted that, in March and early April, 'the German and Italian Fascist Air Forces, a good proportion of whom were seasoned veterans, . . . showed a spirit of enterprise in fighter interception by day and night and in reconnaissance. Their night harassing effort was negligible.'

Fuel was eked out until the last great air battle over Italy on 2 April, when 350th Fighter Group P-47s were given two almost simultaneous missions. Eight from the 346th Fighter Squadron were to bomb the Ora rail bridge in the Middle Brenner, whereupon they were to provide area cover for B-25s bombing San Michele All' Adige bridge further south. Sixteen 347th Fighter Squadron P-47s were to escort other B-25s bombing the Brenner.

The 347th rendezvoused at 13.50hrs with 36 B-25s out of Corsica, while the 346th followed a direct route across the Po Valley. At Aviano, 18 Bf109s from II GrC were scrambled at 13.45hrs, to be joined over Aviano by nine 109s from Osoppo. Control advised the leader, Maj Miani, that a large number of medium bombers with fighter escorts was coming from the south. Control gave the estimated interception point, leaving Miani free to attack at his discretion.

The American crews were warned at 14.00hrs of bandits approaching from the Udine area. By 14.15hrs the B-25s and 347th Fighter Squadron were about 35 miles southeast of Ghedi. II GrC's remaining 25 Bf109s — two had been forced to turn back with problems — were just passing Verona, approaching Lake Garda, while the 346th Fighter Squadron was 15 miles southwest

Below:
Gen Mark Clark's plan for the spring offensive, April 1945.

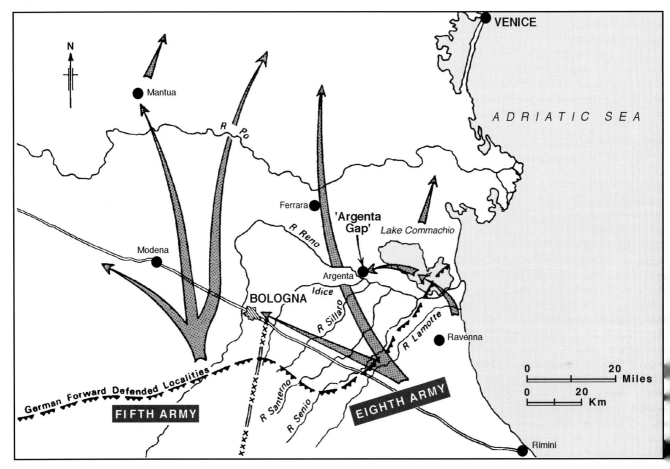

of Villafranca. The two forces made visual contact around 14.20hrs. At that moment, Miani was heard to curse because his airscrew pitch control had jammed. He broke away, ordering Capt Mario Bellagambi to take the lead. There was chaos as some 6 Sq pilots followed Miani, but then Capt Ugo Drago's section poured on the throttle and water methanol injection. Battle commenced in earnest as the pilots split into a series of duels. Capt Heckenkamp, the leader of four P-47s, accounted for three 109s inside 60 seconds and when the dust settled, the Italians had lost 14 109s shot down or damaged beyond repair, with six pilots killed and two wounded; there were no US losses. For all their undoubted bravery, the impact of Mussolini's Italian airmen was best summed up by Kesselring after the war: 'The sudden appearance of small fighter units with Italian crews flying German fast fighter aircraft came as a pleasant surprise, even if it did not mean much.'[6]

*   *   *   *

On 24 January, Mark Clark issued his general plan for the renewed offensive. In outline, Eighth Army was to attack first, supported by 'the major part of all air forces'. Once the Eighth had crossed the Senio and Santerno rivers, the Fifth Army would attack towards Bologna, making its main effort west of Route 65 with a secondary thrust west of Route 64. Eighth Army would continue its main thrust towards Budrio to outflank Bologna, and would mount an amphibious operation in the Lake Comacchio area to open up a way through Argenta to Ferrera.

As the run of the roads through the Apennines made it impossible to concentrate two armies on a single thrust, it is understandable why Clark retained Alexander's 'double-punch' concept, drawing off the German reserves in the east before hurling a sudden blow west of Bologna. By staggering the ground assault, each army could be given maximum air support, and Alexander was confident that MAAF would open wide holes in the Axis defences through which Allied troops would sweep. Concurrently, the air interdiction programme would deny von Vietinghoff all hope of reinforcement or supply. But Mark Clark had his doubts about whether the British could be depended upon 'to carry the ball', especially when it came to forcing a way through the flooded areas around Lake Comacchio. In response, Eighth Army's Planning Staff was attracted to the Via Adriatica, which ran through a narrow gap in the German-induced floods around the village of Argenta and thence to the Po at Ferrara. This thrust line became known as the Argenta Gap.

While planning was taking place, the combined chiefs decided that the Italian campaign had served its purpose. On 2 February, Alexander was informed that the whole Canadian Corps was to move immediately for service in the West. Italy was now to become a holding operation geared to containing German forces, while preparing to take advantage of any weakening or withdrawal of Axis troops. As early as February, even as the Canadians were leaving, German leaders approached the Allies with the suggestion of a surrender in Italy. These negotiations broke down, in part because faith in the Führer was still strong and von Vietinghoff doubted whether his officers and men would collectively obey a call to lay down their arms before they were convinced by events back home that further resistance was useless. Thereafter, unconditional German surrender in Italy could only be brought about by force of arms.

March saw two important changes in Allied air command. AM Slessor was succeeded by AM Sir Guy Garrod as Deputy Air C-in-C and senior British airman on 15 March, and a week later, Maj-Gen John K. Cannon was promoted to lieutenant-general to take over MAAF from Ira Eaker, who was to become USAAF Chief of Staff in Washington. Cannon assumed command on 24 March, the day the US Fifteenth Air Force bombed Berlin for the first time from Mediterranean bases. His place as commander of MATAF and Twelfth Air Force was taken by Gen Chidlaw, who was replaced in his old command of XXII TAC by Brig-Gen Thomas C. Darcy.

With the exception of Garrod, who had come from an air command in southeast Asia, the new commanders were old Mediterranean hands. This showed when it came to planning the air phase of the spring offensive, which was briefer than for any previous Italian operation. It was indicative of both Allied mastery of the air and long experience in welding air and ground into a near perfect team, that MAAF was to issue only one major directive for the whole operation, stretching to just five paragraphs.

Tactical Air Force, charged with the detailed planning, published the final version of what it called Operation 'Wowser' on 7 April. Its purpose was 'the employment of maximum air effort in co-ordination with 15th Army Group during the initial stages of the ground forces' forthcoming spring offensive'.

'Wowser' was straightforward. German defences facing the Eighth Army on the Senio were sited in such depth and built in so strongly that success against them was unlikely unless the garrison could be stunned and demoralised beforehand. It was against these fortifications that the massive Allied bombardment potential was to be deployed — Strategic's heavy bombers, the whole of TAF's medium and fighter-bomber forces, and most of Eighth Army's 1,273 guns.[7]

Timing of the offensive was closely linked with Allied plans elsewhere in Europe. By the end of March, Eisenhower's forces had crossed the Rhine and were beginning to fan out into Germany on a wide front. In the east, Soviet armies were building up on the Oder and Neisse for a major assault on Berlin, while the failure of Hitler's counter-offensive near Lake Balaton brought Marshal Malinovski to the gates of Vienna on 6 April. With these successes still in the making, the disciplined fighting force still available to von Vietinghoff in Italy had to be held down as soon as ground and weather conditions permitted. The date finally chosen for the opening of the offensive was 9 April.

Including reserves, von Vietinghoff had some 349,000 German and 45,000 Italian troops under his command on 9 April. His Army Group held 1,436 pieces of field artillery, around 400 medium anti-tank guns, 450 self-propelled assault guns and 261 serviceable tanks. The Germans' greatest weaknesses were the lack of air support and a supply situation which von Vietinghoff advised Berlin on 6 April was 'below tolerable', due largely to the widespread disruption of rail traffic both in and outside Italy.

Mussolini was making last-ditch efforts to 'disengage from German overlordship', and the most negative effect of the disintegration of the Salo Republic was that it encouraged all partisans to declare open revolt, adding to the burden on the Wehrmacht in its last battle in Italy.

Von Vietinghoff decided to prepare his soldiers for what lay ahead. His surviving Order of the Day for 30 March was shorn of all Nazi rhetoric except for the statutory 'Heil to the Führer' at the end. There were none of the customary references to final victory, and although the Italian theatre was dutifully described as an 'important outpost for the overall conduct of the war', von Vietinghoff was emphatic that German resources on the Eastern and Western fronts were at breaking point. He exhorted his men to trust in themselves and in the nerves of their commanders. 'Come what may' his soldiers must do their duty and hold on. The C-in-C concluded that 'the hour of decision must find us of one mind, and ready with iron determination to fight every superiority with all means in our power'. It is greatly to the credit of his troops that in the face of overwhelming air superiority, they obeyed almost to the letter.

* * * *

'Wowser' did not call for any sustained pre-assault softening-up by the air forces. Throughout March and right up to the beginning of the final drive, air power concentrated on severing Axis lines of communication to deny supplies and prevent escape. By 9 April, every major rail line north of the Po was cut at multiple points. Army Group C was isolated.

Within 'Wowser', Operation 'Buckland' was the united heavy, medium and fighter-bomber support plan for Eighth Army on D-Day and D plus 1. Air and artillery timings for 9 April were geared to the latest time at which the fighter-bombers could attack forward positions with safety — 19.20hrs, one hour before last light. Working back from there, XXII TAC and DAF were to attack targets in the forward areas from 15.20hrs to 19.30hrs. Prior to that, from 14.00hrs the fighter-bombers were to attack communications and German HQs, plus armed recce of all roads leading to the battle area. Meanwhile, the mediums were to attack artillery from 14.50 to 15.20hrs and 15.35 to 15.50hrs.

To start the day's proceedings, heavy bombers were to lay carpets of large fragmentation and GP bombs across the Polish II and British V Corps fronts, beginning at 13.50hrs. The whole programme was to be carefully dovetailed into the artillery plan: as Alexander mentioned in his final dispatch, it was 'no longer appropriate to speak of one service contributing to the success of another, but rather of two methods of applying military power to the same strategic end'.[8]

The Germans anticipated the impending attack but were given no inkling of when or where the blow would fall. Just after midday on 9 April, formations of heavy bombers droned northwards over the Adriatic, to all intents and purposes bound for some distant communications target. But on reaching Cesenatico on the east coast, the flights turned west to begin their run-in on the German Senio River positions.

They were to ring the curtain up on a bravura performance of aerial theatre, and in the front row was Lt-Col S. W. Nicholson, Royal Artillery.

'The long hours of suspense dragged slowly by, eyes turning continually to watches. At last at 13.45hrs, the distant roar of heavy bombers seemed the signal for the first guns to speak. There were the 3.7s firing a line of air-bursts as markers to guide the heavies on to their target . . . A strange hush fell and the silent minutes and seconds ticked slowly by till at 15.20hrs, with a mighty crash, the gun battle began along the whole front. Shells tore into the stop-banks of the Senio from all angles . . . Then the guns were silent, and for ten minutes Thunderbolts, Spitfires and Kittyhawks took charge of the river, zooming up and down with bombs, rockets and machine guns adding their staccato to the hymn of hate. Back came the guns to pound the banks, and again give way to the air. In all, five gun and four air attacks — till at 19.20hrs a sudden silence marked H-hour, broken only by the aircraft coming back for a dummy run to keep enemy heads down and drown the roar of the Crocodiles and Wasps clambering up the near bank to sear with flame the already blasted enemy banks.[9] In their tracks the assaulting infantry, with their kapok bridges, struggled forward to the river in the gathering dusk. 19.30hrs: with a roar the protective barrage opened 400yd behind the river line and held there for 30 minutes, a curtain of steel behind which the infantry completed their grisly task. Fresh platoons leapfrogged through, and at H+40 moved forward with the barrage. There was no stopping now . . .'

The final battle for Italy was on. In two days 1,673 heavy bombers, guided by a carefully worked out system of navigational aids, completely saturated specific target areas opposite the Brits and Poles. After hitting guns and troops opposing the establishment of a bridgehead over the Senio, they returned the second day to 'carpet' crossing sites on the Santerno River.[10] Eighth Army commander Gen McCreery subsequently stated that 'the bombing of the Santerno defences played a most important part in the forcing of this river obstacle', but post-flight euphoria did not mask the fact that such heavy operations from faraway Foggia could hardly have been undertaken without a hitch.

Unprecedented winds on 10 April delayed some formations. A few aiming points were obscured and some of the 1,901 tons of bombs dropped by Fifteenth Air Force fell short. 47th Wing experienced formation difficulties although the same men were leading as the day before. There were near collisions in the crowded sky, and as one unit fell back unexpectedly under the formation, another had to withhold its bombs until the sky was clear, whereupon the bombs fell on the upside of the target area. To make matters worse, an autopilot in the leading aircraft functioned incorrectly. In all, two bombers were lost to flak and three for other reasons, as against six enemy aircraft destroyed and two escort fighters lost.

Over the same two days, 624 medium bombers went for Axis artillery and troop concentrations in closely co-ordinated attacks. They laid thousands of 20lb incendiaries and small fragmentation bombs, first along each side of Highway 9 between the Senio and Santerno, and then north of the Santerno. Immediately afterwards, 740 fighter-bombers came down on command posts, headquarters, gun positions and other crucial points, throwing the enemy into confusion. Everything was fair game; fighter-bombers even attacked dispatch riders, and so overwhelming was Allied air superiority that as many as 15 aircraft would gang up on a single German tank.

The great army fear was that the advance might be held up by an estimated 180 German guns in the immediate assault area. The deal was that if air power would neutralise these guns, ground troops would take care of German infantry and light weapons. As troops watched the carpet of fragmentation bombs being laid, the whole countryside seemed to erupt in clouds of yellow smoke. Evidence from the German side suggested that the first strategic bomber effort caused relatively few casualties. There was no decisive impact on German morale, but what the onslaught did do was sever all telephone communications in the forward area, making it impossible to handle artillery effectively.

'Buckland' having proved its worth, Eighth Army lived up to its end of the bargain, actually exceeding its estimated rate of advance. By the evening of 11 April, Eighth Army had reached the general line of the Santerno and its New Zealanders were across the river. Two days later, troops were moving towards Ferrara, whose capture threatened to encircle the entire German position. After their hard blows ahead of the fighting men, the mediums and heavies returned to the Brenner line on 11 April to prevent the Germans from restoring it to use.

Mark Clark had set 12 April as Fifth Army's D-Day but bad flying weather forced him to postpone the assault by two days. XXII TAC, which had been concentrating on disrupting Axis communications immediately in front of the Fifth Army, now returned to close support. 06.00hrs had been set for H-Hour but as the 14th dawned the airfields were still shrouded in fog. By 08.00hrs the fog had begun to lift and H-Hour was reset for 09.00hrs. From 09.00hrs and continuing all morning, a total of 459 US Thunderbolt and RAF Spitfire and Kittyhawk sorties under XXII TAC operational control were flown. These fighter-bomber and strafing missions eased the way for the ground assault by attacking Axis artillery, and they accompanied the subsequent ground action by bombing and strafing guns, occupied buildings, strongpoints, headquarters and command posts, some by prearrangement and some directed by 'Rover Joe'.

The weight of MAAF effort was switched to the Fifth Army front on 15 April, ushering in the most sustained heavy bomber close-support effort ever undertaken in the Mediterranean. At a conference of Allied air commanders in Rheims on 5 April, ACM Sir Arthur Harris complained that his Bomber Command had practically no more targets left. Two days later, the British chief of air staff warned his American counterpart that further destruction of German cities would magnify the problems facing occupying forces. The RAF then discontinued area bombing and on 16 April, Gen Spaatz sent a personal message to Generals Doolittle and Twining declaring that the Combined Bomber Offensive was over and that the mission of US Strategic Air Forces in Europe was now to be 'direct assistance to the land campaign'.

Although only two days of operations were called for, Strategic Air Force devoted four days to the task: between 15 and 18 April, 4,829 bombers and fighters — of which 2,052 were heavies — struck a variety of targets between Bologna and Highway 9, the main axis of Eighth Army's advance, and Highways 64 and 65, along which the Fifth Army was pouring. Post-attack photographs showed dense concentrations of craters blanketing virtually all assigned sectors, and the overall impact on gun positions, troop concentrations, maintenance installations and communications was described as excellent. But although the tactical employment of so many bombers for so long surprised the Germans, and the absence of their own air force was a source of deep discouragement, Gen Lemelsen's Fourteenth Army remained a united, if shaken, fighting force.

US B-25s flew 126 sorties against reserve areas around Praduro on 15 April, before going against possible escape routes around Bologna. B-25s then expanded operations to cover reserve areas facing the Eighth Army and keep pressure on the Brenner. Meanwhile waves of fighter-bombers, dropping napalm on German ground defences, added 500 sorties to 15 April's aerial tally. Thereafter, air support continued on a massive scale. Allied Air Forces notched up the greatest sustained air attack of the whole Italian campaign between 16 and 19 April. Although hampered on 16 April by low cloud, the Bologna area was hit next day by 751 Strategic Air Force heavy bombers dropping 1,467 tons of bombs, while XXII TAC fighter-bombers flew over 1,200 sorties to maintain round-the-clock pressure on forces facing the Fifth Army. On 18 April, B-24s and B-17s marked their last tactical appearance in the Italian campaign by dropping nearly 1,000 tons of 20lb fragmentation bombs in the Bologna area. All this aerial effort combined with Fifth Army's rapid progress ensured that, within a week, Bologna's fate was sealed.

By 13 April, von Vietinghoff realised that there was to be no amphibious landing in his rear and he rushed down reinforcements to the Argenta Gap. The following day, he made his last appeal to Berlin for authority to conduct an orderly retreat. Allied air forces, he pointed out, had been ceaselessly employed on concentrated, co-ordinated attacks on the main focal point of the battle. By day and night, strongpoints, artillery positions and command posts were being carpeted with bombs. Fighter-bombers were assaulting every discernible target by day and night without respite; they were even flying over low hills undisturbed, keeping weapons out of action and hampering counter-attacks.[11]

German signal communications were continuously smashed, so that commanders were almost completely out of touch with forward units for most of each day and artillery observers were rendered almost entirely ineffectual. Liaison officers took hours to cover the shortest distances, and daylight movement of even the smallest reserves was out of the question. If such moves were recklessly made, units were destroyed before they could make contact with the enemy. Withdrawal in such circumstances made excellent military sense. But Hitler's condemning to death in absentia of commanders of encircled 'fortresses' who surrendered to the Russians ensured that von Vietinghoff's application was doomed to failure.

Nothing daunted, the Germans tried to increase the problems faced by Eighth Army's V Corps in the Argenta Gap by intensifying their flooding programme. Notwithstanding heavy Allied air attacks since 13 April to soften up the defences, by 17 April the battle had developed into an infantry slogging match. At noon the following day, Allied infantry pulled back to allow DAF Mustangs and Kittyhawks the room to attack but the Germans continued to fight from the rubble well into the afternoon.

The German hold on the Argenta Gap 'shrivelled up' under the weight of flame-throwers, artillery and fighter-bombers, but it was also made untenable as the Allies overran their flanking protection to the east and west. Having broken through swiftly to the east and west of Bologna, Fifth and Eighth Armies linked up for the final drive through the Po Valley.

*   *   *   *

On 9 April 1945, there were 23 German and four Italian divisions against Alexander's 17 positioned at the entrance to the Plain of Lombardy. Yet numbers could not save Axis forces which were denied strategic mobility by orders from Berlin to hold ground. Although Hitler retained his grasp of tactical detail, by now he was applying it to a fantasy world. Von Vietinghoff saw this for himself at the end of January, when his Führer briefed from a table-map on which every division had its flag but none bore any reference to battleworthiness. Notwithstanding his supreme commander's 'estrangement from reality', von Vietinghoff held the line until his forces were about to be encircled. Steeling himself to defy Berlin, he put Herbstnebel into effect and then ordered a general withdrawal from the Bologna area in order to save enough troops for a stand in the foothills of the Alps.

It all came too late. The cloying mud of winter having dried, the speed of the Allied advance after 20 April meant that delaying lines could not be held. Hounded from the air, German field staffs had to change headquarters so often that communications between army, corps and divisions were soon interrupted and in many cases lost. With fuel and ammunition running steadily shorter, Axis troops struggled back as best they could. On 23 April, Air Observation Post aircraft reported vast German convoys moving north towards the Po on practically every road, and fighter-bombers under 'Rover' control needed no urging to get amongst

them. Between 21 and 24 April, no fewer than 5,876 Axis vehicles were destroyed, the peak of 2,347 occurring on 23 April.

When the Germans reached the Po, the commanders discovered to their dismay no sign of the promised smooth crossing. Prime targets for both DAF and XXII TAC were the Po crossings, especially those from Bodneo to Ostiglia, and from Polesella to Rovio and Adria, where the biggest concentrations were observed. According to Gen Baumgartner, Commander Po Crossings, pontoon bridges that had survived to the end of March were destroyed from the air, as were other bridges and ferries still under construction. Night intruders kept the pressure on, forcing the abandonment of everything from cart-horses to artillery pieces and leaving many troops with no alternative but to attempt to swim across the river.

Allied air strove to maximise blocks north of the Po to hinder the retreat of any enemy formations that might get across the river. All railway lines including the Brenner now being a shambles, emphasis was placed on road bridges over the Adige and Brenta rivers in northeastern Italy. This assignment was given to Strategic Air Force and, under the code-name Operation 'Corncob' on 20 and 23 April, the heavies knocked out all nine road bridges over the Adige apart from one at Cararzere, which the mediums took care of on 24 April. With the bridges destroyed, Germans north of the Po attempted to use 31 ferry crossings over the Adige, but patrolling DAF and SAF fighters made any large-scale crossings virtually impossible. The last aircraft to drop bombs at night in the Italian campaign was a No 55 Squadron Boston captained by Plt Off M. Vracaric, who bombed a road/rail crossing near Gemona at 22.30hrs on 30 April. Yet important though these escape denial operations were, in the opinion of Gen von Senger:

'It was the bombing of the River Po crossings that finished us. We could have withdrawn successfully with normal rearguard action despite the heavy pressure, but owing to the destruction of the ferries and river crossings we lost all our equipment. North of the river we were no longer an army.'[12]

The scenes which greeted Allied units as they closed up to the Po confirmed how great the German disaster had been. Some 54,000 German troops surrendered by 24 April, while round-the-clock air attack and increasingly heavy artillery fire, as more and more guns came into range, created funeral pyres of burnt-out and twisted vehicles at all crossing sites and along the roads leading up to them. The great air interdiction campaign stretching back to July 1944 ensured that the Po and attendant Reno and Panaro rivers became graveyards for von Vietinghoff's divisions.

*   *   *   *

Throughout April 1945, the great change in Allied aerial emphasis was to support the land battle at the direct expense of Axis communications, which had taken pride of place for the previous six months. Although almost the whole air effort was now concentrated within the narrow confines of the battle area, the MAAF monthly sortie rate soared to 65,959, the equivalent of

2,199 sorties per 24 hours. 4,007 air reconnaissance sorties played a crucial part in locating targets, whereupon 48,310 tons of bombs were dropped. On the debit side, 402 aircraft were lost.

When it became clear that the Po front was collapsing, Gen von Pohl ordered all his units to withdraw. Tactical Reconnaissance Gruppe 11 was ordered to Bolzano but all aircraft were destroyed on the ground before they could leave. Of the two long-range reconnaissance Staffeln of FAGr122 ordered to Innsbruck, two aircraft got to Bolzano and six reached Innsbruck. Out of the 25 or thereabouts night ground-attack aircraft belonging to NSGr9, five FW190s and 15 Ju87s reached Innsbruck, the rest being destroyed at base. Ground personnel of Kommando Sommer reached Lienze on their way to Bolzano — their only remaining Ar234 landed on the autobahn near Munich. The Italian fighter gruppi would have been withdrawn to Innsbruck and Bolzano had not their aircrew been arrested by partisans. A large number of flak guns were left over from the collapsing defence of the Brenner and the Po débâcle but, with the Luftwaffe no longer capable of operating to any good purpose, capitulation appeared to be the best option.

Final victory was won by a well-balanced air/land team which was unbeatable. Speedy Allied ground and air attack left Axis divisions in Italy cut off, unable to reinforce each other and incapable of carrying out a sustained operation. The entire German forces, which by then had little or no fuel, could neither move troops nor receive supplies by road. In the opinion of General Warlimont close to Hitler's HQ, 'the practically immobile Army Group disintegrated . . . Appeals from Supreme Headquarters for 'fanatical resistance' went unheeded because there was no one to hear them.'[13]

On 2 May, von Vietinghoff surrendered unconditionally on his own initiative to Field Marshal Alexander. Maj Edward Gabor of the 345th Fighter Squadron, brought down that day when his P-47 was hit by light flak while strafing near Udine, became the last casualty of the Italian air war.

Notes to Chapter 15

1. While Ira Eaker was in the US in November 1944, it was put to him that the Fifteenth Air Force be converted to Superfortresses. On his return to Italy, he tasked General Twining with making an immediate study of the airfield and logistic problems associated with converting between five and eight groups to the B-29. On 25 November, at a conference in Cannes of all AAF commanders in the European and Mediterranean theatres, it was decided that initial B-29 conversions would take place in Italy, but none were actioned before VE-Day.
2. Even though virtually all Allied landing craft had been withdrawn.
3. Kesselring, op.cit, p.220.
4. 205 Group was now fully equipped with Liberators: the last Mediterranean operation by the ever-faithful Wellingtons took place on the night of 13/14 March 1945. The Lightnings and Mustangs not only escorted their own heavies but also covered some of Tactical's operations and undertook armed reconnaissance, all by day.
5. They were manned and maintained by some 164,000 US and 79,000 British personnel plus other Allied contingents.
6. Kesselring, op.cit, p.220.
7. Ironically, as the war drew to a close, over-lavish air expenditure in February and March brought air commanders up against logistic shortfalls. The first shortages were in 4.5in flares, and then 500lb bombs became critical supply items. By the end of March, both 500lb and 1,000lb bombs were having to be rationed.
8. The Italian Campaign, 12 December 1944 to 2 May 1945. Report to the Combined Chiefs of Staff, p.13.
9. The Crocodile, and its smaller version the Wasp, were flame-throwing tanks. Upwards of 140 were used on the Senio.
10. The Santerno targets areas — known as 'Pig' and 'Whistle' — were only 2,000yd from front-line troops, and high hopes were placed on a system of red star marker shells put down by the army to indicate the targets. As the 205 Group Master Bomber sighted and identified them as correct, he advised his visual markers who added three green target indicators. The main force then dropped into the 'reds' and 'greens'.
11. It was, of course, the light bombers that operated at night.
12. Interrogation Report, 4 May 1945.
13. Warlimont, op.cit, p.505.

AFTERTHOUGHTS

'Wars begin where you will, but they do not end where you please.'
Machiavelli

By 1944 the Luftwaffe was playing little meaningful role in Italian skies, and the situation only got worse. On 1 April 1945, the Allies had 12,482 aircraft in theatre, of which 4,393 were front-line types — as against some 130 serviceable Axis aircraft which were often forced, (like the Argentinians during the 1982 Falklands campaign) to operate at the limits of their range. The consequences were witnessed by a young Scots Guards officer, later to become the distinguished historian, Sir Michael Howard. On landing at Salerno, he saw one German aircraft which bombed wildly and then disappeared:

'That was the only hostile aircraft I saw in 18 months of campaigning up the length of Italy. All the training we had received . . . about protection against the air was completely forgotten. Our armies simply ploughed up Italy in nose-to-tail convoys. Had the Germans been able to allocate one-quarter of their air resources to the close co-operation with their army that they had previously, the Italian campaign would have been a great deal tougher even that it was.'[1]

Yet the going was tough enough in all conscience. After Salerno it took 20 months of arduous campaigning, costing 313,495 Allied casualties including future US Senate leader Bob Dole, before the Germans were forced to surrender. The Germans lost 336,650 over the same period, which is surprising given that the Allies were

Black Nan, a B-24H belonging to the 464th Bomb Group, going down after being hit by 88mm flak on 9 April 1945. Lt E. F. Walsh was the only survivor. *Author's Collection*

always attacking.[2] Allied air power made the difference. From September 1943 to May 1945, over 865,000 Allied operational sorties were flown, delivering over half a million bombs after January 1944. But it cost 8,011 aircraft, some carrying up to eight aircrew. Waging an offensive air war proved to be much more expensive and wasteful than fighting a defensive one against no air force to speak of. It was all in marked contrast to Operation 'Desert Storm' which saw a major military power crushed for the loss of 22 Allied aircraft and 366 US Army casualties.[3]

The following broad conclusions can be drawn from the Italian antithesis of 'Desert Storm'. First, there was the importance of selecting and maintaining the aim of the campaign. Gen John Harding, Alexander's chief of staff from January 1944, believed that 'the diversion of troops from Italy to the south of France in the autumn of 1944 was the biggest strategic blunder of the war'.[4] It is arguable that Mark Clark's diversion three months earlier to free Rome was the weak link in an otherwise admirable air-land campaign: it lost the 1944 'weather window' and extended the Italian campaign by a year. Either way, both instances proved that immense air power could only do so much to offset inappropriate tactics or wishful strategy. Far too often, as Tedder signalled to Portal even before the landing at Salerno, 'there is a tendency to consider the Italian chicken as being already in the pot, whereas in fact it is not yet hatched.'[5]

The key to air success lay in the quality of inter-Allied co-operation. The official British history declared:

'The air contribution to the final offensive in Italy was a masterpiece of co-operation not only with the Allied armies but within the air forces themselves. There were the problems of co-ordinating British and American air efforts and the equally complex co-ordination between types of aircraft: day and night-bombers, day-fighters and intruders, strategic bombers tasked for the land battle, and tactical aircraft. Air war with its great flexibility is a highly complex business which can only be controlled by clear, simple directives and close liaison between the various staffs.'[6]

On the ground, three factors were of paramount tactical importance in the conduct of operations in Italy: terrain, weather and the exceptional skill of German commanders in meshing these natural features with the employment of battlefield troops in blocking operations. German staffs became adept at taking advantage of Italy's numerous mountains, rivers and canals to plan defensive lines, and when bad weather reduced or suspended Allied air activity, this too was exploited for regrouping, or the acceleration of withdrawals which were often better co-ordinated than the Allied pursuit. German prowess in defence was all the more noteworthy as their troops rarely saw any of their own aircraft.

Kesselring and his commanders often commented on the overwhelming nature of Allied air superiority but they never let it crush them mentally. 'Smiling Albert' possessed immense authority and ability, and he was to prove an outstanding C-in-C despite lacking a conventional background for the role. Even his long-time opponent Harold Alexander felt moved to write after the

war that although Kesselring was 'often out-manoeuvred he never accepted defeat and . . . though he could be out-thought, he could only with the greatest difficulty be out-fought.'[7]

Notwithstanding subsequent technological developments, mountains, rivers, foliage, foul weather and human flair remain potent frictions in the workings of war.

*   *   *   *

Allied Air Forces in Italy had three main tasks — to keep enemy aircraft out of the air, to assist the army by close air support and interdiction, and to support the strategic air offensive against the German war machine.[8] Experience of these revealed much about what air power could and could not do.

First, air superiority. When the last Luftwaffe chief of staff, Gen Karl Koller, addressed the question 'Why We Lost the War', he concluded that, 'what was decisive in itself was the loss of air supremacy . . . If our air supremacy had been kept up from the beginning, we would not have been defeated in the Mediterranean area.'[9]

Although Kesselring had relatively few air defence aircraft at his disposal in 1944, the Allies still lost 713 aircraft that year totally destroyed to flak. The 3,206 flak guns manned by the Axis in Italy on 29 March 1945 often forced Allied aircraft to fly far higher than they would have wished, degrading bombing accuracies, or to go instead for easier, less crucial objectives. Just as RAF Tornados in 1991 were forced to alter their tactics in the face of Iraqi ground defences, the imaginative and audacious use of flak in Italy proved that air superiority involves more than just shiny aeroplanes.

Second, close air support. Established air power wisdom is that 'whoever controls the air generally controls the surface'.[10] Well, up to a point. Though air supremacy was gained from the outset of the Italian campaign and was never lost, 'the bald truth is that it did not avail to achieve swift victory. Without it, no invasion would have been possible; with it, the ultimate result was certain, but the way, nevertheless, long and hard.'[11]

Even after a year of miserable hard slog, fighting and retreating under a canopy of hostile air power, Axis forces tended to contain the Allies rather than the other way around. Although, by the end of the campaign, the Allies were operating a sophisticated system of air-ground co-operation that could deal with anything except poor weather, the idea that superior air power could in some way be a substitute for hard fighting on the ground was beguiling but illusory. But the converse was equally true: an army by itself could not defeat a highly organised and disciplined army operating in terrain more suited to defence than attack. In sum, air and land needed each other then, and still do today.

Third, interdiction. The aim of air interdiction is to destroy, disrupt, neutralise or delay an enemy's military potential before it can be brought to bear effectively on friendly forces. During the first week of 'Strangle' in March 1944, the Allies cut every railway from the north in at least two places; thereafter, they averaged 25 cuts a day, reducing daily capacity from 80,000 to 4,000 tons. Later on in mid-1944, within three days of the start of an Anglo-US medium bomber campaign, all 23 bridges across the Po had been

Above:
Maj Adriano Visconte, CO of I° GrC, photographed a few days before the war's end. Visconte was one of the highest scoring Italian fighter aces, with six ANR claims to add to his 19 in the Regia Aeronautica. That the minuscule ANR fighter force achieved what it did was down to the charisma and courage of men like Maj Visconte. But the tense expression on his face and personal submachine gun reflected the fact that his more immediate threat was at ground level. Notwithstanding his gallantry in the air, Visconte was executed in Milan by partisans on 29 April. The moral for today is simple. NATO bomber pilots operating against far-flung places like Iraq are not countering life-or-death threats to their homeland, whereas men like Visconte, whose very existence is tied to the survival of the regime they serve, fight to the death long after logic tells them they are beaten. Notwithstanding any apparent strategic or technological advantages, there can be no sure-fire winner in a contest between a pilot who has everything to live for and an opponent who has nothing to lose.
Author's Collection

rendered unusable. AM Guy Garrod could fairly claim in his final dispatch that 'air power was the major factor in causing the enemy to be . . . desperately short of all those things which are required to wage modern war successfully'.

But this told only half the story. Kesselring's troops survived on 4,000 tons a day in static defence, while the 19 German divisions south of the Po were kept supplied by ferry and pontoon bridges erected at night and dismantled by day in much the same cunning fashion as the Viet Cong obviated US interdiction in Vietnam. In other words, large-scale air interdiction on its own could not make the Germans withdraw. It did deny German commanders the freedom to deploy their major forces except under darkness, but the interdiction campaign in Italy never forced the Germans to retreat. Only ground-attack did that, but thereafter interdiction, by severing communications, paralysing mobility and cutting off supplies by isolating the battlefield, turned an orderly withdrawal into a rout.

From Alexander's viewpoint, the presence of Strategic Air Force units on his Italian airfields throughout 1944 was more of a liability than an asset. Heavy bombers had to be supplied and maintained from in-theatre resources, but strategic bombing appeared to have no direct relation to the military operations for which he was responsible. Yet Alexander was guilty of short-termism. Fifty-one crude and synthetic oil plants lay within range of Foggia-based heavy bombers, accounting for around 75% of Germany's total production. When Alex's 1945 spring offensive opened, the Germans' only real shortage was one of fuel. Far-flung operations by the Fifteenth Air Force made a major contribution to the Allied offensive against Axis oil production which eventually crippled enemy activities on all fronts.

Although nearly one million Axis troops were still under arms in Italy and Austria in May 1945, they could not maintain the fight against the Allied war machine when oxen had to be harnessed to lorries and a thousand cigarettes were the reward for any soldier fortunate enough to bring back a can of petrol from patrol. The combined strategic air offensive from north and south brought the walls tumbling down on the crucial centre of gravity — Reich infrastructure — and in so doing had as much impact on the outcome of the struggle in Italy as any amount of tactical armament.

Which leads to the thorny question of motivation. The key element in the aerial assault on Pantelleria in May and June 1943 was not the ratio of bombs to concrete but morale: if the island had been held by Japanese or German troops, it is arguable that it would not have been taken without a long and bloody struggle. The subsequent failure of 'obliteration' attacks against Cassino town and Monastery cannot be explained by delays in ground troops following up the aerial bombardment. Heavy bombing of German mountain positions south of Bologna months later did not prevent follow-up infantry being halted by small arms and mortar fire from the very weapon pits that had just been pounded by heavy bombers enjoying complete freedom from interference and favourable weather conditions. The Germans expected heavy bombing, they prepared for it and were determined to resist its impact. Consequently, they suffered fewer casualties and withstood the heaviest bombing raids with less loss of morale and fighting capacity than had been expected.

Air power was most definitely used as a psychological weapon during the Italian campaign, but the psychological impact of bombing was to be as dependent on the quality and leadership of who was being dropped on, as the destructive effect of what was being dropped.

*   *   *   *

The RAF's founder, Lord Trenchard, said that all land battles are confusion and muddle, and the job of airmen is to accentuate that confusion and muddle to a point where it gets beyond an enemy's capacity to control. This happened in Italy, but if Allied 'Army plus Air Force' eventually brought victory, the campaign showed that the underdog can survive, hold ground and even inflict massive damage despite being completely dominated from the air. In other words, while air forces had long since won overwhelming air superiority, it took much longer to garner the fruits of that supremacy.

The great difference between the British and American approach in Italy was that the British, harking back to World War 1, fought more cautiously. This gave the spur to the use of material rather than men in British battles, epitomised by the close army/air cooperation which developed in great strides throughout the campaign. But whereas American commanders such as Mark Clark appeared to hold life less dearly, the same is not true today. In the 10 days of fighting up to 23 April 1945, the US Fifth Army congratulated itself on the relatively light casualty total of 5,272. Cut to Somalia almost 50 years later: when 18 crack US soldiers died there in one disastrous night in October 1993 — the intervention force of which they were part pulled out.

The disturbing thought for today is that while a modern enemy would eventually be defeated by numerically comparable professional forces enjoying massive air superiority, it would take time, especially if the terrain was as rugged at that in Italy or a skilful opponent was willing to misuse hostages or die the suicide bomber's death. It is far from clear whether democratic public opinion today would give its politicians and commanders anything like the time given to Allied leaders between 1943-45. If CNN had been in Italy, the Allies may have given up before Kesselring.

To put it another way, thousands of men died in Italy, and thousands of folks back home were willing to let them die, because they were fighting for issues that were deemed worth dying for. In any foreseeable conflict, maintenance of the popular and political will back home is going to be every bit as crucial as the triumph of air power.

Notes to Chapter 16

1. Howard, M.; 'The Concept of Air Power'; Air Power History, Winter 1995, Vol 42, No 4, pp.7–11.
2. Jackson, op.cit, Vol VI, Pt III, pp.334–35.
3. US military aviation lost 14 aircraft from 29,393 combat sorties. Eight other coalition Tornados were lost — six British, one Saudi and one Italian.
4. Shepperd, op.cit, p.x.
5. Tedder, op.cit, p.462.
6. Jackson, op.cit, p.366.
7. Ibid; p.39.
8. 'Operations from Italian Bases — Priority of Tasks', Allied Command Mediterranean Theatre. 69, 31 October 1943.
9. Air Ministry; The Rise and Fall of the German Air Force; p.407.
10. Meilinger, P. S.; Ten Propositions Regarding Air Power; p.3.
11. Richards and Saunders, op.cit, p.365.

SELECT BIBLIOGRAPHY

Air Historical Branch (AHB) Narratives
The Sicilian Campaign
The Italian Campaign 1943-1945, vols I and II

Official Histories
The Mediterranean and Middle East
    vol III; Playfair, I. S. O.; HMSO 1954.
    vol V; Molony, C. J. C.; HMSO, 1973.
    vol VI. Pt II; Jackson, W. and Gleave, T. P.; HMSO, 1987.
Craven, W. H. and Cate, J. L.; The Army Air Forces in World War II; University of Chicago Press, 1949.
Hinsley, F. H.; British Intelligence in the Second World War; HMSO, 1981.

Phillips N. C.; The History of New Zealand in the Second World War, The Sangro to Cassino.
Prasad (ed.); Indian Armed Forces History, Campaign in Italy;

General Histories
Arena, N.; Air War in North Italy 1943-1945; STEM Mucchi, 1975.
Baumbach, W.; Broken Swastika; 1960
Beale, N., D'Amico, F. and Valentini, G.; Air War Italy 1944-45; Airlife, 1996.
Bekker, C.; The Luftwaffe War Diaries; Macdonald, 1967
Bennett, R.; Ultra and Mediterranean Strategy 1941-1945; Hamish Hamilton, 1989.

Birdsall, S.; Log of the Liberators; Doubleday, 1973.

Bragadin, M. A.; Italian Navy in World War II; US Naval Institute, 1957.

Brookes, A. J.; Photo Reconnaissance; Ian Allan, 1975.

Bryant, A.; Triumph in the West; Collins, 1959.

Buckley, C.; Road to Rome; Hodder and Stoughton, 1945.

Butcher, H.; My Three Years With Eisenhower; Simon and Schuster, 1946.

Churchill, W. S.; The Second World War; Cassell, 1951.

Clark, M.; Calculated Risk; Harrap, 1951.

Copp, D. S.; Forged In Fire; Doubleday, 1982.

D'Amico, F.; and Valentini, G.; The Messerschmitt 109 in Italian Service, 1934-1945; Monogram, 1985.

Deakin, F. W.; The Last Days of Mussolini; Penguin, 1962.

D'Este, C.; World War II in the Mediterranean 1942-1945; Algonquin Books of Chapel Hill, 1990.

Detwiler, D. S.; (Ed), World War II German Military Studies; Garland Publishing Inc, 1979.

Douhet, G.; The Command of the Air; Faber and Faber, 1943.

Duke, N.; Test Pilot; Allan Wingate, 1953.

Duncan Smith, W. G. G., Spitfire Into Battle; John Murray, 1981.

Ellis, J.; Cassino; Andre Deutsch, 1984.

Ethell, J. L.; Wings of War; Greenhill Books, 1994.

Franks, N. (ed); The War Diaries of Neville Duke; Grub Street, 1995.

Graham, D.; and Bidwell, S.; Tug of War, The Battle for Italy 1943-1945; Hodder and Stoughton, 1986.

Green, W.; Warplanes of the Third Reich; Macdonald, 1970.

Hallion, R. P.; Strike from the Sky: The History of Battlefield Air Attack 1911-1945; Shrewsbury Airlife Publications, 1989.

Hamilton, N.; Monty, Master of the Battlefield; Hamish Hamilton, 1983.

Healey, D.; The Time of My Life; Michael Joseph, 1989.

Heller, J.; Catch-22; Vintage, 1994.

Hess, W. N.; P-47 Thunderbolt at War; Ian Allan, 1976.

____; A-20 Boston at War; Ian Allan, 1979.

Hibbert, C.; Anzio; Purnells, 1970.

Hicks W. E.; The 97th Bombardment Group, World War 2; Dissertation, University of Kentucky, 1961.

Howard, M.; The Mediterranean Strategy in the Second World War; Greenhill Books, 1993.

Infield, G. B.; Disaster at Bari; Robert Hale, 1974.

Kesselring, A.; The Memoirs; William Kimber, 1953.

Kurowski, F.; History of the Fallschirm Panzerkorps Hermann Göring; Fedorowicz Publishing, 1995.

Lamb, R.; War in Italy, 1943-1945; John Murray, 1993.

Lewin, R.; Rommel as Military Commander; Batsford, 1968.

____; Ultra Goes to War; Hutchinson, 1978.

Linklater, E.; The Campaign in Italy; HMSO, 1951.

Macdonald P.; Through Darkness to Light; Pentland Press, 1990.

Macksey, K.; Kesselring; Greenhill, 1996

Majdalany, F.; Cassino; Longmans, Green & Co, 1957.

Mark, E.; Aerial Interdiction in Three Wars; Center for Air Force History, 1994. McDowell, E. R.; and Hess, W. N.; Checkertail Clan, The 325th Fighter Group in North Africa and Italy; Aero Publications, 1969.

McMillan, R.; Twenty Angels over Rome; London, 1944.

Meilinger, P. S.; Ten Propositions Regarding Air Power; US Air Force History and Museums Program, 1995.

Mets, D. R.; Master of Airpower — General Carl A Spaatz; Presidio Press, 1988.

Milligan, S.; Mussolini, His Part in My Downfall; Penguin, 1984.

Millington, G.; The Unseen Eye; Panther, 1965.

Murray, W.; Strategy for Defeat, The Luftwaffe 1933–1945; Air University Press, 1983.

North, J. (ed); The Alexander Memoirs 1940-1945; Cassell, 1962.

Nowarra, H.; Heinkel He111; Jane's, 1980.

Orange, V.; Coningham; Methuen, 1990.

Owen, R.; The Desert Air Force; Hutchinson, 1948.

Prien, J.; Jagdgeschwader 53; Schiffer, 1998.

Richards, D. and Saunders, H. St G.; Royal Air Force 1939-1945,

vols 2 and 3; HMSO, 1975.

Robichon, J.; Le Corps Expéditionnaire Français en Italie, 1943–44; Presses de la Cité, 1981.

Rust, K. C.; Twelfth Air Force Story; Historical Aviation Album, 1975.

____; Fifteenth Air Force Story; Historical Aviation Album, 1976.

Sallager, F. M.; Operation Strangle; RAND Corporation Report R-851-PR, 1972.

Scrivener, J.; Inside Rome with the Germans; NY, 1954.

Scutts, J.; Messerschmitt Bf109: the operational record; Airlife, 1996.

Senger und Etterlin, F.; Neither Fear Nor Hope; Presidio Press, 1989.

Shepperd, G. A.; The Italian Campaign 1943–45; Arthur Barker, 1968.

Slessor, J.; The Central Blue; Cassell, 1956.

Tedder, Lord; Air Power in War; Hodder and Stoughton, 1948.

____; With Prejudice; Cassell, 1966.

Terraine, J.; The Right of the Line; Hodder and Stoughton, 1985.

Trevelyan, R.; Rome '44; Hodder and Stoughton, 1983.

Turner, J. F.; VCs of the Air; Harrap, 1961.

Vietinghoff, H.; The Campaign in Italy; 1947.

Wakefield, K.; The Fighting Grasshoppers; Midland Counties, 1990.

Wallace, R.; The Italian Campaign; Time-Life Books, 1978.

Warlimont, W.; Inside Hitler's Headquarters 1939–45; Weidenfeld & Nicolson, 1964.

Wells, H. G.; The War in the Air; 1908.

Wörpel, D.; A Hostile Sky.

MAGAZINE ARTICLES

Holden Reid, B.; 'The Italian Campaign, 1943-45: A Reappraisal of Allied Generalship'; The Journal of Strategic Studies, pp.128-161, March 1990.

Howard, M.; 'The Concept of Air Power'; Air Power History, Winter 1995, Vol 42, No 4.

Montgomery, P.; 'Beaufighter Ban Yan'; Aircraft Illustrated, January 1970.

____; 'Italianesque'; Aircraft Illustrated, July 1970.